Early Acclaim

Back to the Summit

"Back to the Summit" records the amazing story of Omer Rains, a person who in spite of having to overcome one challenge after another during his lifetime, has left us with a legacy of legislative and humanitarian achievements that few of his generation can match. I got to know Omer particularly well during the 2000 Presidential Campaign when I was the nominee of the Natural Law Party, the Reform Party and, in New York, of the Independence Party. Little did I know then that he would face his greatest challenge of all less than two years later when death stared him in the face. But fighter that he is, once again he rose to the occasion and today continues to leave his mark helping others both here at home and throughout the developing world. **We can all learn profound lessons from this book.**

Dr. John Hagelin
Internationally Renowned Particle Physicist
3-Time Candidate for President of the U.S.
National Director, Transcendental Meditation Program
President, Global Union of Scientists for Peace
Author, "Manual for a Perfect Government"

"Back to the Summit" illustrates how in America one can still overcome great obstacles given enough will power, determination, and tenacity. The way in which Omer Rains overcame a paralyzing near death experience is **as inspirational as any story can be."**

John C. Malone
Chairman, Liberty Media
Chairman, Liberty Global Inc.
CEO, Discovery Holding Company
Former Pres. & CEO, Tele-Communications Inc. (TCI)

I first met Omer Rains on Mount Everest in 1995. At age 55, he was remarkably fit. Seven years later, while seemingly still active and fit, Omer was unexpectedly struck down by a ruptured brain aneurysm and stroke. Only through a series of miracles and intense personal willpower was he able to survive and later recover. I am Nepalese—a Sherpa—and Omer's inspirational and **heroic story** of recovery is a moving one both in my native land of Nepal and in other countries where he does untold humanitarian work. Today, Omer retains his ties to Nepal through frequent visitations as Chairman of READ which built the library in which I received my own education, including my ability to read and write in English. He is one of my heroes. This book is a **must read** for anyone with a loved one who has ever suffered a near death experience.

Kaji Sherpa
Former Holder of World Record
Fastest Ascent of Mount Everest

Omer Rains was a law student of mine many, many years back. Little did I know then the life challenges he had already overcome in order to even attend – much less excel – in college. It was a bit ironic when later, as Chancellor of the University of California (Berkeley) and in a classic reversal of roles, I would annually visit Omer in his capacity as a California State Senator on behalf of the University. Omer's story, told in "Back to the Summit," is **not just the inspirational story** of how he survived a near fatal brain aneurysm, **but of his humanitarian efforts** to help others around the world to acquire literacy and, thus, education. **This book truly speaks to a life well led.**

Ira Michael Heyman
Emeritus Professor of Law, University of California (Berkeley)
Former Chancellor, University of California (Berkeley)
Former Secretary, Smithsonian Institution (Washington, D.C.)

Reading "Back to the Summit" causes me to feel good about my own life and my chosen profession of medicine. However, it also tells **a story of powers beyond medicine**. As the primary treating physician after Omer Rains initially survived a brain aneurysm and stroke, I can attest to the fact that there is no adequate medical explanation for him being alive today and for the remarkable recovery he made. **This book should be an inspiration for anyone who has ever suffered, or may in the future suffer, a life threatening challenge.**

Dr. David Dozier (ret.)
Chief Treating Neurologist of Omer Rains

Omer Rains was one of my prized patients. My specialty is in working with people who have suffered a stroke and/or a brain injury, as was the case with Omer. His book "Back to the Summit" chronicles how someone with sufficient inner-strength, determination and resolve can recover from a paralytic state to the point that today he leads more than a full and complete life, primarily in the service of others. I'm pleased to have been able to play a role in his recovery process. But the person who deserves most of the credit is Omer himself. "Back to the Summit" is an inspiring book about an inspiring person. If you've ever been faced with a physical challenge, **read this book. It may help you find your own pathway to recovery.**

Waleed Al-Oboudi, MOT, OTR/L
Internationally acclaimed in field of occupational therapy and rehabilitation
Occupational Therapy Professional of the Year
Originator of Neuro-Integrative Functional Rehabilitation and Habitation
(NEURO-IFRAH)

The recovery of Omer Rains from a near death experience, and the way in which it was accomplished by drawing on prior life experiences, is **an amazing story**. One of the very early environmental leaders in the U.S., today Omer takes his message throughout the world. I have had the pleasure of working with READ Global, of which Omer serves as Chairman of the International Board. That Omer can today do the work he does in multiple countries, often in challenging conditions, is a testament to his drive to help those less advantaged than those of us in the developed world. To read "Back to the Summit" is to be truly inspired.

Gunter Pauli
Founder, Zero Emissions Research and Initiatives (ZERI)
Author of 16 books, including "The Blue Economy"

Omer Rains met my brother, Bill, in the Amazon over 25 years ago, and I have known him almost as long. Every step of Omer's life has been a testament to his fortitude and to his determination to make a difference. **We can all learn much from "Back to the Summit,"** a book that tells the story of a man who thinks, breathes and lives life to the fullest. As an actor, writer and producer, I can attest that **even here in Hollywood, the entertainment capital of the world, it would be difficult to write a more inspiring script.**

Deborah Raffin
Actor; writer; producer

"Back to the Summit" is **a riveting read**. How Omer Rains came back from a near death experience and dedicated his life to helping others undeniably has **a powerful spiritual undertone**. Raised in a spiritual setting in the 1940s, it is my belief that Omer's early religious surroundings played a major role in his amazing recovery. As one of his doctors told him: "The only explanation for the recovery you've made is that The Creator is not finished with you yet." That explanation resonates with me, and perhaps speaks in large measure to the way in which Omer today selflessly helps people in need here at home and in many other parts of the world.

Rev. Ernest Chu
Director, The Soul Currency Institute
Best Selling Author, "Soul Currency"

Omer Rains, Chairman of READ Global, is dedicated to promoting literacy and creating jobs in rural and remote parts of the developing world. It is only because of Omer that in my own village of Ullon, West Bengal, India that we now have the "Oceanic Library." Indeed, the Oceanic Library is a tribute to a person who survived a near-death experience and is now renown in the developing world for his work to help impoverished villages where few people know how to read or write. **He is truly helping to change the world. "Back to the Summit" tells how Omer was inspired to commit his life to such humanitarian efforts.**

Kapilanda Mondal
CEO & Secretary, VSSU (Ullon, India)

BACK TO THE SUMMIT

*How One Man Defied Death & Paralysis
to Again Lead a Full Life of Service to Others*

SEN. OMER RAINS

NEW YORK

BACK TO THE SUMMIT
How One Man Defied Death & Paralysis
to Again Lead a Full Life of Service to Others

by SEN. OMER RAINS

ISBN 978-1-61448-094-5 Paperback
ISBN 978-1-61448-095-2 Hard Cover
ISBN 978-1-61448-096-9 eBook

Library of Congress Control Number: 2011937116

Published by:
MORGAN JAMES PUBLISHING
The Entrepreneurial Publisher
5 Penn Plaza, 23rd Floor
New York City, New York 10001
(212) 655-5470 Office
(516) 908-4496 Fax
www.MorganJamesPublishing.com

Cover Design by:
Jerry Dorris
jerry@style-matters.com

Interior Design by:
Bonnie Bushman
bbushman@bresnan.net

Priorities

By Mother Teresa

(Copied from a wall outside an orphanage in Calcutta, India and since then always carried by the author in his wallet)

People are often unreasonable, illogical and self-centered.
Forgive them anyway.
If you are kind, people may accuse you of having selfish, ulterior motives.
Be kind anyway.

If you are successful, you will win some false friends and some true enemies.
Succeed anyway.
If you are honest and frank, people may cheat you.
Be honest and frank anyway.

What you spend your life building, someone may destroy overnight.
Build anyway.
If you find serenity and happiness, people may be jealous.
Be happy anyway.

The good you do today, people will often forget tomorrow.
Do good anyway.
Give the world the best you have and it may never be enough.
Give the world the best you've got anyway.

You see, in the final analysis, it is between you and God.
It was never between you and them anyway.

Table of Contents

Foreword & Acknowledgement

In writing this book I was determined to avoid the type of deceit and fictionalized writing characterized by James Frey's novel "A Million Little Pieces." I was also determined to avoid the type of hyperbole that apparently wormed its way into Greg Mortenson's "Three Cups of Tea." I admire greatly the work that Greg Mortenson has done in Pakistan and Afghanistan, but Mortenson's defense that inaccuracies in his book resulted from the book being ghost written is not to my mind satisfactory. The very fear of inaccuracies, distortions and exaggerations are among the many reasons that I refused to retain the services of a ghost writer, although many offered. This book could only have been accurately written by me. Thus, it is my own work-product and I take personal responsibility for every word in it.

I have been blessed to have led an extraordinary life, a life that certainly does not require hyperbole. That does not mean that it's been all good. In fact, as this book will illustrate, although my peaks have been very high, my valleys have also been very low. I have actually chosen to emphasize the challenges I've encountered in life because most of us learn more from our failures or hardships than from our successes. I'm personally convinced that my personal struggles and challenges in large measure account for me being able to tell the story of one who cheated death in a way that has for years baffled numerous doctors and other medical practitioners.

Finally, I would be remiss if I failed to mention how deeply indebted I am to Suzanne and Robert Murray of "StyleMatters." Suzanne was especially instrumental in making recommendations for the structure of the book, and in making effective suggestions for various flashbacks and flash-forwards, a methodology which I ended up utilizing. The knowledge and expertise of StyleMatters caused me to change my approach more than once and the manuscript was definitely improved by the suggestions received and, more times than not, adopted.

Omer L. Rains
March 1, 2011

Introduction

The remarkable life story of Omer Rains and of his amazing recovery from a near death experience that left him paralyzed to the point that he was told by doctors that he might never walk again is one that should inspire anyone who has ever been faced with such a challenge. Raised in spiritual surroundings from a young age, nature has always been Omer's cathedral. Perhaps that is why he signs his letters with the Lakota Sioux phrase "Mitayuke Oyasin"—a prayer of oneness and harmony with all forms of life and nature, stressing how each and everything in the magical hoop of life is connected.

Striking out on his own at age fifteen, these are the words of a man who has dedicated his life to public and humanitarian service, who has fought continually to protect nature and the environment as well as individuals and groups who could not adequately defend themselves. Repeatedly overcoming obstacles, he achieved one milestone after another—athletically, academically, professionally. Then, at the height of a lifetime of achievement, he was faced with the battle of all battles fighting for his own life and dignity in the face of a paralyzing brain aneurysm and stroke.

Rains' book, "Back to the Summit," is first and foremost the story of a man whom doctors thought would never walk again (assuming he was even able to survive his stroke and aneurysm), who suffered through two divorces, as well as numerous professional and outdoor challenges that would be daunting to most "mortals." Yet each time his back was to the wall, Rains found the physical and emotional strength to pull himself up by his own bootstraps and take one step, and another, and still another, until he was able to conquer whatever obstacle was blocking his path. Calling on life experiences, he was determined to recover from this greatest of all challenges in spite of the condition in which he found himself. Even though there were friends along the way, ultimately he knew that he would have to fight yet another battle pretty much on his own.

Long before being struck down, Omer had won the respect, admiration and friendship not only of his California Senate constituents, but of notables ranging from Charlton Heston to Martin Luther King, Jr., from Jimmy Carter to Ronald Reagan.

As Rains admits in his book, his life has been that of an "adrenalin junkie," someone who would climb great mountains on several continents, raft and kayak some of the world's most dangerous rivers, jump out of airplanes from great altitudes and, yes, even do aerobatic wing-walking. An archaeological and anthropological buff, he has also spent a lifetime as a traveler and student of the world, spending time with and helping people from Nicaragua to the Sunderban delta area of India. His lifetime mantra has been "never quit exploring."

Personally, I first met Omer shortly after his stroke and after his return to Lake Tahoe where he would ultimately recover. Once he defiantly came to again walk and engage in other life activities, he became a frequent visitor to my house, and loved to participate in the song circles, play reads and other such events I frequently hosted. As we got to know each other, I tried several times to persuade him to help me with READ Global, a program I founded in Nepal in 1991 with the goal of promoting literacy and slowing the out-migration of rural inhabitants to cities by making rural villages viable places for people to live, learn and prosper. Rural Education and Development (READ) Global constructs library community centers, provides books in the local language from pre-school to adult, seeds businesses to fully sustain and support them, and then links these centers with groups providing everything from literacy training to microcredit, to health/HIV, and to job creation.

Even though READ epitomized the type of work that Omer had done throughout his adult life, during the period that he was still recovering from his aneurysm and stroke he found it necessary to turn me down. Then, one day he asked my adventure travel company, Myths and Mountains, to arrange an itinerary for him to visit the only region of the world he had not previously visited—basically the former French Indo-China (Vietnam, Laos, and Cambodia), plus Myanmar (Burma).

At the end of a long and rigorous trip of exploration and study, Omer agreed to rendezvous with me in Nepal—a country he knew rather well from prior mountaineering trips. On this occasion, Omer and I traveled to see some of the READ Centers in rural and remote parts of the country. He was clearly moved by what he saw and by the people he met. So, at an extremely critical time for READ, Omer agreed to join our Board and began immediately to help recruit a new, highly professional Board. This man who did not feel he could take on yet another obligation was to become Chairman of the Board of READ Global, a leading spokesperson for our international non-profit organization, and an integral part of READ's subsequent expansion from Nepal into India and Bhutan.

Be assured, the reader of this book will be inspired to fight on and never give up—whatever the challenge faced in life. As for me, I say Mitayuke Oyasin, Omer! I am proud to be one of the "relations" in your own remarkable "hoop of life."

Dr. Antonia (Toni) Neubauer
President, Myths and Mountains and
Founder, Rural Education and Development (READ) Global

1

A Shattered Life

Five *days after I was admitted to Sutter General Hospital in Sacramento, California, and as I slowly came out of a coma, I heard a voice. The sound seemed to come from the left and seemed to be speaking to me. But who was speaking to me and why?*

I struggled to open my eyes, and when they fluttered open, my surroundings—whatever they were—were hazy, cloudy.

"My father was a minister back in Illinois," the voice said to me. "And my mother's maiden name was …" The voice told me a bit about his childhood back in the Midwest. I couldn't understand why.

As the voice continued to tell me things about his life, I began to detect that there were things—lots of things—attached to me, uncomfortable things. I was able to move my eyes slightly to the left, and then I saw him: a man was standing next to where I was lying. A fairly tall man but with a soft and soothing voice.

The man was looking at me. He identified himself as Dr. James Turner.

"Well, Omer, I have told you a bit about myself," he said. "Now can you tell me a few things about you? Where were you born, Omer?"

It was a simple question—rudimentary really. But I struggled to find the answer.

Finally I mumbled, "I think it was in Missouri."

"Can you tell me the name of the town in Missouri?" the man asked.

"Um, it may have been Barnett," I answered.

"What was your mother's maiden name, Omer?" the man asked.

"Damn it, what's wrong with me?" I thought. "These are simple questions. Why is it so hard to answer them?"

"What did your father do for a living?" he continued.

Did I answer? I don't really know whether I did or not, but of this I am sure: I was becoming more and more aware of my surroundings and of the numerous wires attached to my body—to my chest, my right arm, my left arm, my head. An IV drip. A catheter. I think the man introduced himself as a doctor, didn't he?

As the interrogation progressed, several others came to my bedside, intent on looking at me and examining me. Doctors? Nurses?

I was advised that I was in critical condition and in intensive care. This must be the reason so many things are hooked up to me, I thought. But why I was there and what they were monitoring was still unclear.

"My wife, Judy, can answer all of these questions," I told the doctor. "No, no, that's not right. I think my wife's name is Diana or something like that. I'm having a hard time with these questions."

"No, I want to get this information from you," Dr. Turner explained as he continued to ask me more questions.

A day later, another doctor who would attend to me with great regularity over the next month as I remained in critical condition in intensive care, a Dr. David Dozier, broke the news of what had happened to me. I had suffered a ruptured brain aneurysm and an associated hemorrhagic stroke. The doctors couldn't understand from a medical standpoint why I hadn't died on the spot when the artery feeding blood to my brain burst.

Dr. Dozier recounted my admittance to the hospital, the desperate measures that had been taken to save my life, the prolonged operation involving numerous physicians and nurses, and the new procedure that had saved my life—at least temporarily—developed and tried for the first time in Northern California on me. The primary doctor who led the surgical team was the only person on staff having been trained in London in the new procedure. As it turned out, this particular doctor got on a plane, as scheduled, the day after he saved my life. He was, and remains to me, a beneficent phantom.

The artery that had burst in my head was the one that feeds blood to the brain. The new surgical procedure conducted by the phantom doctor, and assisted by several other physicians and nurses, was intended to stop the flow of blood that was spilling over the brain.

During the next several days of my hospitalization in ICU, as new nurses, technicians and orderlies came to assist or monitor me, they would invariably ask the same question: "Where is your zipper?" At first I didn't know what they meant. But I learned that the normal procedure for my condition was to remove the skullcap, to clip the aneurysm, to then put the skullcap back on and sew it up. None of the nurses had ever seen a coiled embolism like mine.

The procedure, as I understand it, went something like this: In the hope of stopping the flow of blood across my brain that resulted from the arterial rupture, the surgeons had begun by making a very small incision in the area of my groin. In an operation that lasted several hours, the medical team carefully threaded platinum coils through arterial veins all the way up to and through my heart and then through the carotid artery in my neck. This artery, as it turns out, provides a sufficiently large passageway to the brain so that the surgeons were able to thread the coils through my carotid artery up to the spot in my brain where the artery had burst. Without blood my brain would die, but with an unmediated flow of blood coursing through my cranium, even if I lived I was at best to be left in a vegetative state.

During the procedure the doctors were able to find the exact spot from which the blood was spilling, and it was here that they inserted the platinum coils to prevent any more blood from escaping. The first time they tried this part of the procedure, the coils dislodged. The second time, however, they hit it spot on and the coils stayed in place—in effect plugging the leaking artery. They remain there today.

Was it enough of a miracle to save my life? They weren't sure. If so, would I ever be able to talk again? Would I ever be able to walk or even move again? Would I have any ability whatever to again reason or to understand? Would I remember my idyllic childhood in Missouri where my grandfather was once respected as the unofficial town Mayor? Would I recall the ex-wife, Judy, who had stalked me for the majority of my adult life? Or the three beautiful children that had resulted from my two marriages, the earlier one to Judy and the current one to Diana? Would I be able to describe the many years I spent serving in the California Senate working for civil rights and environmental protection, or the time when I was startled from sleep in a client's house in Pakistan and sharply interrogated by over sixty town elders and Taliban sympathizers on United States policy, because my "friend" had misrepresented me as a currently serving U.S. Senator?

Would I ever again be the person who had climbed great mountains, rafted mighty rivers, dined and danced in the White House and flown on Air Force One—or would I instead remain in the worst of hells as but an atrophied replica of my former self?

Who could be sure, but lying in bed week after week in critical condition and unable to really move any part of my body, but with an almost eidetic memory that thank God had not betrayed me, I was allowed to think long and hard and reflect upon the amazing life I had led and that I was determined to live once again. But how? I had to start at the beginning.

2

Barnett

*"There is always one moment in childhood when
the door opens and lets the childhood in."*
— Graham Greene

I was born in Barnett, a small town in the northern Ozarks of Missouri. The population of Barnett was and is 200, at least according to the local populace. The sign at the edge of town then said "Population 200" and today, as I write this, I believe it still says "Population 200." I don't believe there were actually 200 people in town during the years I lived there, but in the State of Missouri I'm told that in order to get any roadwork done a village has to have at least 200 people so the citizens of Barnett always had a sign saying population 200. There were no paved roads at that time in Barnett, but the dirt roads were always graded and easy to walk, ride or drive on if one was lucky enough to have an automobile, but not many people did. In fact, Barnett did not even have electricity or running water in those days.

I was born September 25, 1941. To today's youth, that was somewhere between the discovery of fire and the development of the Blackberry. However, to my generation, this was just a few months before we entered WW II. Having been born five years before the first of the "Baby Boomers," my age group—driven by the principle of individual freedom—came to be known as the "Beat Generation." For better or worse, this was the generation that was to lead the counterculture revolution of the late 1950s and early 60s.

My mother had been born and raised in Barnett and her parents, Omer Emanuel Cochran and Tracy Sullivan Cochran, had lived in and around Barnett their entire lives. Needless to say, my rather unusual first name results from being named after my maternal grandfather. One of his ancestors, and thus one of mine, had come through the Cumberland Gap with Daniel Boone in the early part of our country's history and settled around what was then the French fur trapping center of St. Louis. Omer is not an uncommon name in France, and in every French speaking nation there are cities by the name of St. Omer. Although my mother's family was not French, but rather of Scots, Irish, English and Viking descent, the name, with an Anglicized pronunciation (with emphasis on the first syllable so that it sounds like Homer without the "h"), originated in the family at that time—almost certainly because of the proximity to the French speaking fur trappers in the area in which my ancestors had settled before moving further west.

My father was born and raised in the city of Versailles, Missouri, approximately twenty miles to the west of Barnett. His mother, whose maiden name was Golda Widener Mohler, came principally from a Dutch family, the Wideners, who also had come to the New World approximately 200 years earlier.

I was truly blessed not only to have wonderful grandparents, but also to get to know them extremely well. In fact, I even got to know some of my great-grandparents, as they were still alive at the time of my birth and for several years thereafter. One of my most prized possessions is a photograph of me, at approximately six months of age, sitting on my ninety-five-year-old great-Grandfather Cochran's lap in a rocking chair on his front porch in Barnett.

My family also had a strong military history, going back to the Revolutionary War and continuing right up through Vietnam. Two of my Grandfather Cochran's brothers also lived in Barnett. Both had been severely wounded in trench warfare during World War I and bore the results of those wounds. One was named Boone (after Daniel Boone) and the other Abe (after Abraham Lincoln). They were frequent visitors to our home and I got to know them well—well enough that I knew I didn't want to go to war unless it was for an awfully good cause.

Versailles, though a small town of approximately 6,000 people, was the county seat of Morgan County, Missouri, and my Grandfather Rains was seemingly the most prominent merchant in town. Although not wealthy by standards of America in general, he certainly was by Versailles standards. He owned several businesses and most of the buildings around the town square. Each year, he bought a new Oldsmobile '98. As a result, my father was able to attend college although he did not complete his studies— something he always regretted.

Most of the Rains' were outstanding athletes. My father was no exception. He excelled in baseball and while in college, was signed to a professional baseball contract. In those days, the 1930's, professional sports at the highest level (e.g., major league baseball) did not extend west beyond St. Louis. In fact it was not until 1958 that the New York Giants moved to San Francisco and the Brooklyn Dodgers moved to Los Angeles. Without commercial airlines, almost all travel was by bus or train and the players played for small salaries and lived while on the road in flea-bitten hotels. Out west, in large and growing cities along the Pacific Coast, there existed a professional league that was not considered part of the major leagues. However, it was a training ground for players who often ended up in the major leagues. As it turned out, before finishing college, my father had an opportunity to go west and play for the San Francisco Seals. This was still several years before my birth. While there he met and played with Joe, Vince and Dominic DiMaggio, Lefty O'Doul, and many others who were later to become household names in the major leagues.

My brother, Roy, four years older than me, was actually born in San Francisco in 1937. Shortly thereafter, however, my father was signed to a contract by the St. Louis Cardinals causing a return to Missouri. But my mother and father never forgot the lights of the big city and the "streets paved with gold in California," and they always dreamed of one day returning to California. As it turned out, my father threw his arm away and, as a result, his career with the Cardinals (the famous "Gas-House Gang") was not long lived.

When I was born a few years later, war had already erupted in Europe and it was increasingly evident that America also would soon be drawn into WW II. Shortly after the bombing of Pearl Harbor and when I was but a few months old, my father was assigned to Fort Leonard Wood near Rolla, Missouri and he was subsequently assigned to manage a munitions plant in Ft. Leavenworth, Kansas. As a result, due to the war effort, I seldom saw my father during the first five years of my life. My mother, my brother and I lived with my grandparents Cochran in Barnett. As a result, my grandpa Cochran truly became my father as well as my grandfather. As it turned out, I never became particularly close to my father, and my grandfather played a far greater role than did my father in my development. On those rare occasions when my father was around he was very demanding of my mother and generally spoke to her in a rude manner. Both parents had considerable native intelligence, but the demeaning way that Dad sometimes treated Mom was a matter that was to become more and more critical to our family life as the years went by. This caused constant dissension between my father and my brother and me and, in large measure, explains why my brother eventually entered the Navy at age seventeen and why I, in turn, left home when I was fifteen.

My mother, on the other hand, was a truly beautiful woman and loving mother, throughout life making sacrifices for my brother and for me. There wasn't anything she wouldn't do for one of her children. In retrospect, that was one of the things my father couldn't stand. He was jealous of the attention she gave her two sons, and wanted her to devote full time to him. Loving my mother as I did, that behavior always ate at me and was the cause of frequent disputes between my father and I as the years went by.

Living in Barnett—small town America—during those years was truly a blessing and I can't imagine a young child having a happier and healthier life than did I. Again, by the standards of the big city, everyone in Barnett was poor. But the Cochran's were probably as well off as any family there and my grandpa Cochran was always looked upon as the community leader. He was often referred to as the "Mayor," although I don't believe an election was ever held. If a dispute arose in town the disputing parties almost invariably came to my grandfather to resolve it and they seemed to always respect whatever decision he made or whatever he recommended. I don't know that I've ever known a greater man than my grandpa Cochran. I certainly know that I have never loved a man more than my grandfather.

It was seldom that my grandfather would go any place without taking me with him. We were absolutely inseparable. I would beg him to put me on the back of the farm animals for a ride. My brother, my cousin and I were especially fond of riding "Black Betsy," a sway-backed cow that lived on Grandpa's farm. Special fun was had when my grandpa would put me on the back of pigs that had been wallowing in the mud and laughing his head off as I tried to stay on. Of course, I would invariably fall off into the mud and I didn't mind it a bit. However, my mother would scream bloody murder when we returned home.

Life in Barnett for me, other than when I was with my grandpa, pretty much revolved around the town church. There was just one church in town called the Barnett Union Church. Because Barnett was part of the "Bible Belt," everyone in town was Protestant and just about everyone in town went to church every Sunday. However, not everyone was of the same denomination. Many of the farms outside of town had been settled by Amish, Mennonites, and Brethren. Their horse and buggy lifestyles were a curious aspect of the landscape.

However in Barnett itself, we had principally Baptists, Methodists, Presbyterians and Lutherans. As a result, the preachers "rode circuit." Although the congregation would remain the same every Sunday, the preacher would change. Each of the preachers would go from village to village, town to town, rotating on a weekly basis.

My grandmother was the most active member of the church, regardless of who the preacher was going to be on any given Sunday. She was the organist/pianist, the choir director and was almost constantly involved in every church activity. Since I was being raised by my grandmother and grandfather as well as my mother during those early years, it seemed like I was almost always at the church as well.

My grandfather was a man of extraordinary integrity and I am sure that is why he enjoyed the respect he enjoyed in the community. I loved to sit on my grandpa's lap on our front porch and swing in the porch swing. We would sometimes do it for hours and he would regale me with stories of Brar' Bear, Brar' Rabbit, and the like. He could really spin a story. In fact, I've never met anyone who could spin a better story.

Unlike my Methodist grandmother, my Grandfather Cochran did not attend church, and every Sunday afternoon regardless of who the preacher was, my grandma would have the preacher over for Sunday dinner. It seemed that every one of the circuit-riding preachers loved chicken so usually we would have chicken dinner on Sundays. One of my favorite memories is that as my grandfather and I would swing on the porch, we would be on the lookout for the preacher. When my grandfather saw the preacher's car turn coming toward the house, he would say: "Well, Omer, here comes one of those chicken-eaters. We'd better get in and get started or there won't be any left for us."

Religion was equally important when we took the "long" trip to Versailles. My grandmother and Grandfather Rains, also Methodist, may not have been as involved in their church as was my Grandma Cochran, but they had religious paraphernalia and signs with Christian sayings every place one looked. Moreover, if you used profanity in any of granddad Rains' establishments, you were asked to leave and not return. Everyone in town knew the rule, so they really minded their p's and q's when they came into any of his places. Since he had the only recreation business in town (pool tables, bowling alley, dart boards, pin-ball machines, etc.), it was probably the most orderly such place in all of America, certainly of those I've ever frequented. The very threat of never being able to return had an especially marked effect on the testosterone-charged teenagers who acted like absolute choir boys in "Roy's Play Center."

Grandma Cochran was an amazing cook and we ate as well as people could possibly eat. She also wrote the weekly "gossip column" for all of the small towns around Barnett. Although we lived in "town", my grandfather had a farm cared for by a caretaker just a few miles out of Barnett. As a result, we also always had fresh meat, which my grandfather would butcher. In fact, we had a smokehouse right outside the back door of the house and near the water pump. My mother and my grandmother were absolute sticklers for cleanliness so it seemed as though I was always having baths. Without running water, this was not the easy task it otherwise would have been. We would have to pump the water in big tubs, bring it inside the house, heat the water, and then bathe in these tubs.

The outhouse was some distance away from the house for logical reasons, and in the wintertime it was often a bit treacherous to get there because of snow and ice. We didn't have toilet paper during the war years, so catalogues (usually Montgomery Wards or Spiegel's) would be used to conduct business. If all the catalogue paper was gone, corn cobs were stacked in the corner. What a luxury it was when we would go visit my grandparents in Versailles because they had running water, electricity, flush toilets, and other conveniences with which I otherwise would have been completely unfamiliar. They even had a one-party telephone line.

In Barnett where I was better than 95% of the time, we read at night by kerosene lamps or by candlelight and occasionally could pick up the Grand Old Opry, the Lone Ranger, the Green Hornet, and most importantly, at least to my grandpa, the weather report on a transistor radio which occasionally even worked. We had a telephone of sorts hanging on the wall that one had to crank before using. When a call was incoming it was like listening to the Morse code because just about everybody in town was on the same circuit. Therefore, you had to listen to how many short rings and how many long rings occurred, and in what order, to determine whether or not the call was intended for us. However, I don't think it really mattered because everyone in town listened in to whomever the call was intended for anyway. There are no secrets in a small town.

My grandfather himself built the house in which he and my grandmother lived their entire married lives. In fact, as the story goes, they put off their wedding until he was able to finish the house. The house today looks just as it did when I lived there except for the fact that it now has electricity, running water and the outhouse has been removed. It is strong and sturdy and really quite nice. Whenever I go back to visit my "hometown," I always stop in and see the family who now lives there because they knew my grandparents, my parents, and even remember me as a young lad.

Across the street from that house was a large shed-like barn. Inside the barn was kept almost all the mechanical equipment in the entire region around Barnett. It was all owned by my Grandpa Cochran. He had tractors, threshing machines, hay bailers, and the like.

Thinking back, that probably explains why on my grandparents' large household property stood a gasoline pump. It was not for commercial use, but was solely for use by my grandfather. The tanker trucks would come by occasionally to refill the gas tank. Since gasoline was closely rationed throughout the country during WW II, my strong suspicion is that Grandpa's gas pump was important to the Government because all agricultural activity in the area, except that done by the Amish, seemingly relied on use of his equipment and machinery.

As a result, when harvest season came about, his equipment was used to harvest almost all of the crops in the surrounding area. Even though the farms were individually owned, the harvest was done in a collective fashion. That is, all of the farmers would get together to harvest one person's crops, and once that was done they would move on to the next farm. In this way, each person helped the others and, in turn, received much needed help. By the same token, all of the wives would get together each day and collectively fix an enormous meal so that at mid-day the harvester's would all come in from the fields for a large meal

By the time I was five, I was allowed to ride a horse and serve as a water boy during harvest time, taking water from one horse drawn wagon and worker to another. When I wasn't doing that, my grandpa would sit me somewhere near him on top of one of the machines, though in a safe spot and always near him so he could keep an eye on me.

There was but one school in Barnett in those days and it was a one-room schoolhouse. Attending a one-room schoolhouse turned out to be an enormous advantage, one that I probably didn't appreciate until we later moved from Missouri to California. Because grades 1 through 8 were all together, a young lad who listened could pick up information being taught to those in grades much higher and through an osmotic process, if no other, I think I learned a great deal early on that otherwise would not have been accessible.

Also, although we had no library in town, a mobile truck would come through town once a month with quite a good array of books. That was a very important day for me and I always so looked forward to it. I would check out as many books as I possibly could and I developed a lifetime habit of reading early on. I read every book on sports that I could get my hands on and, for whatever reason, I also had a voracious appetite to learn about American Indians, so I also read every book I could get my hands on concerning Native Americans. That may well be the genesis of my interest in trying to help not only American Indians, but also indigenous peoples throughout the world, something that I have done throughout my life. I'm sure it influenced my current involvement as Chairman of the Board of READ (Rural Education and Development) Global, an international not-for-profit organization which builds libraries, economic development projects, and women's empowerment centers in lesser developed nations and where illiteracy is wide-spread.

Another influence was found in the attic/playroom of my Grandparents Rains' house in Versailles. I discovered there early on every edition of National Geographic ever published starting in the 1880s. I would spend hours on end looking at the pictures and reading the articles. I was especially fascinated by those that focused on exotic and faraway places where the people looked different, ate strange (to me) foods, and wore peculiar but beautiful clothes. I dreamed of someday visiting those places, a dream that was to become true—far beyond my wildest dreams.

There actually came a time during my first year in school when for a short period we moved to the city of Independence, a community near Kansas City, Missouri, where my father opened a pool hall. This was just shortly after the end of WW II and Harry Truman, from Independence, was President of the United States, having been sworn in after the death of Franklin D. Roosevelt. Those were more peaceful, quiet, and tranquil times than we know today, and I still remember President Truman taking daily strolls by the pool hall when he was not in Washington D.C. My father, an ardent Republican, was vociferously anti-Truman, but he was unfailingly polite, as was everyone when the President came by.

From Independence, I would frequently ride the train alone to visit my grandparents in Barnett. The Rock Island Line went to and through Barnett. My mother would scrub me clean and dress me in my best clothes. Boarding the train, bag lunch in hand, the friendly conductors would give assurance that my parents need not worry. The whistle would blow and off we would go. Travel was fun and I don't remember ever being worried about traveling by myself and that has been true throughout my life. That may be the result of those early, exciting trips on the Rock Island Line.

We, as Americans, in those days didn't think in terms of assassination, terrorism, or any of the other man-caused tragedies that so plague society today. Our period in

Independence was rather short lived because my father's business venture proved less than successful. As a result, we moved back to Barnett where I remained with my mother, my grandparents and occasionally my father for the remaining years until we moved to California when I was in the fourth grade.

Even though the war was now over and my father's wartime obligations concluded, he still was not around all that much. He had purchased a truck and began to make long haul deliveries of grain to different parts of the country, principally to Texas where effects of the Dust Bowl were still being felt. So, but for the brief period when we were living in the Independence/Kansas City area, I led my carefree early life in Barnett. Because of the relative isolation of Barnett, and because it was in the Bible Belt, I really had never been exposed to African-Americans (except for a maid—an absolutely delightful and wonderful woman who was employed by my grandparents Rains in Versailles), to Latinos, to Asians or from a religious standpoint, to Jews, Muslims, or Hindus. In other words, although Barnett was in many ways an idyllic place in which to grow up, it was not a true reflection of America—not then, not now, not ever.

Though I suppose everyone in Barnett was dirt poor by the standards of urban America, none of us realized it. During the time when I grew up, a young boy could dig in the dirt, admire the animals and bird life and always have lots of time to read books. The reason for this is that we were not surrounded by modern distractions.

It was better than a two mile walk to our one room school house if we went by street. Therefore, from my grandparents' house, my brother and I and a few others would cut across the back way down a steep hollow and up an embankment and cut the distance approximately in half. In the wintertime the snow was often deep and it was a very difficult trek, but we still usually took the shorter path, having snowball fights along the way.

The only real danger in Barnett was that the aforementioned Rock Island Railroad Line went through town. It was a lifeline in that it provided transportation to cities north and south and, of greater significance, it was the way in which grain was taken from the silos in Barnett to markets where it was sold. As young mischief makers, we would often sneak down underneath the Rock Island platform at the depot and smoke grapevine. If caught, we got in major trouble. A couple of times when no one was looking, we were able to jump aboard Rock Island pump cars and pump up and down the track traveling more distance than prudent. If we were caught we would again be in major trouble and I would end up with a spanking and being grounded for doing something I knew I wasn't supposed to be doing. But it was so much fun, it was worth the punishment.

Politeness was something else that was part of growing up in small town America. I don't recall ever addressing an older man other than as "Sir" or a woman other than as "Ma'am." "Excuse me," "thank you," and "you're welcome" were always required. To this day, people will often chuckle because the habit is so ingrained that I still generally address people this way, often even when addressing people much younger than am I. In fact, I even do it when I'm speaking to my dog, a Weimaraner named Spartacus.

Finally, I can't overlook the fact that my grandpa would often take me fishing down near Bagnall Dam where the Osage River was dammed to create the Lake of the Ozarks. That was truly memorable because it was usually just the two of us and we invariably caught fish. Actually, he would usually let me think that I had caught the fish although he was almost always the one who actually reeled it in or netted it. My grandpa had a strong and historic identity with the Lake of the Ozarks because, as I later learned, he drilled virtually all of the water wells around the Lake during its early years and to this day there are photographs all over central Missouri of my grandfather and his drilling rig drilling for water long before I was born.

3
The Move West

"Childhood is a promise that is never kept."
— Ken Hill

From my parents standpoint, possibly the worst decision they ever made was to move our family from Barnett to California where the "streets were paved with gold." Finishing my third year in school, we packed up our old Green Hudson Hornet with virtually all of our possessions. My mother, father, brother, and I crammed in as best we could in a car loaded with different types of items (mainly clothes) and we headed west across the plains and into the western deserts. I remember how incredibly hot it was and, of course, we did not have air conditioning in those days. When we got to Las Vegas it was approximately one hundred and twenty degrees. The heat was stifling and, although we did not have much money, my father bought tickets for us to a movie theatre and we watched the same double feature, cartoon and Movietone news all day long. When night fell we proceeded across the deserts of Nevada and California, finally arriving in the city of Gardena, California where we stayed a brief time with a relative. We were not there long because my father had an offer of employment in Bakersfield, California. An uncle of Dad's had a large butane and propane operation in Grand Island, Nebraska and he had lined up a job for Dad with the butane/propane dealer in Bakersfield.

In my opinion, Bakersfield is a hellhole of a place to live. Given all the places I've ever lived, I would have to say it was far and away the least desirable. However, it was my first exposure to life in the "big city." Bakersfield wasn't really that large by modern day standards (in those days less than 100,000 people), but to a young boy coming from Barnett, Missouri it was huge.

We actually didn't initially live in Bakersfield itself, but rather in an area called Rexland Acres, about five miles south of Bakersfield and just a few miles from a small town called Greenfield. Rexland Acres was quite a poor area and many of the people who lived there were itinerant laborers. Rexland Acres was surrounded in those days by agricultural crops, primarily cotton. That first summer at age eleven I began to work in the cotton fields picking cotton. It was incredibly hot and hard work. To pick the cotton I would have to drape the cotton bag around my neck and drag it between my legs as I went row by row picking the cotton. You were paid strictly by the amount of cotton you picked based upon the weigh machine that you would take your bag to when it was full. For a young lad, eleven years of age, it was tough even to carry the bag when it was full, much less to lift it. Picking cotton by hand means getting your hands deeply scarred every day because of the sharp thorns surrounding the cotton balls. Again, the heat was searing. It is very common for Bakersfield to exceed 110 degrees in the summer. I had never experienced such hard work, but it was something to which I was to become accustomed in the years to come. I have mixed feelings about the field laborer "career" on which I was embarking that summer because it was so hard and in many ways prevented me from having much of a childhood after I arrived in Bakersfield. On the other hand, I certainly learned to appreciate the value of hard work and the assumption of responsibility at an early age.

From that summer, when I was eleven years of age to the present day, except for periods of disability, I have never been without a job. The cotton picking which I did for approximately two years was backbreaking, hard, stoop labor, especially for a little boy in unbelievable heat. When I was about thirteen, I "graduated" to grape picking out near Arvin to the southeast of Bakersfield in vineyards owned by the DiGiorgio family. My father would drive me each morning to a designated spot where I would wait for a truck from the vineyard that came to pick up all of the laborers for the day. We would climb up on the bed of the truck and hold on for dear life as it sped out to the farm several miles away. There, I worked almost exclusively with winos and with illegal immigrants. After the grape vineyards came working at the potato sheds in Wasco and Shafter to the north of Bakersfield where I would stack one-hundred-pound bags of potatoes on dollies, usually five at a time, and then load them on trucks. We actually called the job "trucking" potatoes. I was still not sixteen, though I did have false identification which allowed me to get many of these jobs in violation of California Labor laws.

I can't recall ever having but one job at a time during those years. Generally, I was working two or three at the same time. I also worked as a box boy at a supermarket and for a janitorial service cleaning offices and toilets at night, in addition to doing yard work for anyone who would hire me, delivering the town paper known as the "Bakersfield Californian" and selling the L.A. Times door to door every Sunday morning.

As for school in Bakersfield, I first entered Greenfield Elementary School, the closest school to Rexland Acres. I was picked up every morning by a bus and returned from school along with other kids from the Rexland Acres area in the afternoon. Rexland Acres and Greenfield, in those days, were very poor areas. When I entered Greenfield Elementary School I had as classmates for the first time in my life a number of minority students. Within the first week, my best friends were Clement Hernandez, a Latino, and Floyd Hester, an African American, along with a friend I had met in Rexland Acres, Tommy Gilbert. It was a logical union of friendship, as a common love of sports had brought us together. My father was in a state of shock. Although he had some good traits, he also had some very bad traits. Perhaps the worst was that he was an extreme bigot and could not understand how I could befriend an African American or a Latino. My father and I had never had a very good relationship, but his constant denigration of my friends because of their race accentuated the rift that was becoming increasingly wide between us.

I excelled in every way at Greenfield and my favorite teacher of all time was the fourth grade teacher I had my very first year at Greenfield. She had a great impact on my life. Her name was Mrs. Benoit and I clearly was the teacher's pet. The school, though poor, owned two instruments and had a relatively good music teacher. Mrs. Benoit persuaded the school to allow me to take cornet and trumpet lessons at school's expense, with lessons given by the music teacher. I did so and became rather accomplished and ended up playing in the Kern County Honor Band for the last three years of elementary school (sixth, seventh, and eighth grades). I was also the drum major for our band and we marched in all of the parades held in and around the Bakersfield area.

Probably due to the fact that I was academically ahead of what students were studying in California because of the experience in my one room Missouri schoolhouse, Mrs. Benoit recommended that I skip the fifth grade and go directly from the fourth to the sixth grade. As it was, however, I was considerably younger than my classmates throughout my school years. During the seventh grade I was Vice-President of the Student Body and during the eighth grade I was Student Body President. I also captained the school football, basketball, and softball teams. Graduation night I received awards for being both the outstanding student and the outstanding athlete in the school. My parents were obviously very proud. I really do attribute a lot of my success at Greenfield to Mrs. Benoit, who seemed to realize that I responded very well to praise and also realized that I had a rebellious streak that she knew how to avoid.

That rebellious streak, however, has not always served me well.

The high school I entered upon graduation from Greenfield had historically been known as Kern County Union High School. At one time it was the largest high school in the nation with over five thousand students. The school would bus students in from all over Kern County. Some of the students had daily bus rides well in excess of one or two hours each way. Bakersfield Junior College was also historically situated on the high school campus. Therefore, when I entered Bakersfield High School (the name changed the year before I arrived), it was an environment unlike any I had ever been exposed to.

Bakersfield itself was a strange town, at least for California. It was as though it had been transplanted out of the south in the 50s. Bakersfield had an incredibly wealthy, but limited, number of people who in effect ran the town. The vast majority of people, however, were extremely poor. There was virtually no middle class in the city in those days. The children of the very wealthy participated in activities that I had heard of, but never participated in: golf, tennis, skiing, and so on. Most of their families belonged to country clubs and social organizations. It was a real eye opener. I didn't resent it and don't remember ever being envious of their wealth and opportunities. But for the first time I became acutely aware of the economic differences between people in our country.

When I was not working I participated in sports activities and that made it fairly easy for me to make friends and to be accepted as "one of the guys." One day shortly after entering high school, I had a bad cold or the flu and my parents thought I should stay home for a day or two. When I was well enough to return to school my father wrote a note excusing my absence due to ill health which I was to take to school. Probably because of all of the jobs I had already held, usually working with people much older than me, I had acquired "street smarts" well beyond my years. Thus, realizing that I might want to play hooky from time to time, I carefully copied my father's hand-written excuse and took it to school with me. As it was my first absence, the school attendance office called my father to verify my illness and to confirm that he had written an excuse for me. He confirmed that he had and the administration filed the excuse to use as an exemplar of my father's writing. Since, in fact, it was in my own writing, for all the rest of my years at Bakersfield High School (BHS), whenever I wanted to cut school I simply did and thereafter wrote a letter of excuse, always signing my father's name to it. Frequently, the school was suspicious and I would see the attendance officer take the initial letter out to compare the signatures—but they always matched.

Bakersfield High School had an incredibly rich and extensive sports program and a rather remarkable sports history. Sports were so very important to my life that, notwithstanding the work that I did outside of school, I managed to play freshman football, basketball, and baseball.

If one reviews the past one hundred years of high school football in California, it would be difficult if not impossible to find a high school program with the success that Bakersfield High School has enjoyed. A very recent graduate at the time I entered high school was Frank Gifford, later an all-pro and Hall of Fame halfback for the New York Giants. Our coach was an ex-pro tackle named Paul Briggs. He was a giant of a man standing over six feet five inches tall and weighing over 285 pounds. His coaching methods were brutal, but he put out great teams year after year. Workouts were rugged, especially in the intense Bakersfield heat. And Briggs didn't believe in water breaks. If you asked for water, you were called a pussy.

One day during practice I was lazily leaning on a blocking dummy listening as an assistant coach gave a talk when I was crushed—really crushed, brutally hard—to the ground from behind. Briggs had given me a cross body block from behind (in football called a "clip"). I'm a skinny thirteen-year-old kid and he had put all of his 285 pounds into the block and I felt like I had been cut in two. After some while on the ground in pain, I managed to slowly get up but I hurt—for days. Briggs said he was setting an example that no one was to loaf or that consequences would be suffered. The best thing that Briggs ever taught me was to walk fast and to take stairs. He correctly pointed out that taking stairs rather than elevators (I don't recall escalators or moving walkways existing in those days) was an easy way to get exercise because it didn't seem like exercise at all—just going someplace you had to go anyway. Since then taking stairs became a lifelong habit and I preach it to young people all the time. Occasionally one even listens.

I was also the starting first baseman on the BHS frosh baseball team. When we were not in game mode, we would often take batting practice. Each hitter would take three cuts and then "lay one down" (bunt). Those not up at bat could be wherever they wanted to be in the field. One day during batting practice I was over by third base rather than on the first base side. After each hitter took his three cuts, I would charge the plate knowing that a bunt was coming. I would scoop up the ball and fire it to whoever was covering first base at the time.

Our largest, most powerful and gifted player was a teammate named Richard Edwards. When up at bat one day, Edwards hit three towering drives deep to the outfield. Anticipating the bunt, I charged in full speed from the third base side. The next thing I remember I was in an ambulance. Edwards, rather than laying down a bunt, had swung away hitting a powerful line drive that, before I could even react, struck me right between the eyes, smashing my nose all over my face and knocking me out.

I suffered a serious concussion and was in the hospital several days. Cosmetically, the doctors did a pretty good job of putting my nose back in place. However the septum was badly deviated. Nevertheless, a week after being released from the hospital, I was back in the starting lineup and that summer played on an undefeated all-star team representing Kern County.

As it turned out, this was to be but the first of many injuries and broken bones suffered over the course of an active sports life: broken nose (again) and loss of one tooth (football); broken fingers (baseball); chipped bones in knee and ankle plus serious hematoma (crazed horse); ruptured Achilles tendon (tennis); frostbite of toes (mountaineering); broken clavicle and shoulder and six busted rubs (rock climbing); torn meniscus and ligaments (skiing); and serious abrasions (whitewater rafting). Scars? Yes, but none that are disfiguring and most are not even all that visible. Anyway, scars are just tattoos that come with a better story.

Obviously, mine has not been a Club-Med life, nor would I ever want it to be. My great ambition in life at that point in time was to be a major league baseball player but given my various jobs, fitting practice in after school became impossible. As my father was not doing well financially (to put it mildly), I was constantly on the lookout for odd jobs and taking one whenever and wherever I could.

California did have child labor laws in effect, but they were generally honored in the breach. Nevertheless, I would sometimes be asked for identification when I was applying for jobs. When I was fourteen, I met a Mexican-American who said that he could get me false ID for a small price. I agreed. What he brought me was a real driver's license with two numbers carefully cut out and transposed making it appear, unless one looked very carefully, that I was six years older than in fact was the case. Thus, when I was fifteen "my" license listed me as twenty-one. Already close to six feet in height, to be sure I was fairly tall for my age. However, I looked fifteen—not twenty-one. Nevertheless, I used that license for years and years not only when seeking employment, but I also don't recall ever being turned down at a bar although some liquor stores did get suspicious when I tried to buy alcohol. In the latter case, I would simply go outside and pay a wino a buck or two to go in and buy for my friends and me whatever we wanted.

————————

When I was fifteen, my parents decided to move to Huntington Beach, California, where my father had an opportunity to work for Chevron Oil Company. From a financial standpoint, that was the smartest thing my father ever did. My father, having worked a short period of time for the Butane/Propane Company had thereafter gone into the insurance business in Bakersfield. Saying he was not successful would again be quite an understatement. Although we lived in Rexland Acres for approximately three years, we thereafter had moved into an apartment in East Bakersfield. In fact, during my last year at Greenfield Elementary School, I had to take multiple busses to get to the bus stop where the Greenfield Union school bus would pick me up. This would take me several hours, and I did it only because I was the student body president and wanted to attend that school during my final year.

However, because my father was so unsuccessful in his business endeavors, we were constantly moving, usually due to eviction for failure to pay rent. For one year we lived at a motel, all four of us in one room. We had a large cardboard box in the middle of the room where all of our clothes were kept. The job opportunity with Chevron, where Dad became a land and mineral acquisition agent, was easily the best job he ever had and allowed my parents to enjoy financial security for the first time in their adult lives. On the other hand the move to Huntington Beach caused a family rupture. My brother had previously left home to join the navy, principally because of conflicts he had with my father.

By the same token, when my parents decided to move south to Huntington Beach, I told them I was not going—and I didn't. I was fifteen years old at the time. As a result, from age fifteen on, I lived on my own. This broke my mother's heart, but she realized I was resolute and when I was determined to do something, I did it. She was at a loss as to what to do. She cried and cried but at the end of the day she decided, correctly so, that a commitment was a commitment and when she agreed to marry my father it was "unto death do us part." They were married sixty-six years before they were separated by death.

As for me, since I was holding several jobs at the time, I did have some income and managed to rent a small apartment only a few blocks from Bakersfield High School where I lived during my last two years of high school.

My one big regret about the decision I had made is that I could no longer participate in organized high school sports programs to the extent they required attendance at daily practice sessions after school—and they all did. Living on my own necessitated working at jobs pretty much full time when not in school or otherwise screwing off.

In adult life I have often joked about my childhood ambition of being a professional baseball player and that I had everything going for me (pause) "except sufficient ability." That always brings a laugh. But obviously there was a lot more to it than that. Although I have continued pretty much throughout life to be a weekend sports warrior, due to the necessity of working organized daily participation in football, basketball, baseball or anything else became an impossibility during the latter part of my high school years. It was one of many forks in the road of my life.

4
Paralysis

The day I came out of a coma at Sutter General Hospital having had a near fatal brain aneurysm and associated hemorrhagic stroke, Dr. Turner had asked me a simple question: "What did your father do for a living?"

I don't recall whether or not I answered, but I know for certain that answering that question would not have been easy under any circumstance, even if my brain had not just been rendered nearly useless—even if I was sitting in the sunshine taking a cup of tea on the verandah or more likely playing a game of tennis with my good friend George, or just hiking along with my dog in the wilderness where I always managed to rediscover my spirit.

The question of what my father did for a living was a difficult one because my father was always changing jobs. False starts, failed attempts, and mediocre outcomes were commonplace for my father. Disappointment and upheaval—for Mom, my brother and I—were the norm. What was a bitter, former professional baseball player like my father supposed to do? Could he escape the inevitable tide of feeling washed up if he just kept trying some other way to make a living? Could he outrun the feeling of failure when it tried to find him if he hid behind a briefcase or on a cross-country sojourn to the land where "the streets were paved with gold?"

I might not have minded all the forays to nowhere if my father had spoken kindly or tenderly to my mother. My mother was the most beautiful creature I had ever known and I could not stand the abusive way in which my father spoke to her.

But on the day that Dr. Turner welcomed me back to consciousness with a test of my faculties, I had been stripped of far too many basic capacities to remember how much anger I carried towards my father. I had lost the ability to feed myself, to write my own name, to move my limbs, and to take care of my basic bodily functions—really to do anything.

27

In the first sixty-one years of my life, I had served in the California Senate; authored historic and far-reaching legislation; befriended Steve McQueen, Johnny Cash, Charlton Heston, and Evel Kneivel among others; met with Menachem Begin and Anwar Sadat during the Camp David Accords; consulted for the South African Constitutional Revision Commission; dined and danced in the White House; and flown on Air Force One. Yet, all I had experienced or accomplished to that date really did not matter. After so many days and nights in a coma due to my aneurysm and stroke, it was entirely possible—even probable I was told—that I would never leave my bed again.[1]

I was struck by the irony of the situation as I reflected back on the crazy and reckless things I had done in life, including those of my truly wild years in high school.

---

1   To learn more about overcoming brain injuries and paralysis, visit www.backtothesummit.com

5

Wild Oats and the Victory Bell

"Sooner or later, everyone has to sow wild oats.
Generally the sooner the better."
— Omer Rains

My best friend during most of my high school years was named Bentley Varner. Bentley had been lifting weights since he was a young boy. As a result, he was far and away the strongest person at Bakersfield High. He also had an extraordinarily heavy beard for his age and had a receding hair line as well. He looked thirty or more if he looked a day.

For some reason and in some way Bentley and I became close to several members of the Veterans of Foreign Wars (VFW) in Bakersfield. I suspect this relationship developed because of a job Bentley had as the head trainer of a new gym that opened in Bakersfield that was attended by several members of the VFW. In any event, many of them clearly took a liking to us and we were always welcome at the VFW hall even though we were not veterans. The back room of the VFW hall was the only room I knew of in Bakersfield that showed pornographic films. Probably because it was the VFW, the police never took steps to close it down.

Pornography may be common today, but it certainly wasn't in the 1950s. Given the opportunity, Bentley and I decided we could make some money showing pornographic films and members of the VFW allowed us to take two of the films out. The father of a friend of ours owned a small theater in Bakersfield. The theater did not show pornographic films but it did have projectors that we found we could use. Another acquaintance came from a very wealthy family and his parents were to be out of town for two weeks and, during that time, he was living alone in an impressively large house.

29

Therefore, we did a trial run showing the films on the projector in a large extended living room area of the home. Everything went well during the trial run so we decided to show the movies, one dollar per ticket, to friends and associates in the high school and college community in Bakersfield. Before we knew it we had sold hundreds and hundreds of tickets. The night of the showing the house was completely packed. People were in every room drinking beer and hard liquor, as well. Cars were parked in the neighborhood for blocks and blocks away.

Perhaps predictably, given the ruckus that was being caused and the traffic congestion in the area, the cops were called during the midst of the movie showing. Most of us got away with Bentley and me scooping up the money on our way out.

However, the cops did manage to apprehend a few of those present. One was a foreign exchange student from France. He was whisked out of the country the next day without even giving him the chance to say goodbye to his American family, much less to the rest of us. He was nineteen, much older than other high school students. I remember being quite angry at what I thought to be an overreaction on the part of the authorities. However, I later learned that he had, unbeknownst to his American foreign exchange family, also been boning the family's daughter.

As for Bentley and me, we made some very good money that night but felt that we had lost a good friend. As I remember, much of the money we made that night we blew on booze at a bar in Bakersfield called Renee's. The rest of the money we put aside to help fund a jaunt we proposed to take down to Tijuana, Mexico that summer.

———————

The early part of that summer, when I was fifteen and Bentley was sixteen, we worked together for Geophysical Service, Inc. (GSI), a subsidiary of Texas Instruments. Our jobs were strictly manual labor as "Jug Hustlers" laying out heavy cable with attached "jugs" designed to provide seismic information after explosions were set off. After the detonations, we would reel the one-hundred-pound cables in. Work was in connection with the search for likely oil fields in the desert-like areas to the north and to the west of Bakersfield. Temperatures in the summer often exceeded 110 degrees. Near the end of the summer, GSI packed up and headed off for another job in Louisiana. Bentley and I had planned all summer on taking our trip to Tijuana whenever GSI moved on. As it turned out we thought we could earn a few extra bucks by picking grapes for a couple of days out at DiGiorgio's, the huge grape operation near Arvin where I had previously done some work.

Bentley had access to a 1951 Nash owned by his parents. The car looked like an upside down bathtub but had the advantage of seats that folded down into beds. We drove out one day to an isolated store and parking lot midway between Bakersfield and Arvin. It was a spot I knew well for anyone seeking field work. Bentley and I got out of the car and mingled with the large group of men who had gathered there. As the only non-Latinos, we were looked at rather quizzically. As the others did not speak English and we didn't speak Spanish, we just nodded and smiled.

Pretty soon, a large flatbed truck pulled up. Three men were in the cab. The one who seemed to be the boss got out and said first in Spanish, later repeated in English— "who wants to work today?" Although neither Bentley nor I understood more than a few words of Spanish at the time, when we saw every hand go up, ours shot up as well. The boss began to point at certain of the men picking and choosing who would work that day. Though early in the day, some of the men were already drunk and wreaked of cheap wine. The boss seemed to have a keen eye, but when he looked at Bentley and me, he was genuinely curious. He asked in English: "Do you fellows really want to do this work?" When we said yes, he said "OK, climb aboard." We quickly jumped on the flatbed and soon we were holding on for dear life as the truck sped off to the vineyards several miles away.

Once at the worksite, the boss cleverly separated the two of us by one row. We were then told to begin harvesting the grapes, being careful to not damage them. From prior experience I knew that working in the grape vineyards was miserable, hard, hot stoop labor, but I don't think Bentley did. We didn't even know what we were being paid. However, I was sure it was below minimum wage as virtually all the workers were illegal and they weren't about to complain.

After several hours, a cluster of grapes came flying across the row and hit me on my stooped over back—and then another. I heard Bentley's laugh. I straightened up, saw him and fired back and thus like the irresponsible punks we were, the two of us started firing bunches of grapes back and forth at each other. Pretty soon the foreman saw us and came riding up on a horse. Before he could say "you're fired" Bentley said "we quit." We got a ride back to the pick-up point, jumped into the 1951 Nash and early the following morning we were off to Tijuana.

Before leaving, and knowing that I would blow whatever money I took with me on women and booze, I carefully counted out what I felt I could take knowing that my rent would be due upon my return. The trip down to Tijuana was uneventful, Bentley and I just telling jokes, BS-ing and laughing most of the way. Arriving in Tijuana or "TJ," we checked into the Motel León, a cheap motel across from the Fronton Palacio. We immediately began to hit the bars, clubs, and brothels, which were usually one and the same. After two nights, when we were down to our last few dollars, we ended up at the "Bum-Bum Club." A prostitute named Maria approached me but I immediately told her I had no more dinero. She said (in quite passable English) "That's OK. I like you because you are so young." It was about two o'clock in the morning and the place was still jumping. But rather than move on to better heeled customers, Maria kept playing around with me.

Though Maria spoke passable English, I wasn't sure that she understood me when I kept telling her that I had no money. Finally, she said "I understand, I understand— believe me, I understand. I get off work in less than an hour. I want you to come to my home. There is no charge and I will have a woman for your friend."

Maria told me that her home wasn't far from the club and she drew me a map showing me how to get there. Leaving the club, Bentley and I, both drunk as skunks, discussed whether or not we should go. We barely had enough reasoning power between the two of us to even consider whether or not this was a set-up to get us rolled. But I finally said "What the hell do we have to lose except maybe our lives—we have no money." So about three o'clock a.m. we went down a street that was reasonably well lit and following the map found a house that fit the description Maria had given me.

Not really knowing what to expect, I went to the front door and knocked. When the door opened there stood Maria who gave me a big hug and motioned us in. She led us initially to the kitchen. The house, though of cheap construction, was surprisingly large and it seemed that relatives or friends—who knows—were asleep on couches, beds, in chairs and so on in every room. When we followed Maria into the kitchen, she introduced us to another woman who spoke only Spanish. Her friend took Bentley by the hand and led him into another room. Maria told me to follow her into her bedroom. A man was lying on a cot that had been diagonally placed across the doorway. First Maria and then I stepped over the man to get into her room. She then closed the door.

Maria immediately began to undress me saying "you may think you know about sex, but I don't think you know half of what I'm going to teach you tonight." She was right.

Eventually I fell asleep absolutely exhausted. A few hours later Maria and I were awakened by Bentley who felt we should leave. Maria said "No, we will all take a shower and then I will take you boys out for breakfast." I couldn't believe my ears. First, free sex and now treating us to breakfast? But true to her word, off to breakfast we went, returning to our motel just in time to gather up the little money we had hidden in our room to cover our motel room. As for Maria, she was not only a great teacher, but she was one of the nicest of people I've ever met.

––––––––––

When I turned sixteen, I also purchased my first car. It was the car I would take on my truancy trips hiking in the Sierra's or swimming in the Kern River. From outward appearances, it was a beauty. It was a 1955 Chevrolet, turquoise in color with a Tijuana rolled and pleated interior, a louvered hood, and really bright pink, purple, black and white pin-striped blazes on the outside. The knob on the end of the gearshift was from a Budweiser keg. When class-mates saw the car, they would "ooh and aah." On the other hand, the motor was a mess. The fellow from whom I had purchased the car had done most of the engine work himself. He had jerry-rigged almost every part of the engine and under the hood everything was pretty much held together by glue, spit, rubber bands, and paper clips. It was constantly breaking down. In other words, although the car looked good and girls were certainly attracted to it (my main objective during those years), trying to keep it running with very limited funds was a nightmare. The nightmare notwithstanding, the car looked so cool that all of my friends called it Omer's "pussy wagon." Regrettably, however, I don't think I was quite the Lothario some thought me to be.

Another thing about the car was that the tires were absolutely bald. In fact, on two of the tires the rubber had completely worn through in places all the way to the inner tubes. In one of several high school era incidents of which I'm not at all proud, I cut school one day (a frequent high school occurrence I must admit). Knowing that I had to get good tires or I was going to have a blow-out, maybe at high speed, I decided to walk about the school grounds in broad daylight looking for a car that had good tires the same size as mine. I realized that to pull off what I had in mind, I had to be so brazen and open about it that it wouldn't immediately arouse suspicion. I walked cockily along hoping that if anyone observed me they would believe that I must have obtained a pass to be out of class on some sort of legitimate project.

In front of Harvey Auditorium, I came across a spanking new Chevrolet. The tires were the right size and looked like they didn't have more than a few hundred miles on them. So back I went to my apartment, removed the jack from my trunk, walked brazenly back to campus jack in hand, and there I proceeded to jack up the new car. I knew I had to work fast because truant officers were always on the lookout for students cutting class at BHS and, in any event, classes would be letting out in about forty-five minutes. First I jacked up one side on the front of the car and took the tire off. Then I jacked up the other side, took that tire off as well, and put the car back down resting on its front axle and back tires. I then rolled those two tires as quickly as I could back to my apartment a few blocks away, placed the new tires in my garage, and returned for the back tires.

Time was really short now, but I managed to now jack the back end of the car up, again one side at a time, and to get the back two tires off. I then let the car down now resting only on axles. As I started to roll these two tires away, the class bell rang letting classes out and I rolled the tires as quickly as I could while still trying to maintain a confident and nonchalant appearance. Beads of sweat and the black scuff marks on my white t-shirt from my criminal work certainly would have given me away had I been stopped and interrogated. Luckily, I was not. Back at my place with the garage door closed, I was then able to leisurely place "my" new tires on the spiffy "wagon." Now I really was in business!

———————

Frequently I would just cut school and on my own drive up the Kern River Canyon. I always had books with me and I had two favorite and isolated spots on the Kern River where I could read and from time to time dive into the river to cool off. If I knew I was going to cut school in advance I would take a bathing suit. If not, I would just strip off and dive in butt-naked to swim across the river to a spot on the far side where I could not be seen even by cars going up or down the canyon road. I had a watertight bag that I could use in swimming across the river in which I would carry not just the book I had with me, but also some food to snack on. I would leave my clothes stacked neatly on the road side of the river, generally under a shady tree. Once, however, some girls came upon my clothes. Laughingly, they took off running with them. By the time I swam across the river and got to my gutless wonder of a car they were long gone. Needless to say, I never saw those clothes again.

I would carry reading material everywhere I went. For example, during these trips up the Kern River Canyon and on many other occasions I remember reading on my own (i.e., not assigned for any class) Jack Kerouac's *On the Road*, Voltaire's *Candide*, Miller's *Tropic of Cancer*, Cervante's *Don Quixote*, Salinger's *The Catcher in the Rye*, Tolstoy's *War and Peace*, Huxley's *Brave New World*, Orwell's *1984* and *Animal Farm*, and the Tibetan Book of the Dead. Kerouac's *On the Road* had a particularly profound effect on me during those years, and the only book I recall reading as a fifteen or sixteen-year-old kid that was clearly over my head was the *Tibetan Book of the Dead*. Having re-read it in later years, once I became much more versed in Buddhist philosophy, I realize just how little I did understand back in high school when I first read it.

The fact is that I have made a life-long habit of reading books, newspapers, magazines, and so on and so forth. There is never a time—never—when I am without reading material. As a result, if I am ever stuck in a line or in an environment where perhaps most people would twiddle their thumbs, almost invariably I can be found reading. I have often thought back on my high school years and I have come to the realization that, even though I didn't know it at the time, I was actually involved in effect in a self-education program. Therefore, when I frequently skipped classes, sometimes going into the wilderness alone, I would actually be receiving an education that in many ways was far deeper and more profound than had I been on campus and in class.

The other important aspect of always having material to read is that I can honestly say that with all of the ups and downs I have had in life, I cannot recall ever being bored. When I hear people, generally young people, say "I'm so bored," it inspires me to tell them to "acquire a love of reading and you will never be bored."

I've also had a lifelong love of music—most all kinds, but especially classical, folk, and ethnic. Classical? Yes. One day during high school I heard classical music being played in a record store. I was hooked—first on classical music and not long thereafter on opera as well. I began to read about and listen to the music of Bach, Beethoven, Mozart, Verdi, Copland, Brahms, Wagner, Haydn, Dvorak, Vivaldi, Tchaikovsky, and others. This struck most of my friends as strange. I may have been the only person in my high school class who listened primarily to music of the Masters. That didn't bother me at all. Marching to the beat of my own drum, I've never felt the need to be a conformist. To this day, most visitors to my home find classical music playing in the background.

During football season in my senior year, our high school team (known as the "Drillers") was undefeated going into our final game against traditional rival East Bakersfield High School (EB). The winner of the annual match between the two high schools took possession of a victory bell and held it throughout the following year. As EB had won the 1957 game, the bell was kept somewhere on the EB campus. The week before the "big game," I drove alone over to EB, parked about a block from campus and began to explore the campus area trying to determine where the bell might be kept. As I approached the shop building, I saw it inside mounted on a large trailer.

With instructors and approximately one hundred students mulling about and working on various projects, I walked in and keeping the most calm and confident demeanor possible under the circumstances, began to do reconnaissance. The building was very large with a high corrugated metal door at the entrance. Glass windows surrounded most of the interior. They were too high to open from ground level. When the bell rang between classes and students started scurrying out, I climbed up on a bench, unlocked a window and stuck a piece of cardboard between the window and the sill so that the window did not close completely. Then I exited the building, walked to my car and drove back to my apartment. A friend came over and we placed a temporary trailer hitch on the back of my car.

After dark, accompanied by three others, I again drove to East Bakersfield High. Around the outside of the buildings, the campus was surprisingly well lit. Nevertheless, I drove to the shop building and backed my car up to the door. One of my colleagues and I got out of the car and he gave me a hand boost up to the window level. It opened and I managed to pull myself up and slide inside the building and onto the bench. I jumped down and ran to the chain that raised and lowered the door. Pulling on the chain, I was able to raise the door but at the expense of causing a lot of racket. The others were now out of the car. The door up, we grabbed the tongue of the trailer the bell sat on, and pulled it forward until we could latch it onto the trailer hitch of my car.

I jumped into the driver's seat and the others dived into the car as well. There were speed bumps (we called them "sleeping policemen") throughout the campus area, and the bell began to clang constantly. A carpool of EB students, realizing what was happening, began to give chase. My car was not only a gutless wonder, but was now towing a large and very heavy trailer, so we readied ourselves for a street brawl. However, at that very time we were approaching a train track and the warning signal was on. I gunned the gutless wonder for all it was worth and cleared the track with the trailer, though staying hitched, flying up in the air. When it came down, the bell rang loudly for a good two blocks.

Though my foolish and dangerous push across the track was successful, the chasing vehicle was held up by the train which, customary to Bakersfield in those days, was no doubt over one hundred cars long. By the time they were able to cross the tracks we were long gone.

I drove to my apartment and opened the garage door. We quickly unhitched the trailer and bell and rolled it into my garage. I closed and locked the garage door, and we went out and got drunk, laughing our heads off. The heist was big news the following day in the Bakersfield Californian, the local paper, and people all over town were talking about it. Everyone I overheard speak of it thought it was really funny. However, the two schools did not. The administration at BHS rounded up the usual suspects, myself included. No one talked. Finally, two days before the game was to be held, BHS announced that unless the culprits came forward, the game would be forfeited to EB and the prior games that year would be forfeited as well. Now the matter had gotten out of hand and was no longer a laughing matter—at least not to me.

I met with my fellow miscreants and told them that I intended to disclose everything and take the full rap but only on condition that (1) I did not have to disclose the identity of the others, and (2) that I be allowed to graduate with my class. The others offered to come with me, but I said no—keep your identities quiet. The following day, I went alone to the administration building and laid out the conditions to the Principal, to the Chief Truant Officer, to the Dean of Boys and to the Football Coach. Three of the four were former collegiate or NFL linemen and they were furious. They berated me, pushed me and yelled loudly telling me how, with all my talent, I was wasting my life and along with the others (whoever they were) would never amount to anything. I kept my cool and calmly said "No—if you accept my proposal, I will graduate with my classmates next June, I will become focused and responsible, I will go to and excel in college and thereafter lead a productive and responsible life." After berating me some more and saying that everything I had stated was bullshit, they balked at my conditions and demanded again to know the identities of the others. I stood firm. So did they—at first.

Then, as they fumed, cursed and glared, the impasse was broken by of all people the football coach Paul Briggs, who had more to lose than anyone else as it was his team that was on the verge of having an unbeaten season taken away. When Coach Briggs spoke, people listened—and not just students. His message was: "Look fellows, pushing Omer around won't work. This kid is tough as nails, and he won't break whatever we do by way of threats. I'm sure none of you know this, but I seriously hurt the kid during football practice his freshman year. I knew immediately that I had done the wrong thing. Omer could have ratted on me and I probably would have been fired. But the kid just got up and continued with practice, though in obvious pain. I don't think he ever complained to anyone, not even his teammates. I later had him as a student in my sex-ed class, and I got to know him as well as any student I've ever taught. He was full of legitimate, well thought out questions that I often couldn't answer. He absorbs knowledge like a sponge. Do any of you know why he's not playing for me right now? It's because he's supporting himself by working multiple jobs to pay for rent and food. Every other student I've known in his situation has dropped out of school. He hasn't and, in fact, somehow has gotten good grades—especially for someone frequently not at school."

What Briggs may have suspected is that, hell or high water, I was determined to go to college. I don't know who drove the thought into my mind early in life – I assume either my parents or my grandparents – but all of my life I thought in terms of three parts of education: elementary school; high school; and college. Throughout life, it never once occurred to me that I would not go to college, whatever it took.

Briggs continued: "As I see it, here are our options. We can expel him or even turn him over to the police where he might be placed in a juvenile facility for a few days. When he comes out, he will be a local cult hero because most everyone in the community already thinks that what he pulled off was a pretty cool prank. Quite frankly, if it didn't affect my team, I would be thinking the same thing. So if we take that course, the kid may get a juvenile record; my team loses a season of hard-earned success on the field; and the school—those of us in this room—look like jerks of the highest order. So everyone loses.

"Maybe the rest of you don't, but I believe this kid when he says he's going to turn his life around when he gets to college, and I'm sure he will get there. So what do we have to lose by accepting his conditions? Rains graduates next June and maybe does turn his life around. Maybe yes, maybe no, but at least he has a chance. My team plays Friday night and, if we win, completes an undefeated season. And no one is going to call us out for being lenient. In short, let's turn a lose, lose, lose situation, into a win, win, win situation. Rains graduates with his class, the team has a chance to complete an undefeated season, EB gets to have the Victory Bell back—but for only two days because we intend to kick their asses Friday night if we are given the chance."

I don't think the others believed a word I had said about the way in which I intended to transform my life. But whether they chose to believe me or not, they did come to the realization that what Coach Briggs said made sense. In any event, they finally relented and agreed to my conditions. So, absent the names of the others, I proceeded to tell them the entire story and subsequently walked with them to my garage only a few blocks from campus. I unlocked the garage door, and there stood the victory bell covered with the tarp which I had placed over it.

The game was played two days later and the Drillers won, thus completing an undefeated season. Songs and poems started to be written about the victory bell incident, some by students and some by people in the community who continued to look upon it as a pretty cool prank. Seemingly, only a few of the administrators remained stern. However, to their credit they stuck to the deal. I graduated later that school year and they never again asked me to disclose the names of the others. As for my cool looking but gutless car, I got rid of it not long after this incident and resolved that for the rest of my life I would buy only cars that were functional and not for their looks. I have never regretted that decision.

And, as for my fellow miscreants, little did members of the administration involved in my interrogation that day know (actually neither did I) that similar to the last scene in National Lampoons "Animal House," of my prankster colleagues, one would eventually become a medical doctor, one a city manager of several major California cities, one a university professor and, as it turned out, I didn't do half bad either.

6

Marriage and Berkeley

"Let your hopes, not your hurts, shape your future."
— Chinese Proverb

During my senior year of high school, I began to date Judy Reaves. Although Judy and I were often in the same college prep classes, we ran with completely different crowds. Her father, John, was a very successful businessman having the most prominent engineering and surveying firm in Bakersfield and being part owner of a large and successful construction company.

Whatever Judy lacked in native intelligence, she more than made up for through disciplined study habits, daily commitment to homework, and some of the best organizational skills that I, to this day, have ever been around. She was also quite pretty, the head cheerleader, and Miss Bakersfield High School that year. Although she was slightly overweight, it just had the appearance of a wee bit of baby fat and did not really detract from her attractiveness. However her propensity to put on weight was to take on additional significance as the years went by.

By this time, I had already concluded that all families are dysfunctional—certainly my own included—if you look hard enough. On the father's side of Judy's family, she had hard-working down to earth people, almost exclusively from the Central Valley of California. On her mother LuJane's side, however, things were totally bizarre. Judy's maternal grandfather, Lou Barnett, many years before had established a very successful chain of shoe stores. He went by the name of "Daddy Lou" and was even more dictatorial and authoritarian than was my own father. LuJane's mother, from whom Daddy Lou was divorced, insisted on being called "Banny." Subsequently, Daddy Lou had married

40

a much younger and quite nice lady named Marian. Daddy Lou and Marian had two children, Billy and Bobby. Although Billy (Lou in adult life) and Bobby were about twenty years younger than Judy, technically they were her uncle's. That was quite strange in those days.

The Barnett's lived in a beautiful home at Toluca Lake, an enclave principally of movie stars in the LA area. Both Daddy Lou and Banny were substantially overweight, though not grossly so. On the other hand, LuJane had one sister, Jean, who was huge and grossly overweight by any definition of the word. As for LuJane herself, her weight would fluctuate more dramatically than anyone I had ever known. One time she would appear quite overweight and then a week or two later she would appear to be skinny as a rail. Her weight was just constantly yo-yoing up and down. It seemed strange but I didn't think a lot about it at the time. I liked LuJane and it was apparent that she really liked me—in part I'm sure because I was unfailingly polite, having been raised to always say "Yes Sir, yes Ma'am, please, thank you" and the like.

Judy's father, John, as a father is wont to do and with good cause, eyed me suspiciously when I began to date his daughter. I suspect he had checked out my background. As the years went by, however, he and I became as close as two people can be and that was to remain true up to the time of his death several decades later.

Judy had three siblings, a brother, Tom, and two sisters, Joanie and Janet (many years later John and LuJane adopted yet another daughter, Ginny). I never met Janet because she was hit and killed by a car when she ran into a street. This was about a year before Judy and I began dating.

About twenty years before, Daddy Lou had gifted shares of stock in his shoe chain to LuJane and Jean, thus giving them majority control of the corporation. John then sold LuJane's stock and got Jean to go along. He did this to finance his engineering and construction companies. Daddy Lou was enraged and stopped talking to any member of Judy's family. As a result, he had never even seen Janet when he learned of her death. He did, I'm told, attend the funeral and it opened up a partial reconciliation with the family but he still refused to speak to John.

In twenty-first century America, one reads about this type of family from time to time, but fifty years ago it was uniquely bizarre and was to take on added meaning as the years went by. As for Judy and I, we dated throughout our senior year in high school. One thing led to another and eventually we became intimate. Having my own apartment facilitated matters greatly. Unfortunately, John learned of our indiscretions from an elderly neighbor in the apartment building and spoke to me about it. Ironically, it seemed to help the relationship between the two of us. I think his attitude was, knowing that both Judy and I would eventually be attending the University of California (Berkeley), he couldn't do a lot about it so it was better to accept what probably appeared to him to be inevitable and to become as close to me as possible.

Had I led an irresponsible life during my high school years? Hell yes!!! However, I have developed my own theory that sooner or later almost everyone has to sow wild oats. In my opinion, the sooner the better. By the time I entered college, I think I had gotten most all of the wildness out of my system. As a result, perhaps I didn't make the mistakes that some of my classmates made when they left home and, in some cases, actually flunked out of college or otherwise made a mess of their adult lives.

Consciously, I dramatically cut the umbilical cord to those with whom I had associated during my high school years. For the most part, I stopped drinking and never did drugs even though my collegiate years were spent at the drug Mecca of Berkeley. I was now finally ready to apply myself, and to start becoming a responsible citizen.

The summer after my high school graduation I moved into a house with six others on the bluffs near the Bakersfield Junior College campus. There, when my work schedule permitted, I was able to take some college classes that would be required by my destination campus, The University of California. Although there were seven of us under one roof, I seldom saw the others. For the most part, they were ex-army men taking advantage of the GI bill while, like me, holding down full time jobs. Several had been paratroopers in the army. One day they asked me if I would like to do a jump with them the following Sunday.

I planned my schedule accordingly and on the day in question we took off in a rented plane and flew southeast out over the Mojave Desert in California. At about fifteen thousand feet, my friend Bill rechecked my chute and harnessed me up. He told me not to jump until he gave me the signal. He cautioned me to do a full five-second football count—1001, 1002, 1003, 1004, 1005—before pulling the ripcord. I did as instructed and after jumping I went into freefall until I completed my five second count, then pulled hard on the ripcord.

This was 1959 and we were using World War II vintage parachutes. When my chute opened, it was quite the jolt. Thereafter, I glided down, down, down, without much control over anything. The landing on the pancake desert soil was with a significant impact. I later learned that there is a prescribed way of landing rather than just going "thud" as I did on that occasion, but I had not been told that at the time. Nevertheless, what a thrill it had been—I was hooked!

In later years, I was to do many jumps as well as paragliding, and the changes in equipment and fabric, much of it because of space age advances, have been truly dramatic. Today, an experienced paraglider in the right environment and properly outfitted, can ride the currents for hours at a time and has an ability to "steer" that was impossible in the old time parachute versions.

Even before this incident, I had come to the realization that I was an adrenaline junkie. For better or worse, that has always been true and this jump was simply further confirmation of what was becoming increasingly obvious.

———————

Throughout this, the summer of 1959, I worked as a stone/rock mason and hod carrier for Judy's father, John. The subject building was to be a large brick family home on Garnsey Avenue in Bakersfield. Bricks are not ordinarily used anymore in California due to the danger of earthquakes, but John and his team of engineers were able to put together plans that gained approval from the Kern County building department.

This particular job was unique because John had purchased large stones called Palos Verde rock and I would fit them together as I constructed a large stone fireplace in the den of the house. The greater challenge, however, came in doing the brick work. The reason for this was that John had purchased very expensive enlarged bricks for the interior of the house, each a different color for each room in the house. I got the idea of mixing the grout to blend in with the color of the brick. When I showed John what I was doing he loved it and asked me to do it throughout the house, and I did.

Each day after finishing my stone masonry and hod carrying work, I would eat a quick dinner and then shower off all the cement, dust, and debris of the construction job. Then I would report for my night job as a janitor cleaning commercial office buildings in Bakersfield. This was pretty simple work, mostly comprised of emptying ashtrays, dusting and sweeping as well as dumping trash and, of course, cleaning toilets.

When the family home on Garnsey Avenue was finished, John asked me to help out at his engineering and surveying company. The files concerning every project undertaken since the company was founded were in desperate need of reorganization. It was a significant undertaking, and John and his partner, Wilbur Ricketts, were demonstrably pleased with the job I did.

When I entered the University of California it was love at first sight. Berkeley was at the forefront of the cusp of change as we entered the tumultuous 60s and I was drawn inexorably to the campus and college life. I loved the whole academic atmosphere immediately. While I had visited the campus before, matriculating as a student and actually becoming a part of it was an entirely different thing. The academic climate there was unlike anything to which I had ever been exposed. It provided a feeling of activity and energy, something larger than myself, something important.

The years that I attended Berkeley could not have come at a more significant time period. It was an era that would have a powerful, even transformational, impact on the nation—some good, some perhaps not so good. Students were already demonstrating against the House Un-American Activities Committee (HUAC) chaired by Senator Joseph McCarthy. The 50s were ending and the days when people naively believed everything their Government told them, considering it unpatriotic to disobey any government directive or policy—no matter how wrong—were rapidly becoming history.

At the university there was the now famous sit-in at Sproul Hall, a demonstration by students who entered the administration building and blocked the hallways because then Chancellor Clark Kerr had attempted to curtail free speech on campus. The subsequent invasion of the campus by police and National Guard troops using tear gas and batons, while settling the issue as to the physical occupation, tended to bond the rebellious students into a relatively well organized movement against aspects of our culture that truly needed to be changed. What started at Berkeley began to spread to other college campuses across the country. Idealistic young students, often protesting our increasing involvement in Vietnam, and the denial of equal rights to African Americans in many parts of our country, especially in the South, were giving voice to their beliefs.

Students today on every campus in this country enjoy freedoms and rights that directly flow from what started at Berkeley fifty years ago. However at the time such ideals were very controversial and were for the most part unpopular statewide and indeed across America.

My heavy study load and virtually full time employment obligations were necessary to meet financial needs and barely allowed me time to sleep. Therefore, while I was generally sympathetic to these causes, I was not directly involved very much. There was also an incipient environmental movement taking place in which I became involved at that time and remain involved with today. I immediately sensed that it was important, and in the future I would realize just how important. But initially my concentration was on my course work. Even though I had a strong work ethic, like many beginning college students, I had extremely poor study habits. In high school I was as irresponsible and hardheaded as one could possibly be and still live. Studying just didn't fit into the picture very much during high school and I had simply gotten by on native ability, hardly ever doing homework.

Nevertheless, at Berkeley I carried a minimum of fifteen units per semester and sometimes as many as eighteen. I majored in political science with an emphasis on Soviet-American affairs, a popular major as we were in the midst of the cold war. My curriculum was basically a classic Liberal Arts education. The university at that time required each liberal arts student to take a minimum of twelve units of social sciences, twelve units of natural sciences, twelve units of physical sciences such as chemistry and physics, and twelve units of a foreign language (in my case, German).

My interest in both current events and international affairs made my selection as a political science major a relatively easy one. I had been following politics for a long time and the pursuit of "Soviet-American" studies seemed apropos considering the raging "Cold War." Also, I had always been intrigued by politics and as a kid I used to always listen to the political conventions on the radio. I didn't know any other youngster who liked to follow political conventions, but for whatever reason, I did. This was back in the era when nominating conventions weren't scripted and the delegates actually selected the candidates, often after multiple ballots. To me, it seemed as exciting as any major league sporting event.

It's not that I ever planned myself to run for public office. I was just intrigued intellectually by politics. To me it was like a chess game, involving strategy and foresight and a keen understanding of and concern about public policy. It should come as no surprise then that I have been a policy wonk my entire adult life.

From a political standpoint, the first election in which I was actually involved was the Kennedy/Nixon contest in which I did campaign work for John F. Kennedy. I was also inspired to involve myself in the Civil Rights movement and contributed to it every way that I could. This was a noble cause for any caring American in those days and one in which a person could be proud to participate. No job was too small or too demeaning. Licking stamps, attending meetings, and giving speeches, all of it mattered. Of course, my political bent put me further and further at odds with my father, a staunch Republican.

Financially, college was for me an incredible struggle as I received no financial aid from either my parents or from the government. I don't know if my father, during the time I was in college, ever got to the point where he could have helped me financially but, if he did get to that point, he didn't offer and I wasn't about to ask. In fact, I had no aid at all going to college and paid for all of it from my own earnings.

Working one's way through college is indeed possible, but it's not easy. I had saved up some money before college, and I worked all through college. Two other students and I initially rented an apartment on Channing Way near campus. It was as cheap as can be; that is to say squalid. That it was not up to code was readily apparent. When you plugged something in, smoke would come out of the sockets. But at least it was a roof over my head, and I knew that the price couldn't be beat—not in the vicinity of campus.

During my first semester at Cal, I got a job at a bookstore stocking shelves and taking inventory. To coin an Ozark sentiment I was like a fox in the henhouse. I was so at home around books and my love of reading.

For my meals, I had the greatest job ever—"hashing." Hashing is setting tables, serving food, washing dishes and doing cleanup work in general at a sorority house or girls dormitory. The pay is "free" food. Not a bad place to work for a young student with testosterone churning and a weakness for the flesh.

I did whatever I had to do to make ends meet. I recall that later, in the summer of 1965, when I was doing graduate work at the University's law school, I was in Missouri briefly visiting with relatives. My maternal grandmother said how proud my father was for having "put me through college." This seemingly innocuous statement left me stunned and red-faced with anger. I was so angry that I went outside and slammed my fist into a tree, enraged that he had had the audacity to make such a claim. But I held my tongue when I returned to the house and said nothing.

The fact of the matter was that of absolute necessity, I budgeted every penny when I was a college student, for tuition, books, travel, rent, gas, entertainment, everything. I spent less than $1,000 during my first year at Berkeley. That, of course, would be absolutely impossible today but it was an incredible feat then as well. But in life you do what you have to do—and that's what I had to do.

I had been a pretty darn good baseball player and might have gotten a baseball scholarship if I had been able to continue with sports during high school. However, I did have an opportunity for a "walk-on" try-out for the University of California baseball team right before Christmas break during my first year at Cal. After watching me shag fly balls, field grounders, and take batting practice, the coach asked me to come back after Christmas recess suggesting that I might have a chance to get a walk-on scholarship if I showed up for, and performed well, during spring training. However, fate had something different in store for me.

I went to Bakersfield with Judy during the Christmas break. John, Judy's father, had purchased a horse the week before we arrived. John was very concerned because no one had been able to yet ride the horse. It had a good bloodline, but its previous owner had treated it very cruelly. Impressing Judy was probably somewhere on my mind when I saddled up the horse, determined to take him for a ride—even if no one else could. I managed to get aboard, but the horse immediately started bucking like crazy. I stayed on for about three seconds (though it seemed like an eternity) before I was eating dirt. I had always heard that if you fall off a horse, get right back on or you will always be afraid of horses. I did, and it was one of the dumbest things I ever did.

After remounting, the horse stood eerily silent for a moment. I was tense. Suddenly the horse threw his head back into my face and reared up on its hind legs. My left foot came out of the stirrup as the horse toppled over on its left side. My leg was crushed between the hard canal road on which I had saddled the horse and the stirrup with the horse landing on top. The horse struggled to its feet, reared up on its hind legs and stomped down, barely missing my head with his front hoofs. Clearly, he was intent on killing me. I rolled about on the ground desperately trying to cheat death.

For some reason, just as I thought I was a goner, the horse charged down the canal road full speed. About fifty yards down the road, he stopped. Then he turned around and prepared to rush me again. I spotted a lone cottonwood tree not far away, and I pulled myself on the ground toward it as best as I could. I got to the tree just about the same time the horse arrived, once again rearing up and stomping at me time and time again. I kept pulling myself around the tree and, though the hoofs grazed me a couple of times, there was not a direct hit.

Judy was screaming in horror. Her father, John, suddenly appeared with a rifle and fired shots in the air to scare the horse away. Thankfully, it worked. From a hospital in Bakersfield, I was taken to Cowell Hospital on the University campus in the back of a van. I had a severe hematoma on the lower part of my left calf about three inches about the ankle. The hematoma was about four inches wide and was completely black all the way through the leg. I had chipped bones in both my left knee and my left ankle. The doctors gave me the choice to have them removed or not. I decided not to have the operation done, even though I was told that both my knee and my ankle would someday lock up on me. They never have. However, at one point on the inside of my calf there is to this day an exposed nerve that is extremely sensitive when touched as the surface skin and overlaid muscle has been displaced from the bone, thus exposing the nerve which lies next to the bone.

In any event, I did have to spend about three weeks in the hospital with my leg up in a sling. When I got out of the hospital, I was on crutches the rest of the semester which made getting around the widely spread out, hilly Berkeley campus exceedingly difficult. With only ten minutes between classes, to say it was difficult carrying books up and down the hilly pathways of Berkeley would be quite an understatement.

I was very fortunate to have Judy, who would help me in different ways. As I could no longer "hash," as I had done my first semester, Judy brought me food from her sorority house. I also had a friend who was in most of the same classes I was in and he would bring me my homework assignments during the time I was in the hospital. As a result I managed to keep up with my studies fairly well. The bottom line on this accident, however, was the effective end of a prospective college baseball career, and goodbye scholarship opportunity.

Fortunately, at Cal free entertainment was in abundance during those active years. Performers like Joan Baez, Pete Seeger, Malvina Reynolds, Bob Dylan and many others were frequent performers, especially given the importance of the civil rights and anti-war movements. A standout memory was going from time to time to the Pacifica Foundation radio station where we were allowed to sit around on the floor and sing along with such great and inspirational artists.

The mainstay of life at Berkeley, though, was the top of the line academic atmosphere that the university offered. In those days, there were more Nobel Prize Science winners at the University of California than the rest of America academia combined. To this day, in my opinion, the University of California system is the best public post-secondary program in the world. I say this notwithstanding the very real present day budget problems facing the University. I have always been a strong proponent of the state university system, and that's as true today as it was forty-five years ago. Indeed, after graduation I spent many years as a member of the University of California Alumni Council.

In the beginning, my grades at Cal were good, though not extraordinary. However, they did go up each and every year. At the end of my first semester, I had better than a B average and after that they kept getting better. When I later took the law school aptitude test my score was extremely high, and it was apparent based on discussions I had with Deans of Admissions at Berkeley and Harvard that, because of my LSAT score, I would probably be accepted at any law school in the land to which I applied.

However, before that and before entering my senior year in college, at the young age of twenty, I married my high school girlfriend, Judy Reaves. We were married in Bakersfield on August 26, 1961. We set up house in an apartment on Ashby Avenue in Berkeley, not far from the Berkeley/Oakland city line. Throughout law school I worked in an ice-cream store close by called "Botts." I worked there better than forty hours a week and got to take home as much ice-cream as I wanted. For three years that was my primary source of nutrition. Mr. Botts allowed me to set my own hours which was the only way I could fit my job in around my law school classes.

I also sold Collier's Encyclopedias door-to-door during this period. A few of us would go to areas where there were young families, generally communities in the East Bay area such as Walnut Creek, Livermore, Alamo, parts of Oakland, and down to Fremont and Hayward. All over the East Bay. I ended up number one in sales in the Western United States and made a lot of money doing it.

On April 24, 1963 our first child was born. During Judy's pre-natal period, as an anxious father-to-be I had gone with Judy to Alta Bates Hospital for every visit. I interrogated the doctor to an extraordinary degree and I am sure he got tired of my questions. I also wanted to be present for the birth of my child which, though common today, was not then. In fact I was the first father ever allowed in the delivery room at that hospital. We had actually been to the doctor's office earlier the day of the delivery and the doctor said to Judy: "you are just about ready to start dilating, so the baby will probably be born in about a week." As it turned out, the baby was born that night! It was a beautiful baby daughter whom we named Kelly.

Were we set up for a child in our small apartment? Hardly. It called for getting creative. Our apartment was basically furnished with orange crates on which we sat, and wood slats across bricks to house our books. Later we got a dining table which as I recall was a hand-me-down from one of Judy's relatives. I also had a card table inside a closet at which I studied. The closet had a built in dresser and it had maybe five drawers. I pulled the top drawer out and nailed it firmly open so that it could not be opened or shut until I was absolutely satisfied that it was safely secured in place. We put blankets and toys in there, and hung a mobile from the ceiling. That was Kelly's crib. My card table was by the side of it.

As it turned out, from birth on Kelly had a very bad case of colic. It was horrific, non-stop crying. I would take Kelly out driving around at night in the little Metropolitan automobile I had purchased and that, and only that, would make her stop crying. However, as soon as I stopped the car, even for a stop sign or light, she would start bawling again. We needed help. Between school, work and driving Kelly around, I was going without sleep for days on end. Judy was nursing and also taking a full load of classes. We were beside ourselves. Thank God my mother came to the rescue. She came to stay with us at Berkeley. She slept in our only bed with Judy, and I would sleep on the floor in the closet next to Kelly's crib. Having spent the entire month of May and about a week into June with us, I was eternally grateful to my mother. What Kelly had is commonly called "three-month colic" and sure enough, after three months, it just stopped. Were we ever grateful!

Not long thereafter there were some shocking developments in Judy's family. Her mother, LuJane, got caught stealing some minor items. She also had non-prescription drugs as well as prescription drugs in her possession—lots of them! LuJane could easily have afforded anything she stole but, as it turned out, she was both a kleptomaniac and a drug addict. But John, who was very influential in Bakersfield, had been able to prevent charges from being filed against her on multiple prior occasions over the years, and had managed to keep the problem hidden from the rest of the family. But it finally became public when the local newspaper wrote a story about one of her shoplifting episodes.

Thinking back, it had always seemed strange that one time when we would visit Judy's family, her mother would appear quite heavy and then a few weeks later I would see her and she would be quite thin. It turned out that the see-sawing in weight that I had observed during high school and later had resulted from extreme pill taking. She was addicted to both prescription and non-prescription drugs, uppers and downers, and would spend most of the rest of her life in mental institutions.

In early June of 1963 both Judy and I graduated. At the end of our senior year, I sold the Metropolitan and bought a VW Camper. It wasn't really a camper as we think of it today, although it did have a bed as well as an icebox (not a refrigerator but an actual icebox). We bought a Coleman stove that could be used outside of the vehicle. I was able to arrange my work schedule so that after work on Friday evenings, we would take off for Lake Tahoe, Yosemite, or the mother-lode country of California where gold had been first discovered in 1849.

We would camp out all weekend, and drive back to Berkeley on Sunday morning. After Kelly was born, she would of course come with us and I would carry her in a backpack when we went hiking. We always made careful plans so that we would be certain to get back just in time for me to put on my apron and go back to work at Botts.

7

Law School and the Loss of a Loved One

"Law school taught me one thing: how to take two situations that are exactly the same and show how they are different."
— Hart Pomerantz

I had made application to three law schools, UC Berkeley (commonly known as Boalt Hall), Harvard, and Hastings, which is another University of California law school located across the bay in San Francisco. I immediately received an acceptance from Hastings, and they asked for a $120 fee to hold my place. I couldn't afford it. I went to see the Dean of Admissions at Boalt Hall, and I told him that I needed to know if I was going to be accepted at Boalt. He told me that he could not assure me that I would get in, but that it was very likely, and that in fact I would probably be accepted at any law school in the country because of a very high LSAT score. The Dean of Admissions at Harvard told me the same thing when I called and spoke with him by phone. As it turned out, both schools did accept me, but I chose Boalt Hall because I knew that I couldn't even afford to move my family across the country. It is a decision that I have never once regretted.

During law school, we moved into a duplex on McGee Avenue on the other side of the Berkeley campus. The other unit was occupied by a classmate at Boalt, Larry Taggart. Larry and his wife, Billie, became good friends during our law school years. Larry was a very good sailor, and he and I would often study until after midnight and then go sailing in a fourteen-foot Lido sailboat on San Francisco Bay until the wee hours of the morning. As it was night, we would usually be the only people out on the bay. We would navigate by on-shore lights that Larry knew well, and I soon got to know too.

Of course, I was still working at Botts. For extra money I continued with my encyclopedia and insurance selling. In addition, I began to do paid research for some of my law school professors.

My first year at Boalt we had an entering class of 225 students. There were no African-Americans, one Hispanic, and four women. Today, that same school is more than 50% female. This incredible revolution has taken place in a relatively short period of time. It is amazing to now think back to those days and realize just how dramatically things have changed.

During my first week in law school, as I began to look around at my peers I remember thinking that everyone seemed smarter than me, but I soon discovered that everyone else felt the same way. When our grades came out at the end of the first semester, I breathed a huge sigh of relief when I saw that I had done rather well. I started to relax and began to feel more comfortable. However, to the best of my recollection, I was the only law student who also worked pretty much full time—if at all—when not on campus as that was something the law school discouraged.

A great opportunity arose between my second and third years of law school. Judy had gotten her teaching credential and had begun working as a teacher. Although her school year was only for nine months, she got paid for twelve months of the year. We finally had some additional income. I realized that I hadn't taken a break from work since I was eleven years old and as soon as I graduated from law school I would be entering the full-time work force. So we loaded up our camper, including of course our two year old baby, and off we went. We covered forty-four states and six provinces of Canada in ten and a half weeks while traveling over 18,000 miles. We camped out every night except for a period when we stayed with my grandparents in Missouri and I can only recall us eating in a restaurant on two occasions, once in the French Quarter of New Orleans and again in a restaurant in Bar Harbor, Maine. The trip was carefully planned, and we saw almost every historic site, national park, and geographic phenomenon in North America.

One of our stops was back at the home of my grandparents in Missouri. My maternal grandfather, after whom I was named, had been bedridden for years by now and was only semi-conscious most of the time. With my brother in Hawaii in the military, my grandfather had never gotten to see any of his great-grandchildren. When Judy and I arrived and Grandpa saw our daughter, his great-grandchild, something extraordinary happened. With help, he got out of bed and ate at the table for the first time in years. He then began telling Kelly stories he had told me as a child. My grandmother had tears rolling down her face and was in a total state of disbelief. A few days after we left, Grandpa laid down and died.

There were no cell phones back in those days and the family had no way of reaching us as we continued our camping trip across the land, so I didn't find out about Grandpa's death until several weeks later when we returned to Berkeley. I broke down and cried harder than I ever had or have in my life. I felt terrible that I had not been there for the funeral, but I also knew that I had been taught a lesson about the will to live. And I was happy that Grandpa had lived to see a great-grandchild. My grandmother said that after we left he seemed at last contented and had died peacefully. Nevertheless, his passing was a powerful and emotional event in my life.

Early in my third year of law school, major law firms and corporations came to recruit on campus and tried to attract students, offering job opportunities upon graduation. Two things were very important to me. One was where we were to live after graduation. I didn't want to live in a large urban area. I wanted to live in a medium sized community along the coast of California. Monterey, Santa Barbara, and Ventura were the three areas I had in mind. Second, I knew that I wanted to be a litigator—a trial attorney. I didn't want to be a "man in a grey flannel suit," which was what we called corporate lawyers in those days.

Woodruff J. ("Woody") Deem was the Ventura County District Attorney. Woody had a proposition for law students. He said "I want the best and brightest and to get them I am prepared to compete with the biggest and most prestigious law firms in the land. I don't want nine-to-five employees. I want you to work your buns off for at least a three year period. In return I will give you litigation experience that you would not otherwise acquire over a lifetime of private practice."

This sounded good to me. I had previously given some thought to joining the Peace Corp and spoke to Judy about it. Unfortunately, in those days unlike today, a husband and wife team could not join the Peace Corp together. Moreover, in our case that situation was exacerbated by virtue of the fact that we had a child. In any event, after accepting the job with the Ventura County District Attorney's office early in my third year, later that same year I received a letter from the Director of the Peace Corp, completely unsolicited.

The letter was from Jack Hood-Vaughn, who had just recently replaced Sergeant Shriver who was the original Director of the Peace Corp. Vaughn stated that the Peace Corp would be starting a new program in the American Trust Territory of Micronesia and that since Micronesia was a US Trust Territory, the Peace Corp was going to allow a husband and wife team to go together and that the fact that we had a young child would not be an impediment either. It was a chance to fulfill a dream, something that excited me greatly. I called Washington DC and spoke with Mr. Vaughn by phone. It turned out that I had been recommended for the job by one of my law school professors who was very close to Mr. Vaughn.

Faced with this dilemma, I spoke with Woody Deem by phone and he told me that if I did not follow through with my commitment to him, it would leave his office in the lurch and now, late in the school year, he wouldn't be able to recruit the caliber of person he wanted. He actually made me feel quite guilty that I had even thought of reneging on my earlier commitment, so I renewed my commitment to join the Ventura County DA's office upon graduation. Again, as with most—though not all—decisions in my life, I have never had any regrets. I was blessed with two wonderful opportunities. I thought to myself, how lucky can a guy be?

8

Determination

I had been lucky to this point in life, but I knew that I had also achieved quite a bit through sheer determination. If determination had been important in my life, it would be even more important if I was to ever recover.

To be sure, I was determined to walk again even before the medics carried me up the stairs on a gurney to the second floor of my two-story home in Carmichael where I would be confined while I tried to recover from my aneurysm and stroke. I had told Dr. Turner that I would walk again. In thirty days, no less—and I meant it.

I did not arrive home from the hospital in the best of circumstances. In addition to being paralyzed from the neck down on the right side of my body and severely impaired on the left side as well, my marriage was in complete disarray. Several months before my aneurysm occurred, my wife of twenty-five years, Diana, had filed a Petition for Dissolution of Marriage, California's euphemistic way of avoiding use of the word divorce. As a result, I had previously moved into a home that I rented at Lake Tahoe. Diana and our daughter, Jessica, who was attending a private school in Sacramento, continued to live in the Carmichael home.

Although I had not wanted my marriage to end, I had no complaints about living at Lake Tahoe. The picture windows on the back side of my house provided me a clear and unobstructed view of one of the most beautiful lakes in the world (an absolutely spiritual view). Across the street from the front was stunning national forest land with hiking, biking and equestrian terrain covering hundreds of square miles.

I also had the reliable and constant companionship of my dog, Spartacus, an incredibly intelligent, handsome and loving Weimaraner. In addition, nature has always been my place to commune with all things spiritual and I never felt more at home than when hiking in a forest or gazing at a mountain lake or listening to the sounds of a flowing stream. Tahoe provided all of this and more. Then there was the company of my good friend George Galante, who could always be relied upon to challenge me to improve my tennis game or to tackle a steeper slope during ski season.

Yet, returning to Tahoe after my release from the hospital was simply not an immediate option. Due to the seriousness of my condition and concerns over the effects that the altitude of Tahoe might have on my recovery, I was told by the doctors that I must remain near Sacramento, a city which is not much above sea level in altitude. Given my condition and the options available to me, the most logical place for me to return after my aneurysm was to my own home in Carmichael. Thus, that is where I had the medics deliver me upon my release from the hospital.

Specifically, I was hoisted by the medics up the stairs to the master bedroom and placed in the bed where my wife and I had once slept together on a regular basis, where my wife had been sleeping without me since I had moved to Tahoe, and where my wife would, it turns out, continue to sleep upon my return.

Diana and I had been married for twenty-five years and had been together for close to thirty. Some, during the latter years had been hurtful, but during the early years most had been pretty wonderful. We had traveled to exotic and far-off places all over the world, had shared dashing experiences together and, most importantly, had together brought a beautiful daughter into the world.

So the fact that Diana and I slept in the same bed upon my release from the hospital was not itself so strange to me. I was used to the way in which her beautiful blond hair splayed out across her pillow and the feel of her body warmth next to me. What was in fact strange to me—painful really, in a way that pain can still reach a man's heart even when his limbs have no sensation—was the way that Diana would awaken and arise each morning. Like clockwork, she would shower, dress and make herself up for the day, and then leave the house not to be seen again until the evening, nighttime, or even early morning hours—sometimes without as much as saying a word.

I was baffled by Diana's behavior, and I was perplexed, but most of all I was deeply hurt. In my albeit biased opinion, I had been a good husband. Certainly I had my faults and shortcomings, but I had treated her kindly, loved her, supported her, and taken care of her— hadn't I? I did not expect Diana to change her mind and say she wanted to stay married to me, but I could not understand the lack of compassion she evidenced. Over the many weeks I spent recuperating at the Carmichael home, Diana usually did not even extend a simple "how are you?" that one might give to a pained stranger. If ever there was a doubt, it became clear during this period that my marriage was over—for sure.

Of course, I suppose I knew that well before the aneurysm and stroke. I can't deny that the stress of our break-up itself probably contributed to my health crisis. After all, the divorce filing came right after the deaths of my mother and my brother and after confirmation of the affair Diana was having with another man. But when I experienced Diana's absolute withdrawal from me as I lay helpless in our bed—when I watched her scientific ability to detach not just from the man she once loved but from any human being in the condition I was in—I realized for certain that there would be no turning back.

In some bizarre way, Diana's rejection of me made me determined to recover that much more. So many times before in my life, I had to figure out how to make it on my own. If Diana wasn't going to be part of my recovery, then I would simply have to do it myself.

So there I lay in my bed a few mornings after being returned home from the hospital. Diana was out, and I was alone. The house was quiet.

Nothing worked: my right arm, my right leg, my fingers, my feet. Much of my body was paralyzed; the entire body was atrophied, compromised, and sensationless. The loss of muscle mass, tone and definition that I had undergone as a result of being immobilized for over a month shocked me.

But I'd be damned if I was going to lie there, lifeless.

Fuck it, I thought. I'm not going to live like this. One way or the other I've got to get out of bed. Then I must again learn to walk. That will be a beginning.

I didn't have much feeling in my left hand, but I could move it. From the left side of the bed, where I lay, I looked over to the nightstand. It was the same elevation as the bed. And then I did it. I moved my left hand out to the nightstand.

I had once been a person with good muscle tone, but since the aneurysm I had lost most all of that tone. Even if I hadn't been partially paralyzed, my loss of strength from staying in bed all day for weeks on end would have made movement difficult. Nonetheless, I directed all of my energy to pulling and sliding myself to the edge of the bed. Somehow, I managed to succeed in doing so and even to get my left leg partway to the floor so that it was dangling over the edge of the mattress. I started to push on the nightstand with my left hand trying to prop myself up into a sitting position—but I simply couldn't do it.

I'm too weak, I thought, as I fell back on my pillow, exhausted. I laid on my pillow and tried to catch my breath while my left leg still hung off the side of the bed.

I'm just too damn weak.

I tried to push myself up again, only to again fall back.

I'm going to do this today, I thought. I'm going to do it even if it kills me.

I took a different tact, focusing on getting my left leg all the way down to the floor, and I did it! My toes touched the floor. My foot had made contact! Now I needed the rest of my body to follow.

I exerted all of my energy and again solely with my left hand I tried to pull the rest of my body over so that my one lone leg became a whole man standing. It didn't work. My body slid off the bed, with my head nearly whacking the corner of the nightstand. I landed in a pile on the floor.

But it was not defeat—it was victory! I had used my leg and one arm to move. I had gotten one foot on the ground. I had gotten myself off of the bed, no matter the crumpled mass I now lay in.

If I can do this, I thought, I will be able to stand. And that is how I began my journey back.

9

Success as a Prosecutor Marred by Family Addictions

"Power is no blessing in itself, except when it is used to protect the innocent."
— Jonathan Swift

My graduation from Boalt Hall in June 1966 filled me with a new sense of purpose. Next step for law school graduates was the bar exam, a long, tedious test that filled most with trepidation. I took the California bar exam that summer, but because it was almost exclusively essays, it was several months before we got the results. However, in early November 1966 I was notified that I had passed. It was another memorable date. My swearing in ceremony was on December 23, 1966 in San Francisco.

We were now living in Ventura County, having moved there immediately after graduation. I had secured my first job in the legal profession, pending results of the bar exam, as a paid intern in the Ventura County DA's office. There I studied, wrote briefs, did research, and any other legal chore that needed to be done. Our office was the only one of the fifty-eight District Attorney offices in the state that handled its own appeals. The other counties had theirs done by the state's Attorney General so we interns worked on appellate briefs, along with our other responsibilities. At the same time, we were undergoing trial training so that we would be prepared to start prosecuting cases the day after we were sworn in. I was now doing what I had been trained to do, and I knew the experience was invaluable.

My boss and mentor, Woody Deem, was also determined to start the first Consumer Fraud and White Collar crime unit in the state of California. Evidently my dedication was noticed and I was selected by Woody to head up this unit. This was my baptism into legal work above the level of a law clerk. As a result, while awaiting the bar results, I began to develop policies and procedures that would later be replicated by other offices in California, as well as offices elsewhere in the country.

When my internship was finished, I began my actual job as an attorney. My starting salary was approximately $7,000 a year. Obviously, that sounds like a pittance by today's standards, but this was the 1960s. Apartment rents were about $100 per month and gasoline was roughly thirty cents a gallon so this was quite a satisfactory salary for that period of time. My immediate goal was trial experience. I knew that far greater financial rewards would come when I decided to enter private practice.

The DA's staff (attorneys, investigators, and clerical staff) was housed in three cities. The home office was in Ventura, but we also had offices in Oxnard (where most of our investigators were housed), and in Camarillo. In January 1967, one month after being sworn in, I was appointed head of the Camarillo branch of the DA's office. From there, I also began to develop the Consumer Fraud division. In 1968 I transferred to our Oxnard office where I also served as supervisor of our deputy DAs and investigators. Near the end of that year, I became the Major Felony Trial Deputy based in Ventura. I was definitely on a fast track.

Although the branch in Camarillo was the smallest of our offices, it had a very active caseload. It thrust me immediately into the work I had sought. Not only administrative duties, but lots of trials. I was in court every week litigating cases. I wanted litigation experience and I was certainly getting it.

Although things were going well for me professionally, there were some in-law problems that began to develop at or about that time. LuJane, who had bounced from institution to institution, ended up in the Camarillo State Hospital for the Mentally Insane. I would think that such a person would be hard to like, but I truly liked LuJane. She and I had always been close. The hospital where she was confined was only a half hour drive from where we lived in Ventura. I would go out and visit her often, sometimes two to three times a week. Judy, however, never went to see her mother, not even once. I kept prodding her to do so, but to no avail. It broke LuJane's heart, knowing how close to the hospital we lived and that Judy failed to visit her.

Each visit to the state hospital was a sobering experience. Although the hospital grounds were well kept and even beautiful, it was depressing to see the patients walking around heavily medicated and many in an almost zombie-like state. Because I normally wore a suit and tie, everybody I would walk by would call me "Doctor." It was strange at first, but eventually I got used to it.

Finally LuJane was given a trial release from the hospital though with multiple terms and conditions. A few days later while Judy and I were both home reading in the living room, the phone rang. Judy, seated next to the phone, picked it up. I heard her say "Yes, this is Judy Rains." After a brief pause, she said "OK, thank you for calling." She went back to her reading. I asked "Who was that?"

"The San Ysidro California Police Department," she answered.

"The San Ysidro Police department?"

"Yes"

"What about?"

"They found mother today in a motel room near the Mexican border. She had committed suicide," she said as matter-of-factly as if she had said "Mom is coming over for lunch."

I ran over and put my arms around her. But with a stoic expression and a flat voice she said "It's no big deal. It's for the best."

Judy truly had ice in her veins. The experience with her mother's death was very, very strange—and unsettling. There was absolutely no emotion or reaction. She just went back to reading. Later when I tried to discuss it with her, she just said, "I don't want to talk about it."

Before learning of LuJane's problems, I had always thought that Judy's family was the all-American family, but as the old saying goes, "If you look closely enough every family is dysfunctional." Judy's father, John, for years had done everything he could to keep LuJane from being prosecuted for shoplifting and drug abuse and he was extremely embarrassed for the family when her problems were finally exposed. I had become extremely close to both John and LuJane, and I was very saddened by LuJane's death.

This entire episode around LuJane's suicide caused me to focus more closely on certain habits of Judy that I had begun to observe. Although Judy was naturally a wee bit chubby, she was nevertheless quite attractive. I suspected that because obesity ran in her family, Judy began taking pills to deal with her weight. She was an outstanding cook and would often fix really lovely dinners for the children and me, but she herself would eat very little, often just a dollop on her plate. She did in fact start losing weight rather quickly, but she was not anorexic as far as I could tell. Not long thereafter, however, I discovered that she was taking weight control pills—lots of them. I expressed my concerns, but she was very defensive and stated that she was only taking items that were prescription and that she was simply trying to avoid health problems that often resulted from obesity. Rather than start a war, I temporarily allowed this incident to pass though I was extremely concerned.

As for my prosecutorial responsibilities, once I became supervisor of the Oxnard office, I was prosecuting strictly felony cases. One of my other responsibilities was to assign cases to the various deputies and to approve or disapprove of any recommended plea bargain. Cases arose in each and every city in the County, as well in unincorporated areas. The cities included Ventura, Oxnard, Santa Paula, Fillmore, Camarillo, Moorpark, Ojai, Simi Valley, Westlake Village, Thousand Oaks, and Port Hueneme.

I would frequently ride with police officers and sheriff deputies at night to see how they conducted themselves. I saw the good, the bad, and the ugly. Most officers were and are good public servants trying to do a tough job under difficult circumstances. Obviously, there are also some who are not so good.

I worked incredibly long hours. I simply didn't know another lifestyle. Twelve to fourteen hour workdays were not at all unusual. I was by this time getting a lot of media attention and was being invited to speak to numerous civic organizations and service clubs, one of which, Rotary International, I joined and remained a member for seventeen years. The invitations to speak were not by design, it was just happening. A lot of these engagements arose out of the consumer fraud work I was doing. This went on throughout my years with the DA's office. We became deeply involved with investigating pyramid schemes, door-to-door scams, immigration fraud, and the like. We also worked closely with the State Attorney General's office and the Securities and Exchange Commission. We were very active in going after white collar criminals.

About this time, I also began teaching Constitutional Law at the Ventura County Sheriff's Academy. What is unlawful search and seizure? What is "due process?" How can electronic surveillance be done legally? What type of conduct makes evidence inadmissible?

It was very important to me that law enforcement officers be as knowledgeable as possible on such issues.

When it came to trials my practice was to assign cases to my staff of attorneys, reserving for myself certain cases which I wanted to prosecute myself. These included murders, rapes, burglaries, grand theft and so on. They ran the gamut of the California penal code. In three years of continuous trial work, I won all but one jury trial. In all others, convictions were secured. Interestingly enough, I learned more from the one case I lost than from all that I won combined because I replayed the loss in my mind over and over again. That was a lesson never forgotten.

Meanwhile, larger events were taking place in both the world and at home. The Board of Supervisors of Ventura County decided to take a position on the Vietnam War. The five members, all men, were in favor of it and wanted to declare that to be the County's position. I made an appearance before the board and without stating a position on the war – one way or the other – reminded them that it was outrageous and, indeed, ridiculous for a county board to be taking a position—any position—on a matter concerning the foreign policy of our nation. Woody Deem was a strong supporter of the war, and he was very mad when he heard of my appearance. I had enormous respect for the man, but I couldn't see eye to eye with him on this one and I told him so. I said, "If you want my resignation, you've got it." I don't think he was accustomed to anyone speaking to him in that way. He apologized and he never brought the matter up again.

In 1967 we also bought our own home on Linda Vista Street in Ventura. I loved that house. Views are very important to me. We were on a hillside and our picture window offered a panoramic vista of the Pacific Ocean and of the numerous channel islands offshore. These islands are now a national monument, a designation for which I and others successfully fought. Out on the shimmering water, white billowing sails dotted the ocean. Home from a hectic day at the office, I would stretch out in my favorite chair and gaze at the islands and the ocean. I never tire of the many moods of the sea, sometimes calm, other times wind-tossed with white caps and racing clouds. The ocean has always had a tranquilizing effect on me and in many ways I found it then and still find it moving and spiritual.

Our son, Mark, was born on March 30, 1967. Kelly was four at the time. Mark is now a tenured Professor of Hydrology at the University of South Florida in Tampa, and Kelly is an active housewife in San Rafael, California. Mark and his wife, Kai, have two lovely daughters and Kelly and her husband, Colin, have an adventurous and talented son. They are handsome and accomplished families and I am very proud of them although my relationship with Kelly has sometimes been unfortunately strained.

All during this period, my zest for the great outdoors never ceased. Judy's father had a cabin on the White River in the Sierra's. We would take frequent trips to the mountains. There were numerous caves in the region and I have always enjoyed cave exploring or spelunking. So I began to explore each of them. I would often crawl in on my belly in order to go as far as possible. Almost invariably I was alone, so this probably wasn't the most prudent thing to do. However, it has always been part of my lifestyle. Having also developed a love of mountaineering, I climbed Mount Whitney for the first of three times in September of 1963. Mount Whitney is the highest mountain in the lower forty-eight, 14,496 feet high—not a significant elevation by my later standards— but at the time I felt a real sense of accomplishment.

A favorite family activity was always camping. Even when the kids were little, we would take them camping and have a great time. This also has been characteristic of my entire life. When I work, I work hard. When I play, I play hard. No matter how busy I have been, I have always made time for adventure, exploration, and fun, especially outdoors. Nature is and always has been my cathedral.

About this time I began to also coach basketball in the youth league run by the Ventura Recreation Department. The boys I coached were principally nine through twelve year olds. I loved coaching youngsters. I knew basketball well. These kids weren't gifted athletes but that didn't matter. What pleased me most was that I was able to teach them the value of teamwork. Sports can be a gift because the lessons that are learned are invaluable in all aspects of life. In fact, in my opinion, many of life's most important lessons—teamwork, loyalty, drive, working with those of different ethnicities and socio-economic backgrounds, all can be learned through sports.

I had previously gotten to know Johnny Cash who, with his first wife during the mid-60s, was living between Ventura and Ojai. When he and his wife were having problems that eventually led to a divorce, he sought my advice. At that time, I was still a member of the DA's office, so I could not represent him. However, I did refer him to outside counsel.

Johnny was having a lot of problems at the time, not the least of which having to do with heavy drug use. He and his ex-brother-in-law, while camping in the Los

Padres National Forest above Ojai, had accidentally started a forest fire. The Government brought suit against Johnny seeking reimbursement for the expense of containing the fire. Not long thereafter Johnny and his wife divorced and he moved to Hendersonville, Tennessee and later married June Carter Cash.

Johnny was a little bit taller than me, but he was a much bigger boned person. Really larger than life type of guy. I liked him a lot during the short time I knew him, and the way in which he was able to turn his life around was inspiring. To this day, I love the sound of his voice and listen frequently to his recordings.

Because of the proximity of Ventura to Hollywood, I also managed to acquire some other notable Hollywood friends. One of those was Steve McQueen. Like Cash, he was a rugged guy, not too tall and I found that he was in many ways just like his movie persona. Steve was also a pilot and sometimes he kept a mid-30s Pitcairn biplane at the Santa Paula airport in which we would occasionally fly together over to a restaurant on Catalina Island that served Buffalo Burgers—a favorite of Steve's.

In September, 1969, Steve, Bill Dulla, and I were going to fly over to Monache Meadows, a no-abort dirt landing strip on the southwest flank of Mount Whitney. We were planning to fish for golden trout. For some reason, at the last minute, Steve could not go so Bill and I took off alone.

Bill lived in Oxnard and was a very good pilot, even though he wore glasses so thick they looked like bottoms of Coke bottles. Anyway, after landing at Monache Meadows, Bill and I began to hike and fish. After a while we noticed storm clouds, grey and full, racing across the sky. Because I was experienced in the Sierras, I fully understood how quickly storms can develop especially when they are coming from the south. Rushing back to our plane, we were going to attempt to beat the storm. However, we had a hard time getting off the ground and we had to lighten our load by leaving some gear behind.

When we were finally aloft the storm hit us—hard! Pitchfork lightening, the rumble of thunder, strong winds and slashing rain. We searched for a refuge either above or below the weather as we knew it was dangerous. The small Santa Paula airport advised us that we could not land there because of the weather conditions. At Oxnard, to which we had been diverted, they also told us that no landing was possible. The same thing happened at LAX and then at Burbank. Flying at about 15,000 feet and almost out of gas, Bill had a decision to make and he made it. He told the tower at Santa Paula that we were going to have to do a corkscrew landing right down through the storm. He did an incredible job. However we had what at best could be called an out of control landing. My eardrums (as did his) blew out completely because of the rapid, corkscrew descent. I have had problems with hearing ever since, especially in my right ear. If I have a cold or congestion when I fly, it can rupture and bleed. I needed to have rubber tubing surgically implanted in my ear at the time, but Bill and I survived.

As for Steve McQueen, he remained a friend but I did not often see him once I was later elected to public office. I did know that he had contracted cancer. Then one day many years later, I got a sad call from him. He had gone to Mexico for some alternative and quite unconventional treatments that he couldn't get in the United States. He said that he was calling from Juarez, Mexico. He had little hope of surviving much longer and told me so. It was a bittersweet call from a friend that I still often think of, especially when one of his movies is being shown. Steve didn't really have to act. He just had to play himself. He was one of a kind, and I often remember the great times we had together.

———————

As 1969 rolled around, I filed the County's biggest consumer fraud case ever. It involved a man named John Van Geldern and a company called Hydro Ship Building. I wanted to personally prosecute the Van Geldern case as I had spent so much time in working it up, but by this time I was getting a number of attractive offers from law firms in the Ventura County area. When it became clear after awhile that the Van Geldern case wasn't going to go to trial for at least another year, I decided that I would go ahead and take a particularly attractive opportunity to enter private practice. As it turned out, it was two years after I left the DA's office before Van Geldern was ultimately convicted.

10

Private Practice and Public Life

"I find that the harder I work, the more luck I seem to have."
— Thomas Jefferson

At the ripe old age of twenty-seven I finished my days as a prosecutor and went into private practice. I became a Partner in one of the oldest and most prestigious law firms in Ventura County, the firm of Durley & Cearnal which, with my joining, became Durley, Cearnal, & Rains.[2]

The firm had a very interesting history. Originally, it had been Gardner & Durley. Gardner was Erle Stanley Gardner, the author of the Perry Mason books. All of the Perry Mason stories were based on Gardner's actual cases in Ventura County. However, when he began making more money from the sale of his books than from the practice of law, Gardner moved to the Palm Springs/Temecula area and kept writing books the rest of his life. Thereafter, the name of the firm ultimately became Durley & Cearnal and then Durley, Cearnel, & Rains.

One day I walked into a restaurant and a reporter friend of mine, John McCormack, from the Oxnard Press Courier was there. John was sitting with another man named Bill Kehoe. Kehoe was in his mid-sixties, and involved with real estate. He was also an active member of Alcoholics Anonymous though he hadn't had a drink since shortly after his discharge from the army in 1947. During lunch, we had a pleasant talk and Kehoe seemed like a nice person, but I didn't think much more about it at the time.

---

2   One can learn more about my international legal practice and consulting in later chapters and by visiting www.backtothesummit.com and www.senorains.com

However, Kehoe called me a few days later with a minor legal matter, which I took care of for him. Then he brought me another one a few weeks later. I again took care of it. He came to me a third time and said "Omer, most of my investments are overseas. You probably know, at least by name, of my two partners. One is Charlton Heston. The other is Bill Isaacs (at the time Kirk Kerkorian's right hand). Chuck and Bill have estates next to each other on Coldwater Canyon Drive in Beverly Hills. The three of us have rather substantial holdings in Australia and elsewhere in the South Pacific and Asia."

"That's great, so what's the problem?" I asked

"Well, my brother, Jerry, just died of emphysema and I've begun thinking of my own mortality." Bill, like his bother Jerry, smoked like a chimney and he was well aware of the extent to which smoking had detrimental effects on his health.

So Bill, who was over time to become like a father to me, was worried about protecting his wife, Bertie, in the event of his own death. His concerns were not at all with either Heston or Isaacs, but rather with certain parties overseas.

He further told me that a Beverly Hills attorney whose name I believe was Benjamin Held had represented his interests, along with those of Heston and Isaac, for a long time. "I took Held to Australia for six weeks recently so that he would be familiar with all of our holdings. The week after we returned, he dropped over dead from a heart attack. I have come in a short time to like and trust you and to respect your work. I have also discussed you with Chuck (Heston) and Bill. So here's the deal: I want you to come to Australia and the Far East with me. I'm not sure when this will be. It may not be for a year or more. Whenever it is, you will be paid the entire time you're away, so don't worry about your practice."

As a young lawyer, still pretty green behind the ears, I thought I had died and gone to heaven. Although I was now being exposed to all kinds of legal matters including estate planning, probate, tort and negligence cases, and civil litigation, I doubted that I had sufficient all around experience to justify the confidence Bill reposed in me.

Life in the DA's office and life as a partner in a thriving private firm was like moving from the rigidity of the military ranks to the informality of a country club bar. The DA's office is public service and of course that meant it had its rules and its regimentation. Private practice was a lot less hectic and far more lucrative. Having broken out of my narrow, but experience-backed role as a prosecutor, I was by now becoming a well-rounded attorney. So in 1970, soon after Mark Durley passed peacefully away, I decided to open my own firm. This was done with equal measures of dedication, discipline, and most of all just plain old hard work. I was proud of that. Discipline and hard work would now be the key to success with my own law firm. Without the comfort and security of public service or a position in an established firm, I was going to have to rely in large measure on the many good contacts I had made to get my firm up and running. At any rate, ready or not, I wanted to be on my own. The challenge excited me.

I had become involved in a myriad of civic organizations and activities shortly after coming to Ventura. I was especially immersed, as I had been for years, in the environmental movement. I was the Chairman of the Legal Committee of the Los Padres Chapter of the Sierra Club, a founding member of the Environmental Coalition of Ventura County, and of the Citizens to Preserve the Ojai, both of which I had incorporated. Although this was gratifying work, it was all done on a pro bono basis. I have never charged a penny for any work I've done for environmental organizations.

Cases involving environmental preservation were, of course, right up my alley. Some cases particularly stand out. Back in the late 60s and early 70s the environmental movement wasn't a big issue to most people and "green" organizations weren't as strong or as popular as they are today.

In 1971, the Environmental Coalition and the Citizens to Preserve the Ojai (CPO) commenced a major environmental action against US Gypsum, a giant multi-national corporation that wanted to strip mine for phosphates in the Los Padres National Forest. The proposed project was not only going to cause a lot of environmental damage, but it was going to disrupt the only arterial through the national forest between the sea and the Central Valley of California. The damage to the environment was going to include air pollution, harm to several species of birds (including the endangered California Condor), water pollution and wildlife. In short, we were looking at an environmental nightmare.

Gypsum comes out of sedimentary rocks. The mineral is part of the alabaster family and quite toxic. Its primary use is to manufacture plaster and drywall. Eventually, court filings, public protests, and media coverage caused US Gypsum to withdraw its plans. It was a major victory for the environmental movement in the central coast area of California. The case was the impetus for the growth of the Environmental Coalition of Ventura County. In addition, as a result of the knowledge I acquired during that case, I was later to author legislation preventing strip mining in all of California's forests and public land.

Another case, which was actually to become historic, involved the Ventura River. On the west side of the river's mouth is a wooded area called Hobo Jungle. It probably got its name during the depression years when hobos reputedly used to camp there because they could do so without being seen. It is a pretty area, but of greater importance it was a major migratory stop off point for the Monarch butterflies that nested and rested there during their migratory patterns south in the winter and back north in the spring.

Above the river mouth, from Hobo Jungle inland, fish were dying by the thousands. It was suspected that the problem stemmed from a Shell Chemical plant that discharged its toxic effluent directly into the Ventura River. Aided mightily by scientists from the University of California at Santa Barbara (UCSB) and the Environmental Council of Santa Barbara, and after considerable research on my own, I concluded that Shell's actions were in violation of the Rivers and Harbors Act of 1899.

I took the case and spent weeks on end working it up. I then confronted Shell's attorneys whose response was that the law did not apply because the waterways were not "navigable." Their position, and mine as well, was based on the definition of a "navigable waterway." Shell Chemical basically argued that large vessels would have to be involved for the Rivers and Harbors Act to be applicable. My position, which I felt to be well founded, was that if Shell Chemical violated the 1899 act it would be applicable to any waterway, even a shallow one that would not support vessels of any great size.

I took my case, completely worked up, to the United States Department of Justice in Los Angeles. While the attorneys with whom I met appreciated the work effort involved in bringing the case to their attention, they refused to prosecute the case even though they said they agreed with my legal theories. The reason for their position was that even if they won the case it would only result in a $5,000 per incident fine (which is all the 1899 statute called for). To them it was small potatoes and they felt they had more important fish to fry.

Needless to say, I was seriously disappointed but under the circumstance determined to try yet another approach. I decided to file a "Qui Tam" action. A "Qui Tam" action is one whereby if the government refuses to prosecute a matter, then in certain cases and with permission of the court, a private citizen can file suit on behalf of the United States. With this theory in mind I brought suit in the U.S. District Court for the Central District of California in Los Angeles. I pursued the case to a successful conclusion. The win meant that Shell would have to cease and desist polluting the Ventura River and pay a $10,000 fine ($5,000 each for two separate violations that were established). Now

$10,000 is of course peanuts to a huge multinational, but the adverse publicity was widespread and a real black eye for Shell. As a result, Shell decided to close the plant.

This wasn't the only, or even the most, beneficial outcome of the case. We had set a precedent. The Rivers and Harbor Act of 1899 was thereafter able to be used by other environmentalists to get rid of industrial polluters in different parts of the country.

Ironically, the $10,000 which was awarded to me for bringing the action caused friction on the home front. I was determined to split the money—$5,000 to the Environmental Coalition of Ventura County and $5,000 to the Environmental Council of Santa Barbara, the latter of which had enlisted for me the aid of a few scientists at the University of California without whose help I probably could not have successfully prosecuted the case. Judy was adamant that we keep the money for the services I had rendered. She had resented the time I spent working on the case and felt strongly that I was already doing more than my share for the environment. In my opinion, given the fact that I was providing well by this time for my family, her position was one of needless greed so I proceeded to donate the money as originally intended. To my surprise, she wouldn't let the matter drop and brought it up repeatedly for several months.

In any event, cases like this helped break new ground for the environmental movement in this country and I was proud to be in the front lines of that battle.

———————

At the same time, I was becoming increasingly involved in city and regional affairs. I became a member of the Board of Directors of the Greater Ventura Chamber of Commerce and, shortly thereafter, Chairman of the Visitors and Convention Bureau and of several other Chamber committees. Eventually I was to become Vice President of the Chamber. I was also serving as the Ventura County Law Day Chairman, as a coach in the Youth Basketball League, as a sponsor of the Boy Scouts of America, as a member of the Ventura Trade Club and as a patron of the Ventura Concert Series and the Ventura County Master Chorale. I was also one of the original incorporators and directors of "VIA," an umbrella organization designed to assist the Ventura Youth Employment Service, the Ventura Free Clinic, the Ventura Hotline, Horizon of Ventura and the Catacombs Association. In 1971, at the age of twenty-nine, I was the recipient of Ventura's "Distinguished Service Award" presented to its most outstanding citizen.

About this time I was also appointed to the Ventura Planning Commission. Since I was initially the token environmentalist, the votes at first were almost always six to one. When another environmentally conscious member (later the mayor of Ventura, Harriet Kosmo Henson) became a member of the Commission, the votes started going five to two on controversial subjects. Then with the help of a truly fine city management team headed by the City Manager, Ed McCombs, and a quite capable planning director, Roger Barry, one of the longtime members of the commission began to take an interest in sound land use planning. Thus the votes on controversial issues generally were four to three and the "hell with the environment" crowd became nervous. Then after a while the votes began going four to three the other way and I soon found myself serving as Chairman of the Planning Commission, a position I was to hold continuously until I was elected to the California Senate.

Ventura is an old and very historic city, but by the 1970s its downtown area was becoming very run down. However, we were able to turn that around with remarkable rapidity. The truly beautiful Ventura County Courthouse, one of the most historic buildings in Ventura County, was about to be demolished because the County had built a sparkling new courthouse quite some distance from the downtown area. Several of us engaged in an effort to save that building. The first step was to get the building declared a national historic monument. That was accomplished. Then the city of Ventura bought the courthouse from the County for $1 and began a renovation project taking special care that it was earthquake proof. The building was to become the truly beautiful Ventura City Hall.

Next came plans for construction of an archeological museum near Mission San Buenaventura, the Mission being the single most historic building in the County. The museum today follows the development of the area and the contribution and influence of the Chinese and the Native American communities in what is now the thriving downtown area. We developed a Ventura County Museum, and established a lookout point with sensational views above the downtown in an area called Grant Park. We did planning for the Ventura Harbor Village and established "green belts" around the city to preserve its integrity and character and so it would not become part of yet another southern Californian megalopolis.

Some of us were determined that Ventura would have a heart instead of being like Los Angeles, which is actually over one hundred cities tied together. Ventura has a lot of green farmland around it —and we wanted to keep it that way. This was not only to serve as an actual barrier, but the farm land, the product of river alluvium left over thousands of years comprises some of the best and deepest agricultural top soil in the nation. We were assisted in this endeavor by state legislation which allowed agricultural interests to have certain tax advantages if they agreed to keep their land in agriculture a certain period of time rather than sell out to real estate developers.

Eventually the city established a Comprehensive Plan Advisory Committee (CPAC). The city asked me to serve as Chairman. CPAC was formed to generate an updated and comprehensive city plan that would not only lead to the renovation of any and all rundown areas, but also recognize the historic significance of Ventura. Due in large major to the efforts of CPAC and the many fine people who served on that body, Ventura today is a thriving community and the downtown area has multiple indoor and outdoor restaurants and one of the more healthy business environments in the United States.

Make no mistake about it, I loved Ventura then and, though I have not lived there for a long time, I love it today. It has everything, starting with a year-round temperature of 70 to 80 degrees. From a fitness standpoint there isn't much that can't be done in and around Ventura: biking, hiking, running, skateboarding, bodysurfing, sail surfing, boating, fishing, paragliding, beach volleyball and football, swimming, snorkeling offshore around the Channel Islands, rollerblading, and just plain old beach bumming. There are very few places like it in America.

So by the 1970s, I seemed to have it all. I was living where I wanted to live, my business was thriving, and notwithstanding increasing concerns about my wife, I had what I thought to be a good family life with two beautiful children.

In addition, my passion for the great outdoors still burned bright and I would often go hiking as well as hunting, fishing, and camping whenever I could. One of the hunting trips became especially memorable. My father-in-law, John Reaves, had introduced me to a professional guide and mountain-man who lived up in Wyoming. His name was Snooke Moore. In October 1970, two attorney friends of mine and I drove to Wyoming and met up with Snooke and his brother-in-law. We were heading for the mountain country of Wyoming and the Wind River Range of the Rockies. We had permits to hunt both elk and bear.

As it was late October when we started out on horseback, snow had already blanketed the mountains. Travelling by horse quite fast, by the end of the second day we were able to establish our base camp. It had gotten colder and colder the higher we climbed. The first thing that Snooke had us do was cut down a tree to use the log as a sit-down field lavatory. It was a good idea except Snooke failed to remind us that given the weather conditions it was imperative we clear off any residue of black ice before sitting down on the log. Like a little kid sticking his tongue on a railroad track and getting it stuck, I got my butt stuck on the log. It cost me some skin to finally get up. The others had a hoot over that.

With each passing day, and the weather becoming increasingly severe, we were not having success looking for the elusive elk or bear. Near the end of the trip, Snooke set up a plan whereas two men (Snooke and I) would flush the game through a heavily forested area towards the others. Snooke and I dismounted leaving all of our gear, including heavy clothing, on the horses as we didn't expect to be apart from the others for more than an hour or so.

We were huffing and puffing uphill as the snow was quite deep and it was difficult to walk. Snooke and I were probably 100 yards apart when near a ridge I spotted a bull elk up on top. He was a magnificent specimen. I began to unsling my rifle from my shoulder when suddenly his mate, a smaller cow elk appeared and stood beside him, both looking down at me. The bull's female mate also was a sight to behold. By this time I had the bull right between my crosshairs. Snooke, seeing what had developed, started yelling "Shoot. Shoot!"

I was preparing to do just that when a young calf appeared and joined his mother and his father. The family of three stood gazing, their big dark eyes, innocent and unwary. It touched something deep inside me. I was close enough for a sure shot. The bull was right in my crosshairs. Snooke yelled again "Shoot!" But something about this family group would not let me fire. It was something in me. Something mystical, maybe spiritual, that told me I could not do this. I lowered the rifle and have never hunted since that time.

Snooke was upset that I had not taken the shot but there wasn't anything he could do about it. But he and I continued walking in the soft powdery snow which was very difficult. We were sinking down almost to our hips. Snooke was having an even harder time than me because whereas I was six feet tall, he was only five foot six inches at most, and walked with a significant limp (he had lost a battle with a bear many years before). But the worst part is that when we arrived at the point where we were to meet up with the rest of our party they were not there. Snooke was puzzled. He said, "That's funny. They should have been right over that rise."

We climbed to an open area slightly above the forested region from which we had emerged. I have a saying that I commonly use: "There is no such thing as bad weather—just inappropriate clothing." Well to be sure, Snooke and I were inappropriately clothed as we had expected to be separated from the others no more than an hour. By this time dusk was upon us and darkness was closing fast. We definitely were not properly clothed and a storm was about to hit. Several times we fired three shot signals as we had agreed upon, but we heard no answer. The others were clearly not where they were supposed to be. I didn't panic because I knew that Snooke was one of the best outdoorsmen around. He said, "We had better get a fire going."

We were in trouble. It was incredibly cold and the temperature was dropping fast. When we went back to the forested area to fetch firewood, we discovered that everything was soaking wet. With infinite patience, Snooke began to shave tiny slivers from the trees. I followed his lead and did the best I could to help. Eventually we had some dry slivers with which we were able to start a small and very smoky fire. When we got it going we were able to feed it, the damp wood succumbing to the flames, but we had not expected to be out overnight. We simply did not have proper clothing or gear for camping out in what was now a truly vicious, stormy alpine evening. Soon it was brutally cold, with a biting and fierce wind that ravaged any exposed skin and really hurt. If we ventured more than a couple of feet from the fire it was unbearable. Later we were to learn that where we were was the coldest spot in the nation that night.

We continued periodically to fire off three shot signals. We knew we couldn't possibly hike out. It was over fifty miles of rough icy terrain to the nearest town and almost half that distance to our base camp. By the middle of the moonless night a prophetic fear gripped my heart like a bear trap. I was beginning to worry, even though I had clung to the hope that Snooke would get us through this. When Snooke, the experienced mountain man said to me, "We're gonna die tonight," it was me, the tenderfoot, who had to calmly say, "No, we're not."

Nevertheless, I knew that I was feeling the onset of hypothermia and that my core temperature was dropping fast so my words were as much bravado as anything else. Around 3:00 a.m. I said to Snooke, "I have three bullets left. Should I fire them?"

He shrugged. "May as well." His attitude was kind of, we're dead anyway.

I fired off the last three rounds from my 30.6 and lo and behold we got back three answering shots. They sounded as though they came from an area not that far away. As it turned out, our colleagues, at long last, had spotted our fire and were starting toward us.

At about 4:30 a.m., the rest of our party arrived and with them, our horses. The vicious wind had been preventing the sounds of our shots from being carried toward them.

By this time, Snooke and I were not in shape to do much of anything, let alone to get down that mountain. But we had no choice: "Do it or die." There was no moonlight that night and once we moved a few feet away from the fire we couldn't see much of anything. Nevertheless, we had to get back down that slippery, icy trail on horseback. Thank goodness the horses were trail savvy and picked their way downhill without tripping. Something like that would have been fatal because we were coming down narrow icy trails skirting some drops that were over 1,000 feet to the valley floor below. However, Snooke did have a mishap. His horse bolted at one point and ran him face first into a low-hanging branch and broke several bones in his face. It was the type of wound that we could do nothing about until we got back to civilization.

It was a frozen, tired group of hunters who struggled into Snooke's place a full day later. I permanently lost a toenail and feeling in that toe to frostbite on that trip. Other toes and some fingers were also frostbite damaged. And I was lucky that more serious and permanent frostbite did not occur. By this time, I considered myself already an experienced outdoorsman. But that trip certainly did cause me to develop a more healthy respect for Mother Nature as well as a profound sensitivity about life and death, including that of animals.

Elvis

That same year, 1970, Bill Kehoe, Chuck Heston, and I along with our respective wives were invited by Bill Isaac to attend Elvis Presley's debut of the grand opening of the new International Hotel in Las Vegas. Bill, as stated earlier, was Lynn ("Kirk") Kerkorian's right-hand man and was the manager of the International. At the time it opened, it was the largest hotel in the world. Today it is the Las Vegas Hilton.

While I wasn't particularly a fan of Elvis, along with the others, Judy and I eagerly accepted. We had a private front row booth in the theater which can only be described as panoramic. We later learned that Elvis was worried that he wouldn't be able to carry the room as the place was so big.

Elvis performed and it was easy during that performance to see why he was the superstar that he was. He was onstage for almost two hours and by the time he was done he was covered in sweat. As usual, women were screaming and throwing personal items at him, and in his usual fashion he was wiping off the sweat and throwing the towels and the handkerchiefs back to the adoring fans, kissing women and doing the whole, now familiar, repertoire. Elvis put on a terrific show.

As the show ended, a distinguished looking man with an odd white moustache and goatee motioned to us. It was Elvis' manager, Colonel Parker, along with his own entourage. He said, "Would you folks like to meet Elvis?"

Kehoe, an avid fan, said "Oh my God! Of course."

Parker escorted us back to Elvis' dressing room through massive security. We figured that Presley would be absolutely exhausted after such a show but when he answered the door himself, he was in a robe, fresh as a spring morning after having taken what must have been the world's fastest shower.

He invited us into his dressing room, was very gracious to us and was the absolute epitome of a Southern gentleman. Whatever stereotype I had in mind of such a superstar was dashed at that time by his generous and sincere behavior.

Australia

By 1972, my relationship with Bill Kehoe had evolved from that of attorney/client into something akin to father and son, and I had also become close friends with Charlton Heston and Bill Isaac. In August, 1972, I traveled to Australia to meet up with Bill and others who had preceded me to learn firsthand about the group's real estate and other holdings and investments "Down Under." This was the trip that Bill had discussed with me a few years earlier when he and his colleagues first retained my services. Although I initially arrived in Sydney, I continued on to Brisbane, the capital of Queensland, where Bill was awaiting my arrival. The day after I arrived, the Lord Mayor of Brisbane threw a party for us. As could be expected for a party held by the Lord Mayor, a lot of prominent people were present at his truly beautiful home. The party was lively and the two hired bartenders were very busy throughout the evening.

I approached one of the bartenders and asked him if he knew how to make a Lucas Valley Sling, which I had renamed the "Wong-Wong Whoopie," after a stockbroker friend of mine, Kenneth Wong. He looked blankly at me. "What's in it?"

I said, "If you'll let me behind the bar, I'll show you. I need to see if you have all the ingredients." He grinned and motioned for me to come on ahead.

He had everything that was needed and I showed him how to make the drink. The drink was the hit of the party and we had to send out for more and more ingredients.

The next day I mentioned that I wanted to visit the Gold Coast of Australia. One of Bill's local associates, Dick Guetzow, said that he would take me there. When we arrived, it was a beautiful beach and eventually we gravitated to a small pub with bar seats, but no tables. Dick and I sat down on the last two stools at the bar. We ordered a couple of beers and as we sipped them, I heard the door behind me open and close. The man who had entered walked toward the bar but, with no seats available, stood between Dick and me when he asked the bartender: "Say old chap, do you know how to make these Wong-Wong Whoopies? I understand there was a party at the Lord Mayor's house in Brisbane last night and everyone there is talking about them today."

Not knowing if this was a put-on or if he was serious, I swiveled on my stool to look up at him and said, "Are you being serious?" He said, "Sure. Why?" I said, "Well, I'm the person who actually started serving the Wong-Wong Whoopies last night in Brisbane." About this time the bartender said, "Well, what in the world is it?"

Just as I did the night before at the Lord Mayor's house, I said, "I'd be happy to show you if I could come over behind the bar."

"Absolutely. Come on back here."

So here I was again behind the bar mixing drinks, all of which were on the house. Once again they were a hit.

Fast forward ten years when I returned next to the area. Things, of course, were quite different on the Gold Coast as it had truly been discovered, but the pub, greatly enlarged, was still there and was now displaying a neon sign that read "Home of the World Famous Wong-Wong Whoopie."

Entering the door, the owner recognized me and greeted me with a warm smile and a handshake. He said, "You made me a rich man."

"Do I get a cut of the profits?" I asked mirthfully.

"No. But the drinks are again on the house."

Typhoon

Over the years, I had heard and read a lot about the Great Barrier Reef of Australia. It is a natural phenomenon that is off the north-east coast of Queensland. Comprised of 900 coral islands and 2,900 reefs, it's about 2,600 feet wide and runs down the coast for over 1,600 miles, forming the greatest natural barrier reef and breakwater in the world.

Bill Kehoe and I and some others, all older and prominent Australian business leaders, decided to take a boat trip from Cairns north of Brisbane, inside The Great Barrier Reef, then west through the Torres Strait to Darwin in the Northern Territory. After leaving Darwin, we went around Turkey Island and up to Port Moresby, New Guinea.

Our vessel was a converted World War II American PT boat. The skipper, Gordon Oke, was as the Australians say, "a great bloke." He worked the boat with a couple of young deckhands.

We were having a fine time fishing and sightseeing… with no knowledge of a major typhoon brewing in the Pacific. We had no satellite communications back then and we were unaware of the developing typhoon. We were on our way back to Cairns on the outside of the Great Barrier Reef when the Category 5 typhoon hit with a force that none of us had ever seen—including Gordon. I had to help Gordon and his hands secure the older men to their bunks as the vessel was tossed about violently. One of the men was hit by a runaway refrigerator which had crushed his chest.

At the height of the storm's fury, with winds howling at close to 150 miles per hour, we were in serious danger of capsizing. The skipper had to fight the helm to keep the bow heading into the waves to avoid broaching broadside. If this happened we would definitely capsize. We would climb a mountainous wave, slide down the other side and the bow would dig into the base of the next wave as we started to climb again. Gordon was making for the historic but tiny inlet of Cooktown on the northern Queensland coast. Meanwhile the Australian Air Force was out looking for us, although we didn't know it at the time.

We finally limped into Cooktown, north of Cairns. There the injured, including Bill Kehoe, were helicoptered out to the hospital in Townsville. But I wanted to continue the adventure, even if alone, so I rented a car and headed to Brisbane about three days drive to the south. I was as fascinated as a school kid by the unusual flora, fauna and wildlife of Queensland. This area like most of Australia is dry and the rivers are seasonal. However, there is one area, known as the Atherton Tablelands that is truly unique—not just in this area, but in all of Australia.

At times the Atherton Tablelands appear mystical with twisted, oddly shaped eucalyptus trees, along with dry acacia bushes which fill the grasslands often peeking out of a shroud of whiteness. There were literally thousands of kangaroos and wallabies. As a tourist I thought they were wonderful, but I did realize that the Australians look upon them as a nuisance, much like our farmers regard gophers and rabbits. Once in the Tablelands, I also spotted lots of dingoes, a type of wild dog found only in Australia. They are mangy looking creatures as they skulk about the bush looking at you out of the sides of their eyes.

Leaving the Tablelands, I also saw a lot of emus, which look much like ostriches. They bound along areas that are relatively flat, looking awkward and graceful at the same time.

In any event, when I finally got to Bill and Bertie's house in Brisbane, Bill was out of the hospital so this was good. When I left Australia, I continued on to Singapore, Kuala Lumpur, Bangkok, and Hong Kong before returning to the States. Those were all pre-planned stops except for Kuala Lumpur which occurred by happenchance.

Cobra Dancing

On my flight leaving Sydney for Singapore I met a young Malaysian couple, Steven and Sweet Leong. They had just graduated from college in Australia and were on their way home to Kuala Lumpur (KL). Although I am usually engrossed in a book when I fly, I began chatting with Steven and Sweet and we really hit it off. They asked me to visit them in Kuala Lumpur after I finished my business for the Kehoe-Heston group in Singapore. I said that I would consider it and provided them with the phone number of the historic Raffles Hotel at which I had reservations in Singapore. The next day I received a call at the hotel from the Leong's again asking me to visit and telling me that Steven's parents, with whom they lived in Kuala Lumpur (KL), would also like to meet me.

So I decided to go. Steven and Sweet met me at the KL airport and took me to the parent's home. It was quite large and comfortable. We spent a day touring KL and its immediate environs. The second evening Steve said that he had a surprise in store for me. He wondered if I would like to see some cobra dancing and listen to a snake oil salesman well outside of town in a wilderness area. He didn't use the term "snake oil salesman" in the slang way we use it. He meant it literally. I said, "Sure, let's go."

Arriving at the site, we found ourselves in the midst of a large group of men. They were intently listening to a man who was holding a cobra snake in his hands and standing in the midst of over twenty large baskets. I suspected, correctly as it turned out, that snakes were inside each basket.

Although I couldn't understand what the man was saying, Steve was translating for me. The man was trying to sell snake oil, venom, and pellets made of some sort of snake ingredients that he claimed to be unique in the world.

As he spoke he kept looking at me. I initially assumed that was simply because I was not only taller than most around me, but I was the only white face in the crowd. He kept talking about the power of the pellets, how they provided incredible courage, stamina, and dexterity to anyone who ingested them.

The "Preacher" as I began to refer to him, motioned for me to come forward to show the others that they need not be afraid of the snakes. Steve said it would be OK and by this time I had gotten to know Steve sufficiently well to know that he was a level-headed guy. So I went up to the Preacher and with water that he gave me I swallowed two of the pellets, each about the size of a gumball.

The Preacher then took the lids off all of the baskets and began to play a flute-type instrument. I was starting to become disoriented and began to see visions of snakes slithering out of baskets and raising their heads. Whatever the ingredients in the pellets, clearly they were having a hallucinogenic effect on me. Soon it appeared that the snakes were all around me. They were. I heard the men who were gathered around gasp as they moved further—much further—away. I began to step between the snakes, doing so to the sound of the music. I don't know how long this went on, but I do remember everything as being very rhythmic as the cobras raised and lowered themselves and as I "danced" among them.

I had never hallucinated before as I had never done drugs. Steve drove us home afterwards, but I don't remember much of anything else after we left until the following morning when I awakened after a long sleep. It was then that Steve told me of the events of the preceding night including the fact that the "Preacher" had sold all of his products to those present after they witnessed me "bravely" dance with the snakes.

Birthing

There was one more thing I wanted to do in KL. That was to visit the famous Batu Caves. The series of caves, which constitute one of the most popular Hindu shrines in the world, lie about fifteen miles outside of KL.

My last day in KL, Steve had a job interview. I asked him to drop me off on his way to the interview on the road to Batu. Backpack full of water and basic food, I began to hitchhike toward the caves. Soon I was picked up by a truck driver on the outskirts of town. Although the driver didn't speak English, he understood where I wanted to go and he took me about three-fourths of the way there before he turned off toward his own destination. I thanked him and began to hike in the direction he pointed.

About a mile further on I noticed a woman on the other side of the road going in the same direction as me. She had on a traditionally long dress and was carrying crops on top of her head. I noticed that she was stumbling and moving very slowly. She was also moaning and although I was slightly behind her, it was apparent that she was in pain.

All of a sudden she cried out, dropped the basket from her head and squatted beside the road. Wanting to help, I started to move quickly toward her. Suddenly several women who had been working in the fields began to gather around the squatting woman. They brusquely shooed me away. Then I realized why. The squatting woman was giving birth to a baby.

I was fascinated, and respectfully kept to myself a substantial distance away on the other side of the road. The woman's anguished cries went on for perhaps another fifteen minutes or so. More women had arrived, tightly closing the circle around the woman. Then I heard the wailing of a baby. The birth had been successful.

As I saw some of the women wiping the baby off, I continued on my way to the shrine. But I couldn't get out of my mind the suffering of the woman who had given birth to her baby without medical help in the most primitive of conditions while tending to her chores in the field.

When I later related this story to others, they were not at all surprised and did not find the story to be very unusual. It was a fairly common incident in that part of the world some forty years ago.

As the years went by and as I travelled elsewhere in Asia, Africa, and certain parts of Latin America, I was to learn time and time again the ordeals through which people in much of the world go as they lead their daily lives.

But this had been an introduction to the world as it exists in many of those places still today and as it existed in much of our own country before the 1900s—not all that long ago.

11

Divorce and Its Aftermath

"Love, the quest; marriage, the conquest; divorce, the inquest."
— Helen Rowland

During my travels to the South Pacific and Asia, the law office had run smoothly and the domestic clients had received competent professional assistance from other attorneys I had hired. True to the arrangement, Kehoe, Heston, and Isaac handsomely compensated me for the time I was gone. I felt guilty accepting their check because I really had not done all that much by way of actual legal work during my time abroad. However, they were happy with my services and performance and were insistent that I accept the full amount that had been agreed upon in advance.

So here I was, still a relatively young attorney, representing great clients, making a difference, and earning more money than I had ever dreamed of. We had two beautiful children and a nice home that was virtually paid for in full. The future couldn't have looked much brighter.

Being cash-heavy literally for the first time in my life, the first thing I did was pay down what remained of the mortgage so it was all but eliminated. Then Judy, who was not usually a spendthrift, began asking for all sorts of things—a new car, new appliances, new furniture, carpeting measured, made and cut specifically for the living room of our home, and a number of other items. For the most part, these were simply to replace rather nice things we had purchased just a few years before. Strange, but I didn't dwell on it.

Judy was also undergoing troublesome personal changes, seemingly more serious than before. She went on a very strict diet and hardly ate anything at all. She did start losing weight, a life-long concern of hers given her family history and her own propensity to gain weight. At first I just attributed this loss to her dieting. However, I then started coming across amphetamines and other pills. I was alarmed and confronted her. She was angry and demanded to have them back. Instead, I flushed them down the toilet. She was enraged. Because of her mother's addictive history, I was deeply concerned. However, when I tried to discuss it with Judy, she just withdrew and became angry.

Not long after I returned from Australia, Judy informed me that she intended to have a tubal ligation. I was baffled and hurt. We had always discussed having four children and I didn't understand why she wanted to take this action. When she told me that she had already scheduled the procedure, I asked her for what date. The date she gave me was one on which I was to give a speech in LA. I told her I would cancel the speech in order to be with her, even though it would be on very short notice. She was adamant that I not do so, saying that it was a female thing, and medically a minor matter in any event. She had also said that she had specifically scheduled the procedure for when I would be out of town because she didn't want me worrying about it. As it turns out there was a lot more involved than she told me, but I didn't know it at the time.

One afternoon as I returned from work, I stretched out for my customary end of day meltdown, martini and relaxation before dinner in my favorite chair looking out at the marvelous view of the Channel Islands. There, lying on the arm of the chair was an envelope addressed to me from a Beverley Hills attorney. Opening the letter, I learned that my wife of over ten years wanted a divorce. I was shocked! Stunned! Why? Divorce was absolutely alien to me and to the culture in which I was raised. At that time, no one in my family had ever been divorced. Yet when I stopped and thought about it I realized that Judy and I did have serious differences. Evidently, I didn't realize just how deep they were.

When I did gather my wits, I suggested counseling. Reluctantly Judy agreed to go one time. During that visit the counselor asked her, "What is it about Omer that you don't like?" She actually said, "I have no complaints." That of course was obviously not true, but her mind was clearly made up. The die was cast. She wanted out of our marriage.

Not long afterwards, I learned of an affair that Judy had during the time I was overseas. The affair was with a married man, a rather charismatic minister whom we had both met during the US Gypsum matters. I was later to see a letter Judy wrote to the man, a letter that was full of threats to him and saying, among other things, that "I demand that you make me happy, or else." But her lover not only rejected her overtures, he was forced to make drastic changes in his life, leaving his ministry and was forced to move from the community of Ojai in an attempt to save his marriage.

Although Judy and I in retrospect weren't really well suited for each other, like my mother before me, I know that I would have remained in the marriage until I died. Probably out of inertia, habit and commitment. It was simply the way I had been raised.

Years later, and well after Judy and I were divorced, by happenchance I ran into a nurse formerly with the doctor Judy had visited ostensibly for her tubal ligation. As it turned out, the visit was for another procedure; one I would never have endorsed. As she explained to me the real reason for Judy's visit, I was stunned. "What are you talking about? She just went in for a tubal ligation?"

"A tubal ligation was performed, but it was secondary to the procedure. Surely you knew."

"Oh my God. I not only didn't know, but I would have done anything to prevent it. I'm in a state of shock."

───────────

When our divorce decree was published in the local newspaper, the Ventura County Star-Free Press, I got the generational shock of my life. The day the newspaper came out referencing our divorce, I received three phone calls from different women asking me for a date. In my time things like that were not done. But I did begin to date—a lot.

One that seemingly bothered Judy a great deal involved a woman we both had met on an earlier rafting trip down the Colorado River through the Grand Canyon. This lady was a travel editor for a famous New York based national magazine and, when we met her, she was writing a story about the rafting trip. How she heard about my divorce I'm not sure, but she got in touch with me and we started a bi-coastal romance. She was a New Yorker of Hungarian heritage, chic, attractive, and urbane.

Though I had been to New York, I certainly didn't know the city like she did. She showed me New York as only a native New Yorker can. Together we explored every nook and cranny of the city, tasting the food in every enclave of the city: Veal parmigiana in

Little Italy, Moo Goo Gai Pan in Chinatown, Goulash in Hungarian restaurants, soul food in Harlem, as well as draft beer in the most Irish of pubs outside of Dublin.

This lady was an exciting and adventurous person who did things rather instinctively. A few years after we began dating and when I was a delegate to a Democratic Convention in Kansas City, she called me. She said that she was going on assignment to the Bahamas, Haiti and to various countries in Central America. "Why don't you come with me?" she said. "It will be fun."

"But I don't have my passport with me. It's home in California."

This was pre-9/11, so things weren't as strict as they are now. I went to the convention secretary and had her type a letter, which I dictated, advising that I was a member of the California Senate and I was authorized to travel without my passport. The letter was authenticated by March Fong Eu, the California Secretary of State, who was also a delegate to the convention. Country after country allowed my entry with nothing other than that letter and my Senate identification. We had a wonderful trip travelling in the Caribbean and Central America with no passport and yet had no trouble at all. Things were certainly different back in those days.

During this period I also dated the reigning Miss California. We had to sneak around like a couple of adulterers because she was being constantly chaperoned. Off and on, I also dated two rather well known actresses in Hollywood. In retrospect, I realize that all of this dating, in large measure, was a healthy ego booster in the aftermath of my divorce when no doubt my self-esteem felt rather battered.

Now, although I had attended college at Berkeley, a mecca of illegal drug activity and usage, I never once had done drugs up to this point in my life. That remains true to this very day, except that during this period I did try an occasional marijuana cigarette. But after trying marijuana I thought, "What's the big deal about this?" It didn't seem to do anything to me or for me.

But another experience showed me differently. One of the ladies I briefly dated made me a batch of marijuana-laced cookies. Since they were in cookie form and I didn't like cooking, I ate them for lunch—the entire plate at one sitting! The next thing I knew I was sitting in my idling car in the middle of the street in front of her house. How I drove there I don't recall. As a responsible citizen I realized I could have endangered people driving in that condition. Thank God no one was hurt, and I had not hit anything.

The only regret I had with all the women I dated during this period of my life involved the travel editor from New York. When years later I met Diana, the woman who was to be my second wife, I broke up with the New York lady without telling her the reason. As it was, there was no future for us. Either I would have to give up my career or she would have to give up hers. I guess life made the decision for us. But I still felt bad for not being 100% honest and upfront with her.

From a professional standpoint, my firm continued to grow and prosper. Clients of mine wanted to develop the Ventura Harbor at the Ventura Port District. The idea was to mirror Portofino, Italy, which is one of the most picturesque ports in the world.

The whole thing was controversial because although the beautiful port of Ventura had lots of potential, it had been mismanaged for years. And although the taxes kept going up, nothing notable had been developed. For this reason the management of the Port District was always under fire, and the United States Corp of Engineers was constantly having to dredge the harbor. Members of the Harbor Commission were suspected of behind the scenes wheeling and dealing, some involving major corporate interests. When we made our presentation, we did not, in my opinion, have a fair hearing. My views resonated with the public and the publicity for the presentation we made was quite favorable. The public outcry in and around the Ventura community at that time was significant and quite vocal in support of our proposal.

Subsequently, I was shocked to receive an invitation to interview to be General Counsel for the Port District. This was a strange development because I was their worst public enemy. At least that's how I thought they had perceived me. I had caused them a lot of embarrassment. The only rationale I could figure was that if they retained me, it would mollify some in the community who did trust my position. It was kind of like if you hire the enemy they can't hurt you anymore.

The bottom line is that I was, in fact, retained but at the time I insisted that I would accept the position only if there were no longer "secret meetings," and only topics allowed under the state's "Sunshine Laws" would be considered. Sunshine Laws basically require that all public business be done in open and public meetings. The members of the commission agreed to follow my advice and counsel to the letter of the law—and they did.

Within two years, the port was flourishing. It was well on the way to becoming a large marina which featured slips, full marina service, all kinds of restaurants, boutiques, and other amenities. Many Hollywood celebrities came to use the marina, which of course drew even more business. I myself even bought a sailboat in 1973 but could only use it for about a year as whatever leisure time I had was increasingly taken up. I also began to lobby to have the Channel Islands National Park office located at the Port, an effort that was eventually to be successful.

Although the Port District was but one of many clients, representing the District took up about 20% of my time, which was a lot. However, I was being properly compensated for the time spent there and my law firm continued to grow.

A critical juncture of my life happened in late 1973 between Christmas and New Year's. I had lunch with a friend of mine, Republican Congressman Charles Teague. Teague was a very popular Congressman, not for any of his accomplishments because he really didn't have any, but because this man made the supreme effort of flying home to his district all the way across country every single weekend. Talk about long distance commuting. People marveled at it as Teague had done this for over twenty years.

A few days after that fateful lunch, Congressman Teague died. Little did I know that his passing would change my life forever.

12

Pain and Hurt

When *I was finally allowed to leave the hospital, I was taken by ambulance to my home in Carmichael. On a stretcher, the paramedics had carried me upstairs and placed me in my bed on the second floor.*

Friends and family who visited saw but the frail shell of my former self—I had lost almost fifty pounds, my muscles had withered, and I could not walk, get myself to the bathroom, bathe myself, or even feed myself. I must have seemed like but a faint trace of the Omer Rains they once knew—except to my friend George.

George walked through my bedroom door to visit shortly after I was brought home from the hospital. He sat down near my bed, and we talked for a long time. Although my body was still severely impaired from the aneurysm and stroke, my speech, thankfully, had returned pretty much to normal. There were things that George and I said, and things we left unsaid.

I didn't have to tell George how emasculating it was to have to be bathed and fed by a paid caregiver, who came by for a short time each day. She did all she could to help me feel as comfortable as possible under the circumstances. George could see that Diana was absent and that I needed others to do almost everything for me.

I didn't have to tell George these things because he knew me as well as anyone knew me. During the time that I had made Tahoe my principal place of residence, George had challenged me on the tennis courts, the ski slopes, and the bike trails of the Sierra Nevada's. George knew that I was single-minded in my determination to achieve a goal once I had set it. He understood that when put to the test in the name of a good cause, I could be one rebellious trouble-maker until I achieved what I set out to do.

"You know, you're going to get through this," George said to me. "When I broke my back many years ago, they said I would be crippled for the rest of my life. Now doctors look at my x-rays and say 'My God, you have bones like tree trunks'!"

"The body will recover itself," George said. "And with your strength and your determination, you're going to come out of this and be stronger than ever, Omer. I know what a fighter you are. I know how determined you are. You'll do it. I did it, and you'll do it too."

George knew that when I said I would walk again in thirty days, I would do it or die trying.

My twenty-five year marriage to Diana may have ended—or at least soon would. My body may have failed me. But George and many others cared, and they all seemed to believe in me. That meant an awful lot to a partial invalid lying in bed day and night without the use of the right side of his body and only limited use of the left side.

One afternoon in those early days at home in Carmichael, the phone rang. It was a friend of Diana's.

"It's so great that Diana is devoting her life to care for you," she said. If I had been at the edge of the bed, I think I would have fallen off.

Where on earth had anyone gotten the notion that Diana was helping me recover? It became clear that this was how Diana was representing the situation.

My anger stirred. I had not been a perfect husband, but this was the height of absurdity. Diana clearly had no intent or desire to participate in my recovery, and yet she was obviously representing herself as being heavily involved in my daily care. I hung up the phone without saying anything negative, but I was mad as hell. In fact, the phone call reminded me of the time that my Grandma Cochran had said how great it was that my father had put me through college when in fact my father had not paid a single penny toward my education or expenses.

As it turned out, Diana's friend was not the only acquaintance of hers who called during my recovery and indicated how great it was that Diana was tending to me "round the clock." This aberration from the truth spurred me to work even harder to recover. So what if I would have to do it on my own? That had often been the case in my life.

But along with being hurt and angry, I was also confused. How could Diana be so uncaring? So unmoved by the plight of the man she had been with for well over twenty-five years, many of them good ones? I had taken care of her in so many ways, and yet she seemed to feel absolutely nothing for me. I didn't expect her to fall back in love with me, but I couldn't understand how she could sleep next to me in bed and yet remain disengaged on every level. After all, there were other bedrooms in the house. All I really wanted was Diana's kindness to me, one human being to another, but that was not to be.

Had Diana slid from love to loathing of me because I had travelled so much during our marriage and unknowingly let her internal complaints and frustrations build up unmitigated? Did she stay away during my recovery because my decrepit state was simply too much of a burden for her to bear?

It surely couldn't have been easy for her to see how I—the man she had once loved but now wanted to divorce—had become so helpless. It was I who had always taken care of her, but now I could do very little but depend on others to care for me. Where I had once been gone on long trips and more recently been living at Lake Tahoe, I was now once again ever present with her in the home. That must have been a difficult change for Diana, even if it didn't help me understand her coldness to me.

I do not know the reasons that Diana chose to sleep next to me (was it to portray to our daughter that our marriage was okay?) and then disappear for the entirety of the day, often without even extending basic civilities to me. One thing was for sure, however. I was more determined than ever to recover so I could leave the dismaying environment of my once beloved wife and our Carmichael home. I needed the fresh air and natural surroundings of Lake Tahoe. I needed to be able to breathe again. But first, I needed to walk again.

Yes, a new and different environment. After all, wasn't that a key to escaping the funk I was in after my first divorce? My first campaign for elective office had proved to be just the distraction I needed at that time.

13

Elective Office

"The winner ain't the one with the fastest car; it's the one who refuses to lose."
— Dale Earnhardt

With the death of Congressman Teague, as 1974 rolled around the waters in the political cauldron were stirring in the central coast area of California. Robert J. Lagomarsino, the sitting California State Senator from the area, was pressured by then Governor Ronald Reagan, President Gerald Ford, and others to run for Teague's seat in the United States Congress. Lagomarsino, realizing that a Congressional seat would in reality be a step down from his position in the California State Senate, was reluctant.

Lagomarsino was a popular politician from a prominent and wealthy family. His father was one of the founders of what was originally the Bank of Italy, later to become the Bank of America. While I respected and liked Bob personally, as with Teague, I disagreed with him on most issues.

Since it was almost certain that Lagomarsino, a Republican like Teague, would be elected to Congress thus vacating his Senate seat, friends and associates of mine urged me to seek Lagomarsino's Senate seat. My response was initially light-hearted and I mentioned that not only was I too young, but that I had an active law practice and was involved in a myriad of local and state responsibilities including service on the University of California Alumni Council and interest in helping to develop the Master Plan for Higher Education in California.

Another concern that was even more practical was a common belief that no Democrat could carry this very conservative and historically safe Republican district. I thought this to be especially true since, at my young age, a victory however unlikely would make me the youngest person elected to the California Senate up to that point in the 1900s. Nevertheless, many friends kept prodding me, seemingly with the true belief that I could actually carry the district and perhaps that I was the only Democrat who could.

The pressure for me to run continued to mount. More and more voices were encouraging my candidacy and I was frequently being mentioned in the press as a possible candidate. Eventually, I decided that I would indeed throw my hat into the ring. I knew I had a formidable task, and that it was going to be an uphill climb to say the least. But the enormous challenge meant that I would just have to work that much harder—consistent with lifelong habits.

California Senate Districts are incredibly large, much, much larger than those of any other state. The district involved, Senate District 24, was almost twice the size of a Congressional District and had over 1 million people in it.

Every ten years, all state and congressional districts are reapportioned pursuant to provisions of the United States and California Constitutions. Reapportionment is the drawing of district lines for each office and, because of court rulings in the 1960s, they had to be equal in size from a population standpoint. Ronald Reagan had been elected Governor of California in 1966 and, to the chagrin of virtually all elected officials (including Republicans) he vetoed the predictably incumbent oriented reapportionment bill of 1970. By so doing, the matter ended up before the California Supreme Court. The court appointed a "Master" to establish parameters that would avoid the usual "gerrymandering," so that reapportionment would be done more in accordance with county and city boundaries and other communities of interest. Gerrymandering, named after a former Governor of Massachusetts, is the method by which incumbents draw lines to insure their reelection or by which one party draws lines to insure its control of one legislative house or another until the next reapportionment is required. The court, acting in a non-partisan way, was determined to avoid the typical "dragon-like" figures on the map that all too often characterize the various district boundaries throughout the country.

Because of Reagan's veto and the fact that the judicial process moves with glacial speed, the 1970 reapportionment did not go into effect until the 1974 elections. By that time, there had been an enormous spillover of population from Los Angeles County, thus making the 24th Senatorial District incredibly large. In fact, from a population standpoint, it was the largest State Senate District in the state and, therefore, in the nation.

To further complicate matters, although Lagomarsino's unexpired term was in the 24th Senatorial District, with the reapportionment bill taking effect later that same year, the district would change shape and would be renumbered as the 18th Senatorial District. Therefore, it would be necessary for a candidate to win primary elections in two separate Senate Districts and then prevail in general elections in the same two Senate Districts, all within one year. I am not sure this had ever occurred in California history. Four elections in one year!

In any event, my intention in the initial campaign seeking to represent Lagomarsino's unexpired term in the 24th Senate District was to cover the entire district. This would be a difficult feat since it encompassed an area of over 5,000 square miles. No doubt I was going to use up a lot of shoe leather and a lot of gas.

In retrospect, I realize that my decision to run was neither purely political nor practical because my original reasons for not running were indeed valid. Along with other considerations, I believe there were emotional reasons that finally led me to decide to go for it. I was still reeling from the emotional bomb blast of my divorce from Judy. While it was true that I dated actively, I still wallowed in the depths of despair and concern for my children. I needed a distraction. The campaign would prove to be far more than a mere distraction as I worked countless hours during this effort.

To my amazement, by the time I did finally announce my candidacy, the number of people urging me to run had grown to be a small avalanche. The level of support actually stunned me, especially considering that a lot of prominent Republicans were behind me as well.

I had to wait until Lagomarsino actually won the Congressional seat, thus vacating his Senate seat before I could file my Declaration of Intention papers. I did this on February 11, 1974. I made sure that I got prominent people to sign my nomination papers in order to buttress my candidacy with a sense of legitimacy and plausibility.

Governor Reagan scheduled a special election for June to fill Lagomarsino's unexpired term. However, even if I won, I would have to run again in November for the full four year term in the new apportioned 18th Senatorial District. But first I had to win the Democratic nominations.

Reagan set the dates for the two primaries on the same date (ostensibly to save money) so I had to run in two districts and two primaries at the same time. The primary elections were to be on June 4, 1974.

The primaries drew four candidates on the Democratic side as well as four candidates on the Republican side. However, the very heavy favorite was the former Mayor of Santa Barbara and long time State Assemblyman who represented Santa Barbara County, W. Don MacGillivray. Although MacGillivray was a household name in Santa Barbara, he was not really known in Ventura County.

I made some key decisions right from the beginning about how I was going to run my campaign. Some of these decisions caused veteran campaign operatives to think I was crazy. Among other things, I decided to take no corporate or special interest money. I ran what turned out to be possibly the last true grassroots campaign in California history. The campaign cost less than $20,000, an unheard of figure today where the same type of campaign typically runs into the millions of dollars on each side.

My campaign was indeed grassroots in every way. I was a local man extremely active in civic affairs in the district and I had quite a bit of name recognition—though mainly in Ventura County. As it turned out, I did win the Democratic nominations and as expected, MacGillivray won the Republican nominations. Reagan set the date for the run off in the 24th Senate District for July 2. He admitted that this was done for political reasons to help MacGillivray since the students at the University California at Santa Barbara, the only Democratic stronghold in the entire District, would be out for the summer recess. Moreover, July 2, being so close to the July 4 break, would ordinarily call for a lower turnout—something that almost invariably favors Republican candidates.

MacGillivray and I were polar opposites on almost every issue. I was opposed to offshore oil drilling in the Santa Barbara Channel. He was in favor of it. My opposition was based on facts that seemed indisputable to me. In early 1969 the area had suffered what is commonly called "The Blowout at Platform A" in the Santa Barbara Channel. It was a great ecological disaster that fouled the waters and destroyed bird and marine wildlife for miles and miles. The aftereffects lasted for years. I remember that incident so very well as I was there on the beaches helping to clean oil off dying birds. Also, the Platform A incident had a terrible economic impact on the Santa Barbara region, as that region relies so very heavily on tourism.

I argued strongly for alternative sources of energy such as solar, geothermal, developing ocean technologies, wind, biomass conversion, and so on. MacGillivray on the other hand felt that we should increase, not decrease, our dependence on oil as, in his opinion, it was the only reliable source of energy and if this meant drilling in the Santa Barbara Channel, so be it.

I was also in favor of the Equal Rights Amendment (ERA) designed to enshrine in the US Constitution language to ensure that women have rights equal to men, and a number of other issues of importance to women. MacGillivray opposed the ERA.

I was for political reform starting with the disclosure of all campaign contributions. He was opposed to such disclosures. No wonder—considering all of the special interest money he took from those whose identities could not be determined under existing law.

In short, the battle lines could not have been drawn more clearly.

From day one, I walked the District door to door. Talk about retail politics! I ventured into restaurants, barber shops, gift shops and supermarkets. I answered questions whenever asked. I shook hands. And yes, I kissed babies too.

But I made my appeal on every level, speaking to all kinds of organizations: community groups, civic groups, student groups, service groups, Latino groups, to the Elks, Rotarians, the Kiwanis Club, the AARP, the Navy League, and some groups I'd never even heard of before.

I especially courted the editorial staffs of newspapers like the Santa Barbara News Press, the Ventura Star Free Press and the Oxnard Press Courier, as well as TV and radio stations district-wide. Early on, I received a boost from a glowing editorial about me in the Thousand Oaks News Chronicle. This was very helpful since it was in an especially strong Republican area just north of the Los Angeles county line.

The campaign also had the benefit of a huge number of volunteers who carried signs, made phone calls, delivered pamphlets, placed fliers on windshields, and who otherwise campaigned for me. Many of the volunteers were college students in the University of California (Santa Barbara) community who were squarely behind me. Their youthful energy and enthusiasm was invaluable.

A very notable and hardworking volunteer was Roosevelt (Rosie) Grier, the former Los Angeles Rams football player and one of the greatest defensive linemen in NFL history. A dedicated activist, it was Rosie who had been at Robert Kennedy's side when Kennedy was assassinated in 1968. Rosie and I occasionally walked precincts together and that was a benefit because he was so very recognizable.

However, what was really amazing was the number of prominent Republicans who endorsed me. No doubt one reason for my strong Republican support was because, although I was rather progressive on social issues, on fiscal matters I was and am quite conservative. I favor a balanced budget, sunset laws, zero-based budgets, a line-item veto, and so on. That has never changed.

Another reason for this support is that the Republican business community in and around the city of Santa Barbara realized that the area lives or dies on tourism and the economic development of that community goes hand in hand with a healthy environment. By the same token, in Ventura County where I had served as Chairman of the Visitors and Conventions Bureau and as Vice-President of the Greater Ventura Chamber of Commerce, I was close friends with virtually all Republican businessmen in the area.

The entire campaign was retail or grassroots politics at its best. One day a particular supporter and I prepared a newspaper type flier, starting mid-afternoon and working throughout the entire night into the next day. Twenty-four hours straight. It was the one and only mailer we could afford so it had to be well done—and it was.

Month after month, I wore out shoe leather and tire rubber. Since I couldn't afford a driver, I drove everywhere myself covering the 5000-square-mile district. I amassed five speeding tickets during that campaign. After the primary election, the Los Angeles papers referred to me as the "newest and speediest legislator." Fortunately, it was another thirty-five years before I received another moving violation.

As for the issues of the day, I learned that a prevalent maxim in politics couldn't be more true. "The more things change, the more they stay the same." The major issues of the time were much the same as they are today. They were healthcare, the environment, the deteriorating infrastructure, taxation, and the need for education reform.

The one-month period between the primary election and the general election was a whirlwind of activity. On election day I was still going strong, walking precincts. In fact, I didn't stop until the polls closed on July 2. I knew what I was up against. Though MacGillivray had slaughtered Democratic opponents in the past, that just made me work even harder—especially in areas in which he had historically shown his greatest strength.

Although I had started out as a huge underdog, the Ventura Star Free Press took an unscientific poll of reporters from around the district as election day approached and a number of these political observers, actually the vast majority of those asked, felt that I would win. I wondered if many might be getting a distorted view of my strength because of the numerous lawn signs, automobile bumper stickers and other advertising material carrying my name that thanks to the grassroots nature of my campaign were showing up all over the district. In any event, to me it had begun to appear that I might have at least a 50/50 shot.

MacGillivray, of course, had strong financial help from special interests as well as from Republican Party coffers in Sacramento. MacGillivray was getting money from virtually untraceable sources. For example, an organization that was called something like "Citizens for a Greener Environment" turned out to actually be lumber industry money. The pseudonyms used by special interests in funneling money to their favorite politicians were, and are, very creative and almost invariably misleading. The bottom line is that our campaign was dramatically outspent. However, we had known that this would be the case as far back as day one.

After the polls closed on election night, I took a date (later to become my second wife, Diana) to dinner as we awaited the initial results. After dinner, we went to Campaign headquarters. It was a long time before the first results began to trickle in. However, when they did arrive, they first came from Lompoc, a city in northern Santa Barbara County. Lompoc was solid GOP territory and an area in which MacGillivray had always demonstrated overwhelming strength. Yet, I had carried the city and surrounding area, including Vandenberg Air Force Base, decisively. The margin was about 60-40 in my favor. That was amazing! At this point the cautious part of my optimism, and those of my supporters, swelled into full blown confidence. The 60-40 margin would pretty much hold true throughout the entire district.

When MacGillivray made his concession speech that night, he was very combative. He said, "I lost tonight, but we will see how Rains does in a true bare knuckles fight to the finish in November." This was a reference to the newly apportioned 18th Senatorial District in which the next election would be held.

I took the oath of office in the City Council Chambers in Ventura, the old historic courthouse where I had first practiced law as a prosecutor and which I had fought so hard to save from destruction.

Because Santa Barbara County and Ventura County are so distinct and serviced by different media setups, I also took the oath of office that same day in Santa Barbara at the Santa Barbara County Courthouse. The dual oaths were symbolic of my intention to genuinely represent all areas of the District with equal fervor.

A day or two after I was sworn in and before I had gone to Sacramento, I received a phone call from John Reaves, Judy's father.

"Omer, we need to meet in private. This is important."

"OK, John, where and when do you want to meet?"

"I suggest today if your schedule permits. Why don't we meet at Tip's at Castaic Junction?"

"OK, I can be there around three o'clock."

Arriving at the restaurant in mid-afternoon, I immediately saw John, as the restaurant was practically empty. Although John and I had become very close over the years, there was no small talk on this occasion. We warmly shook hands and sat down.

John said, "Omer, thanks for coming on such short notice. I know how busy you are right now, what with your campaign and all. Needless to say, this is about Judy. I am very worried about her. She is not well and is beside herself now that you've been elected to the Senate. She feels that she should be going to Sacramento with you as the Senator's wife. I told her that that isn't realistic and I can't imagine Omer agreeing to a reconciliation given all that you have put him through. I certainly wouldn't were I him."

"John, I would never have initiated a divorce, but there's far too much water under the bridge now."

John agreed and continued, "You do know, don't you, that the fellow that she was having an affair with jilted her?"

"Yes, I know."

"She admits that she went after him with a vengeance in an attempt to destroy his marriage. He has been forced to resign his position. Omer, she's completely lost her bearings and I suspect she's doing drugs. Lord knows I don't want her to end up like LuJane, and I can't imagine you ever wanting to go through what I had to go through with LuJane. I have asked Judy to consider a rehabilitation program. However, she is in complete denial.

"Omer, there is nothing worse than a woman scorned and Judy's now been twice scorned—first by her lover and now by you. When she and I spoke the day after you won the election, she said that if she couldn't be part of the victory then she intended to bring you down."

John continued, "Earlier today when I spoke to her again by phone, she said that she was preparing to make contact with your opponent, or with members of his staff, the Assemblyman up in Santa Barbara whom you will be running against again in November. What are your thoughts?"

"I don't know, John. I know Judy better than anyone else does and I do know how vindictive she can be. So I must simply be prepared for the worst. If the voters want to listen to the allegations of a disgruntled ex-wife, then I will just have to live with it. But she has a problem. She will have to make up some real whoppers. As you know, John, there was never physical abuse, never verbal abuse, she—not I—filed for divorce and I have faithfully made child support payments every single month, and I always will. So let's not focus on me. Whatever will be will be. My real concern is for Kelly and Mark. How can they best be protected? I really don't know what is in their best interest at this point in time. I probably shouldn't have run for office in the first place, but I did, so that's Monday morning quarterbacking."

"I have been thinking about Mark and Kelly too, Omer. First, I don't think you should do anything that might interrupt Judy's relationship with them—at least not at this period in time. She's in a very fragile state and isn't thinking rationally at all. I think her self-esteem is low. She seems to be going through a man a month. Every time I go to Ventura or she comes to Bakersfield I meet another guy. The one she's seeing right now — I think his name is Dale — comes across to me as a "doper." I hope I'm wrong. In any event, if you can monitor her from your end—even if it's by way of information received from mutual friends—I will stay in close touch with her and do the best I can to monitor her and how her conduct is affecting the children from my end."

"Well that's probably about the best we can do for the time being. Hopefully, she will come to her senses if given some time."

"Don't bet on it, Omer. Judy has asked that I stop seeing or, for that matter, even speaking with you. Many of us came down pretty hard on her when she filed for divorce. Grams really read her the riot act. She apparently didn't realize just how close we were to you, though I don't know why she wouldn't have known it. Anyway, I told Judy that I love her, she is my eldest and I will always be there for her. Nevertheless, I also said: "Judy, I've told you before, Omer has been a member of our family now for over twelve years. He is a dear friend whom I not only like, but whom I trust and respect. I fully expect to maintain that friendship. You decided to divorce him for reasons you've never been able or willing to adequately explain to me. OK, that was your decision. Now, you must learn to live with that decision. But don't try to ruin my relationship with Omer or with anyone else."

"I appreciate that, John. Although Judy may make things difficult, I can't think of a single reason why we can't remain as close as we have ever been."

And so ended what had once been an idyllic high school and college romance, a subsequent marriage, and the birth of two amazing children. Judy's assertions, and conduct for several decades after my conversation with John at Castaic Junction and over many decades is almost beyond belief, an albatross with which I have simply had to live.

In parting, John wished me good luck with the upcoming campaign and asked, "How do you feel about it?"

"Well, we beat the guy decisively last week and people seem to think it will be even more decisive in November in the new district. All I know is that I will run every day like I'm behind and won't stop until after the polls close on election day in November."

"If its hard work that counts, Omer, you'll win."

—————

Not long thereafter, I was contacted by Al Jalaty, the Sheriff of Ventura County and a very close friend of mine. Through me, he also knew Judy. Al asked me if I could drop by and see him. I said, "Sure." During that meeting, Al said, "Omer, Judy's been doing drugs and some of my men know it. I've been doing my best to monitor the situation and protect her, but she's been socializing with at least two suspected narcotic users. One is a possible dealer. As a friend, I called her in and told her that I could protect her only so long. I don't know how much good I did, but she seemed really shaken up when she left. I told her that I would be telling you and she begged me not to. I've sat on this for a few weeks wondering whether or not to have this conversation with you. I don't sense that the children are in any immediate danger so I don't think you should do anything now. Let me continue to monitor the situation for a while. I may even have a car go by the Linda Vista house from time to time to see if cars parked in front are any they recognize as belonging to users or peddlers. Hopefully, she has had the fear of God put in her and will start minding her P's and Q's. We will see."

I left his office more worried than ever about Mark and Kelly but not really knowing what to do about it. I went to see an attorney friend of mine and sought his advice. His counsel, similar to Jalaty's, was not to do anything for the time being and to give Judy a bit longer to straighten out her life.

I also spoke again with Judy's father, John, and he was not at all surprised at what Jalaty told me. It confirmed suspicions that he already had. However, his advice was the same as that given by Jalaty and the attorney, Lyman Smith.

After our divorce, along with rejection by her lover, Judy went through a number of men. Finally, she married one of them, but I don't think it lasted very long and she went through yet another divorce. I suspect that her second husband was one that Jalaty had told me about, but of that I can't be sure.

Ultimately, Judy seemed to get her head somewhat straightened out. She went into school administration and eventually married a third time. The fellow she married was another attorney whom I knew primarily because he was the best friend of the fellow who was to become the local Republican Assemblyman, Charles Imbrecht, who himself was to later die of a drug overdose.

John and I were to remain close—in fact, increasingly close, over the years and that was to be the case right up to the time of his death decades later. That absolutely enraged Judy. As the years went by, she became more and more vindictive and began, for lack of a better term, "stalking" me, a situation that would go on continuously — now for over thirty-five years. This was to take many forms as the years went by.

14

Ronald Reagan and the Next Election

*"The race goes not necessarily to the swift nor the battle to the strong,
but that's sure as hell the smart way to bet!"*
— Damon Runyon

Soon after I arrived in Sacramento to take my seat in the Senate, I got an invitation from then Governor Ronald Reagan to join him for a personal visit. Our conversation went much longer than expected. I found him to be every bit the charming, charismatic, sunny fellow he was reported to be and then some. For those who said he was unforgettable, I agree. When he later became President with a "Western White House" in Santa Barbara County, he would refer to me as "my Senator." This remained a standing joke between us in a relationship that was always cordial despite our frequent policy differences—and they were many. However, in spite of our political differences, I came to like him very much and it was apparent that he, in turn, liked me.

Reagan was one of those leaders who delegated almost all responsibilities, although he always took responsibility for his subordinate's actions. Another aspect of his character, perhaps not as well known, is that although he seemed stubbornly ideological in his speeches and his presentations, he was nonetheless quite adept at compromise. It was Ronald Reagan who signed into law the largest tax increase in the history of any state up until that time. More surprisingly, he also signed into law California's Therapeutic Abortion Act.

Marilyn Chapman had been Lagomarsino's secretary and she knew the district and its people very well. In addition, she seemed quite competent. I told her that if she was loyal, she had the job as my lead secretary. She was surprised in that I was a Democrat and Lagomarsino was a Republican. With my election, she had assumed that she would be out of a job. She gladly accepted.

I also hired for the Sacramento office two key campaign staff workers, Ross Pumfrey, who had been instrumental in the student community of Santa Barbara during my campaign and Jim Browning, an Oxnard attorney who himself had previously run unsuccessfully for Congress.

I then hired Bob Borrego to be my Field Coordinator/Administrative Assistant working out of the Ventura County Office. I have always been particularly proud of this appointment because Bob, at the time, became the highest ranking Latino staff person employed by the Senate and his appointment set in motion a diversification program that was later to be followed by other members of the Senate. I hasten to add, however, that Bob wasn't hired simply because he was Latino. He was hired because he was the most qualified person for the job. Shirley Jackson and Joan Province, the latter being one of my former legal secretaries, were hired to help Bob in the Ventura County District Office.

For the Santa Barbara County Office, I hired Mary Margaret Overbey as an Administrative Assistant, to be aided by Rosemarie Fanucchi. A later addition was Jack O'Connell, who himself would eventually be elected first to the Assembly, then to the Senate, and thereafter to the state-wide position of Superintendent of Public Instruction.

George Moscone, provided the name of a candidate, Bruce Rosenthal, to be an administrative aide in Sacramento. In order to bring me up to speed in a hurry I had two campaign staffers, Prem Hunji and Bob Holmes, help me to analyze the 7,000 pending bills so that I had some idea what they were about. 7,000! Why so many? First, California has no limit on the number of bills each member can introduce. Second, legislators like most everyone else, tend to procrastinate and avoid the "heavy lifting" as long as they can. Third, games can be played, often overlooked, when such an avalanche of bills are being voted on in such short order.

Voting in the Senate was very tedious because, unlike the Assembly where voting was computerized, every bill voted on in the Senate needed an individual and oral aye or nay vote. Because this is a time consuming process, the end of the two year session, with such an incredible backlog of bills to be voted on, caused us to work literally day and night on the Senate floor for over a month.

The California Senate does not operate on a seniority system as does Congress. The Democratic majority in the Senate wanted to protect a seat they had not expected to have. As a result, on my very first day, I was appointed Chairman of a new Committee on Political Reform. It was a harbinger of things to come. In addition, I was also appointed to the Senate Judiciary Committee, the Committee on Energy and Public Utilities, and the Committee on Natural Resources and Wildlife.

I also took the opportunity to author a bill popular with the public, but unpopular with my Senate colleagues, that repealed huge pension benefits that otherwise would have gone to defeated or retiring members of the Legislature.

As soon as session ended, I was back to the district full time working toward the November election date in the new district. I was now to learn what MacGillivray meant by a "bare knuckles campaign." As MacGillivray had ties to the power blocks throughout Santa Barbara County, he and his staff went to extremes to try to prevent me from appearing in the Old Spanish Days parade in Santa Barbara, the major event of the year in Santa Barbara, as well as in the Danish Days parade in Solvang, California's touristy traditional Danish village. For the most part, he was unsuccessful in these efforts. That caused MacGillivray and his team to start a personal campaign, working with Judy. She made a number of assertions that were demonstrably false and harmed her credibility more than mine.

She made false statements that I had divorced her, had abandoned the family, and had not made child support payments. All of these comments were not only untrue, but so outrageous and easily disproved that it's difficult to believe they had much effect. MacGillivray ran newspaper ads that his campaign staff prepared containing some of these allegations, but some papers refused to run them when they found, for example, that every single child support payment had been made—no exception. This was to remain true throughout the lives of my children until they became adults.

In fact, I made sure that my secretary mailed the child support payments out well in advance of all due dates so that it would never be possible for Judy to credibly claim that I was shirking responsibilities. As a result, I was never a single day late on child support payments—ever. Nevertheless, these blatant lies thoroughly aggravated me. For the most part, I was able to simply dismiss her from my mind. The exception was when someone would ask me what I thought about Judy making such statements and assertions. My canned response was, to paraphrase Humphrey Bogart, "I actually don't think of her at all unless someone asks me about her."

Admittedly, however, it is very difficult not to think about her from time to time simply because she continues to this day to write letters, to talk to people, and to follow me wherever I am. She is absolutely obsessed and determined at all times to know what I'm doing, who I am meeting with and so on and so forth.

As recently as the very time when I'm writing this book, over thirty-five years after our divorce, an attorney in New York City informed me the first time I met him that my ex-wife, Judy, had been in touch with him. He had no idea how Judy even knew we were having a meeting, and I didn't either. After telling me the ridiculous statements she had made in an attempt to embarrass or discredit me, he asked me if this lady was absolutely cuckoo. I said, "I don't know, but probably so."

Some thirty years after our divorce, she actually had the chutzpah to travel to Huntington Beach, California after my mother and father had died. She informed a neighbor who had access to my parent's home that she was my wife. Thus, she gained access to the home and removed items from it. To this day she has never told me of the incident or what she took without my authorization, or that of the executor, or that of the attorney handling my parent's estate. All we know is that she loaded up her car and trunk and drove off with items that she found to her liking. Although I could have reported the incident to the local police authorities, I did not because of the possibly adverse effects it could have on my two older children.

Insofar as the general election campaign in 1974 was concerned, the assertions seemingly had no effect whatsoever as she was thoroughly discredited and my support remained very strong and stable.

Rather than dwell on negative features, I continued to run a straightforward and positive campaign. Having been successful in grassroots campaigning thus far, I was determined to keep it up. After all, campaigning is about meeting people and telling them who you are and what you are all about.

Whereas some people grouse about places with small populations like New Hampshire having so much prominence in Presidential campaigns, I thoroughly disagree. In small, basically rural New Hampshire, "pressing the flesh" is not only natural but required. Retail politics is necessary and the observant American public can get a good feel for the candidates as they watch them interact and relate with real people in small towns. This is a much better way to evaluate a candidate than having to rely upon slick media ad campaigns, more often than not negative, that are simply run by those candidates able to raise the most money (usually from special interests).

As my grassroots campaign for the November election shifted into high gear, two non-paid pollsters, both PhDs from UCSB were attracted to my campaign. One of them, Timothy Hodson, was later to become a valued member of my Sacramento staff. While they weren't professional pollsters, they knew how to conduct a poll. The results of their polling revealed that for a number of reasons I had a much better than even chance of being re-elected in November for the full four year term. In fact, it appeared that the November election would be even more decisive than the one in July. Consistent with the polling results, I won by a landslide in November.

15

Legislative Life

"No man should be in public office who can't make more money in private life."
— Thomas E. Dewey

So, having been re-elected to the Senate, I finally could breathe and do a proper organizational transition from private to public life. But if I thought running a law practice, campaigning and chairing twelve out of sixteen regional or state commissions was an armful, what I had facing me now was a truck-full. First, I had vowed during the campaign to divest myself of all assets and business interests because I very much wanted to avoid even the perception, much less the reality, of a conflict of interest. Therefore, I needed to sell my law firm to a partner and set up house in such a way that I could live on the Senate salary which was then only about $16,000 a year. Talk about a pay cut!

I was also faced with the task of setting up permanent offices in both counties of the district and, of course, in Sacramento, too. Travel to Sacramento was problematic. It was about a ten hour drive and air travel then was not direct except a few days a week. Also, airfare at that time was about $400 one way and it was not reimbursable, but rather had to be paid out of pocket. (Thank goodness, this rule has since changed.)

As I started my second and initial full four-year term I was now the Senator for the 18th Senatorial District. The Legislature reconvened on December 2 for a new two-year session. In addition to my prior appointments, I was also appointed to chair the Senate Committee on Elections and Reapportionment, as well as the Joint Legislative Committee on Legal Equality.

The Committee on Legal Equality was the only Legislative Committee in the United States that was established solely to deal with women's rights and concerns. Probably the most embarrassing question I was ever asked in public service, and I was asked it repeatedly, was "Why is it that you, a man, Chair this Committee?" The reason the question was embarrassing was that I was forced to admit that after 125 years of statehood, California had never in its history elected a single woman to its Senate. This was fairly amazing, but true.

The makeup of the Senate when I arrived in December of 1974 for the start of the new session was twenty-two Democrats and eighteen Republicans. Due as much as anything to reapportionment, the Democrats had controlled the state Legislature in California for a long period of time. However, until Bill Clinton's election in 1992, California hadn't voted for a Democrat for President since 1944 with the exception of the Johnson/Goldwater election in 1964.

Had California been an independent nation in 1978, it would have had the fifth largest economy in the world. California has the largest agricultural industry in the country, the largest trucking industry, the largest timber industry, the largest tourist industry, the largest high-tech industry, the largest film industry, and so on. In many ways California was (and is) the engine that drives America. California is big business. As a result, California's politicians wield unusual power.

Although the new 18th Senatorial District was slightly smaller from a population standpoint than the former 24th District, I still represented close to one million people. That not only far exceeded any other State Senate District in the United States, but exceeded by far the population of a Congressional seat and, indeed, the entire population of several states.

Not surprisingly, the lobbyists in the state capital of Sacramento are very active. They are commonly referred to as the "Third House." They had and have as much influence at getting legislation passed (or killed) in the Senate and the Assembly as they do in Washington, DC. Some people would probably argue that the influence of the Third House is even greater than that of the Legislature since the special interests that they represent are willing to spend as much money as necessary to satiate the appetite of certain politicians who rely on their largess. In short, the California capital is so important that the same interests with lobbyists in Washington, DC also have lobbyists in Sacramento, and often they are one and the same.

Early in the session I was talking to a very powerful lobbyist. When the conversation got around to the fact that I had closed my law office he exclaimed, "My God, you're going to give up your law firm?" When I looked kind of puzzled he went on. "We can send you all kinds of business, and you won't even have to report it as a contribution on your campaign disclosure forms."

While he didn't actually make an explicit offer, I knew exactly what he meant. Many companies of course hire attorneys on a retainer basis. That is, they pay them money and if some legal matter arises where the firm or company needs them, then they are available to handle it. Of course, there might not be any work at all from that client. Nevertheless, the money continues to flow in.

This meeting and the described discussion disturbed me greatly and I thought long and hard about it until finally I sought the counsel of my friend, George Moscone. My first impulse was to report the lobbyist to the Fair Political Practices Commission (FPPC). George advised me, "Don't do it." The thrust of his advice was that I already had a reputation as a straight shooter, so there was no reason to draw attention to myself, especially in a case where nothing could actually be proven. Word was already around he told me, "Be careful what you say to Rains." So, needless to say, my relationship with the Third House was circumspect almost from day one.

On December 2, the new term started. Jerry Brown had been elected Governor succeeding Ronald Reagan and most Democrats in the Legislature were happy with him in the beginning. He was a sharp and progressive guy and seemed full of promise. But his relationship with the Legislature went into a deep downhill dive during his eight-year tenure as Governor. Although he is quite an intelligent man, he sometimes has the attention span of a gnat. If you were talking to him about an energy program, within forty-five seconds he would be focused on transportation and in another forty-five seconds he would be talking about education reform or something else entirely. It was hard—almost impossible—to have him remain focused, at least it was in those days. Admittedly, this was the Jerry Brown of the 1970s and 80s, and there are those with whom I have spoken more recently who believe that he is a changed man and may now, having been given a second chance, distinguish himself as Governor. I hope this is the case.

In any event, when first elected in 1974, as a Democratic Governor with a Democratic Legislature, Brown had everything going for him. However, as things turned out, the

Legislature overrode more of Jerry Brown's vetoes than all past Governors of California combined. The acrimonious relationship was not healthy for the state.

An important measure that took effect early in my second term was precipitated by the passage of Proposition 9, a ballot measure known as the Political Reform Act of 1974. I had been a strong and vociferous supporter of Prop 9, but most legislators had been opposed to its passage. As it turned out, Prop 9 did pass. Among other things it required the disclosure of those who made campaign contributions and the amount contributed to each candidate for public office. But the new act had other provisions, too. One was that a lobbyist could not spend more than $10 a month on a legislator which theoretically meant he could perhaps take a member of the Legislature out for a cup of coffee but that was about it. Creativity was required to avoid prosecution although there were numerous ways to transfer money for favors without a direct or indirect exchange of money from lobbyist to legislator. Needless to say, the easiest was to get the principal, rather than his lobbyist, to become directly involved with the legislator and this is exactly what happened. To avoid the proscriptions that Prop 9 placed on lobbyists, CEOs of Fortune 500 companies began with regularity to visit the Capitol.

In addition to the passage of Prop 9, another healthy change took place from within the Senate itself. The annual budget battles always involved a great deal of in-fighting. In 1975 there was a revolt. A new group, myself included, with the designation of "Young Turks" emerged informally in the California Senate. The group was concerned with the influence that special interests and one or two members had in the budgeting process. The Young Turks were not necessarily youthful but they did challenge the "Old Guard" who had long standing ties with the moneyed interests.

For those of us on the inside, it was apparent that the policy of some was basically to provide special treatment and show favoritism to those with a "pay to play" mindset. What developed in 1975 in regard to the budget battles was historic. After both the Senate and the Assembly had passed budget bills it was necessary that year, as in all years, for the two houses to appoint conferees to iron out the differences between the two bills. There were three members appointed from the Assembly and three from the Senate. However, heading the process for many years had been a powerful Senate Leader, Randy Collier, commonly known as the "Gray Fox of the Siskiyou's." The Siskiyou's are a remote mountain range in the northwest part of California. That particular district was dominated by the timber interests. Collier had been in the Senate so long he was Chairman of the Senate Finance Committee and, quite frankly, he would end up pretty much drafting the final version of the budget himself. Not surprisingly, more pork went into his district than any other district.

When the budget bill came up for a vote in June, 1975, surprises were in store. The roll call in the Senate is always done alphabetically and Senator Reuben Ayala was always first. When he cast a nay vote for Collier's budget, a silence fell over the assemblage. This did not portend well for Collier or Collier's budget bill. The budget bill as presented did not pass, and Collier was deposed from his long-held position as Chairman of the Finance Committee.

This changing of the guard ushered in a whole new era. Chairmanship of the Finance Committee was taken from Collier and given to a fine senator from the Beverly Hills area, Tony Beilenson. About the same time, I was elected to be the Senate Majority Caucus Chairman. This gave me yet more responsibilities, but I welcomed it because I saw it as an opportunity to professionalize the Caucus staff. Therefore, in my early thirties, approximately twenty years younger than any other member of the Senate at the time, I was the third ranking member of the California Senate. I also assumed the position of Chairman of the Business and Professions Committee. At one time or another, I chaired five standing committees and was a member of multiple others.

Finally, George Moscone took me aside and cautioned me about overloading myself and burning out prematurely. Lt. Governor and Senate colleague during my first term, Mervyn Dymally, had the same advice. While at the time I didn't take their counsel, eventually they proved to be right. What was operating was my lifelong habit of being unable to say no, and another lifetime habit of long hours and hard work. While it was me and my character, I knew that it didn't lead to a well-balanced life. Nevertheless, I did not take steps to change my lifestyle.

One of my committees, The Joint Legislative Committee on Legal Equality was, as indicated, at the time in the vanguard of dealing with women's rights and concerns in America. Realizing the importance of this committee, I undertook a major project and charged the staff with the responsibility of reviewing thousands of codes and statutory provisions to make sure there was no discriminatory gender language or effect in them. It was an enormous job and resulted in my authorship of a package of sixty-eight bills which I managed to shepherd through to the Governor and which were signed into law. Some changes involved the clarification of mere nuances, but many were quite dramatic. Among the provisions of this package were bills ensuring that women had equal rights to all community property in divorce cases. The bills also strengthened

California's "no fault" divorce system. In effect they ensured equal rights for women and brought California into compliance with the Equal Rights Amendment (ERA), a proposed amendment to the United States Constitution ratified by California, but not by a sufficient number of states to become part of the United States Constitution.

For my work on behalf of women's rights, the President of the National Women's Political Caucus stated that "Omer Rains has done more to further the rights of women under the law than any other legislator in California history."

Insofar as the Democratic Caucus was concerned, I made a conscious decision to not only change the composition of the staff but to change the responsibilities of the staff. Historically, the staffs of both the Democratic Caucus and the Republican Caucus focused primarily on electioneering type activities; that is, trying to help candidates of their respective parties to get elected. Questioning the propriety of this conduct, I appointed as Staff Director a lady named Sue Foreman, who had previously worked for me as a Director of the Committee on Legal Equality. Sue and I discussed in depth the fact that members were not able to read each and every bill, as they numbered in the thousands over a two-year period. As a result, members were not always adequately informed of the specific contents of each bill. Therefore, a highly professional, well-credentialed, and educated staff was hired to prepare for distribution to each member of the Caucus a Third Reading Analyses (TRA). The TRAs were to summarize each and every bill and, in so doing, take an even-handed approach —not one that was strictly partisan. In addition the TRAs were to set forth those either in opposition to or in support of the particular piece of legislation. The TRAs became invaluable to the members of the Democratic Caucus and made it possible for members to make more reasoned and considered votes as bills came up for vote. In addition, the Caucus staff was to prepare speeches on substantive issues for members of the Caucus.

All in all, the changes to the Caucus staff operation were initially well received. As a result, when Senator Ken Maddy was later elected Republican Caucus Chair, he made the unusual request to be my seat mate. Ken was a friend but, in addition, he informed me that his own Republican Caucus had come to rely upon the TRAs being provided to the Democratic Caucus members. He wanted to change the direction of the Republican Caucus staff to more closely mirror the responsibilities I had given the Democratic Caucus staff. This worked extremely well and Ken and I became the best of friends. Tragically, Ken's life was prematurely cut short by cancer. It was a great loss.

California, like most states was often in the middle of a budget crisis caused by deficits. When Jerry Brown was elected in 1974, he inherited Reagan's deficit. This was addressed basically by robbing Peter to pay Paul. In 1982, newly elected Governor George Deukmejian inherited the mess from Brown. Deukmejian then left his deficit to Pete Wilson who in turn left it to Gray Davis, who mishandled it so badly that he made history by being recalled, opening the door for the election of Arnold Schwarzenegger. Jerry Brown's recent election, after a twenty-eight-year hiatus, gives him a second chance to deal with a budgetary nightmare that is now worse—far worse — than ever.

Unlike most other states which require a simple majority vote to pass the budget bill, California historically required a two-thirds vote of each house, thus enabling a minority party to hold up passage of the budget bill whenever it wished to do so and it so chose that course of action virtually every year.

Given my fiscal conservatism and my belief in not only having a balanced budget, but also in maintaining a "rainy day reserve" for the state to utilize in the event of unexpected crises, I was deeply bothered by these deficits. Concerned about the state's runaway spending and seeming inability to balance its budget, I began looking into ways that we could become more fiscally responsible. One way was via consolidation of Governmental entities. There are fifty-eight counties in California. At the time there were also 420 cities, more than 1,000 school districts and well over 5,000 "special districts," which include everything from Cemetery Districts to Mosquito Abatement Districts to Water Districts and so on and so forth. All of these entities have their own counsel, independent accountants, general managers, and other staff personnel, all with overlapping authority and with all the needless expense and rich pensions that such duplication implies—at significant cost to the taxpayers. With reorganization, some incredible savings and efficiencies could be achieved in my opinion.

This problem was later exacerbated in 1978 when a new and controversial ballot initiative emerged. It was Proposition 13, which was designed to limit real estate taxes paid by California homeowners. The reason for it was the ever climbing property tax rate in California which truly was out of control. Prop 13, if passed as originally drafted, would limit tax increases for those already owning homes to a maximum of 1% per year. As the years went by a new homeowner living in a tract home right beside a home covered by Prop 13 could have a tax rate double or even triple that of his neighbor with an identical home. This inequality would eventually cause all kinds of problems, social as well as economic. A tax rebellion was truly forming.

While I appreciated the reasons for the revolt, I also recognized that downstream the passage of Prop 13 would become a fiscal nightmare for the state. One of my best friends in the Senate was Peter Behr, a Republican who represented Marin County north to the Oregon border. Peter shared my concerns about Prop 13. With both of us realizing how disastrous and fiscally irresponsible Prop 13 would be in the long term, Peter and I co-authored an alternative which was passed by the Legislature and placed on the ballot along with Prop 13 in June, 1978. Proposition 8, as our legislation was numbered on the ballot, also placed a cap on the tax rate that could be utilized for property tax purposes but did so in a way that would be fiscally responsible.

As it turned out, both Propositions passed, but Prop 13 passed by a larger margin and, as a result, it became law. Its proponents were consumed with the victory of being able to limit property taxes and their focus couldn't be diverted beyond that. They didn't see the huge financial potholes that the proposition left in the road ahead, potholes the citizens of California are falling into this very day.

What predictably did happen downstream was that since cities and counties relied so heavily on real estate taxes, there was immediately an enormous shortfall of revenue. This required a massive bailout of cities and counties by the state of California. But like the Shanghai'ed English sailors of old, when you take the King's money, you are then indebted to the King and must do his service. And so the cities and counties lost most of their independence to the state. This truly hamstrung the cities and counties as more and more control shifted to the State Government in Sacramento. It also caused more and more budgetary games to be played whenever on an annual basis the budget bill came before the Legislature.

In politics, true reform can generally be accomplished only in times of crisis. The one silver lining I saw with the passage of Prop 13 was that my annual arguments in favor of consolidation of governmental entities was called for now more than ever before. In short, "When you have a lemon, make lemonade."

However, when I arrived at my capital office the day after the passage of Prop 13, an extraordinary number of state and local officials, as well as public employee lobbyists, were lined up outside my door. My long-held beliefs about government reorganization were well known and, as a result, I was a prime focus of locally elected officials who wished to simply be bailed out by state money so they could conduct business as usual. In that line were numerous proponents of Prop 13 who had supported it simply for the sake of their own popularity. One prime example was the Mayor of Santa Barbara, again, supposedly a strong supporter of Proposition 13. Yet, his message was, "We can't allow this to hurt Santa Barbara. We are special. You have to help come up with state money for us."

Gritting my teeth in anger, my response was, "You verbally supported it, I assume you voted for it—so now learn to live with it." Nevertheless, a "one-time" massive bailout bill in the amount of $4.4 billion from the state surplus (yes, California then had a surplus) allowed for a stopgap solution supposedly designed to cushion the impact of Prop 13 only until long-term governmental reorganization could be developed and implemented over the course of the following year.

Needless to say in light of the mess that California finds itself in today, no significant and fiscally responsible steps were taken during the following year to address the challenge caused by Prop 13. Rather, all 7,000 plus entities once again came hat in hand the following year saying give us even more. Thus, Assembly Bill 8 was enacted, ostensibly as a permanent plan for funding local services. However, for the most part it accomplished that goal by simply shifting funding from the local to the state level. Sadly, it failed to offer any guarantee of fundamental reform—and did so at what was then the outrageous cost of $4.85 billion for that year alone—almost $500,000,000 more than the year before. Designed to continue indefinitely, it was the most fiscally irresponsible piece of legislation that I was ever asked to vote on. As a result, I voted No! In doing so, I may have been the only Democrat and one of the few members of either house, Republican or Democrat, to express my concerns—and I did so vociferously, arguing again that great change could only occur during moments of crisis and that we should take advantage of this crisis to effect a cost saving and more efficient reorganization of government in California. But with 7,000 locally elected governmental entities in the state begging for money, a bailout by the state not only occurred then but, predictably, it became the norm year after year.

Today, California is an insolvent state and the reason for that can be traced in large measure directly to the passage in 1978 of Proposition 13, and to the Legislature's response thereto. Not surprisingly, in some ways this was the most intensely lobbied bill of my legislative career. It may not have had the array of traditional special interest lobbyists that I saw annually in opposition to my Bottle Bill, but the sheer number of local officials and public employees at every level of government were so thick that it was difficult to even wade through the Capitol corridors.

In explaining my vote against AB 8, I wrote a number of articles forecasting the woes that, in my opinion, would eventually befall the state absent adjusting program and pension levels to meet lower revenue limits and bemoaning the acceptance of the same tired and failed strategies of the past. Specifically, I wrote in one article that, "during a period of increasing fiscal uncertainty, [AB 8] calls for the largest appropriation in the history of this or any other state. In the face of current recessionary trends and other fiscal uncertainties, and with the long-range effects of Proposition 13 still unclear, such extravagant spending commitments pose a serious threat to our future economic well-being."

I concluded by stating that, "by passing AB 8, I believe we missed the perfect opportunity to restructure California government so that it might be more responsive, more efficient; yet less bureaucratic and less costly. Perhaps time will prove me wrong. I truly hope so." Needless to say as one looks at California mired today in insolvency, time did not prove me wrong. I wish it had.

─────────────

Increasingly concerned about the image of the State Legislature, I also consistently voted against legislative pay raises. This didn't make me popular with my colleagues, but in light of the state's budget problems and given the environment that inspired the passage of Proposition 13, I didn't think it was a good idea for us to increase our own salaries thus making an already cynical public that much more untrusting of the Legislature. It wasn't that I didn't believe we deserved a pay raise, because we did. The rate back then had risen to about $17,000 a year and all that was allowed by law was a 5% increase.

One colleague who was really angered by my position in this regard was Jim Mills, President Pro Tem of the Senate. Jim was nearing retirement age and his retirement benefits were adversely affected when pay raises were not granted. So he began a campaign to oust me as the Chairman of the Senate Majority Caucus, but he was unable to do so. In 1978 he attempted to replace me with Senator Wilson from the San Diego area, but that attempt was likewise unsuccessful. Mills' inability to do so shocked the California political establishment since Mills was ostensibly the Leader of the Senate. Eventually, we voted to oust Mills as President Pro Tem, replacing him with Senator David Roberti, a colleague from Hollywood.

I was one of those who had encouraged Roberti to make a run at Mills. In return for my support and with the idea of eventually running for the office of Attorney General, I told David that my support was predicated on me assuming the Chairmanship of every single Senate or Joint Legislative Committee or Sub-Committee that dealt with the administration of either civil or criminal justice in California. There never had been such a consolidation of power, and it would mean giving one person extraordinary control over the making of virtually all laws affecting Californians. I also would be serving on the State Judicial Council, chaired by the Chief Justice of the California Supreme Court, as well as on the California Law Revision Commission. I informed David that, given these appointments, I would relinquish my position as Democratic Caucus Chair. David agreed to all of these conditions, and Roberti replaced Mills as President Pro Tem.

The person who succeeded me as Caucus Chair, Paul Carpenter, pledged to devote his time exclusively to raising money for Democratic candidates. This was unfortunate and to be sure the Caucus became less professional, more partisan, and began to be used by Carpenter in a number of questionable ways. Eventually, Carpenter suffered a felony conviction for his activities. Before he was sentenced, he fled to Costa Rica. However, facing extradition, he was returned to California where he was sentenced to prison and eventually was to die of cancer while still incarcerated.

16
The Red Baron

"Never leave hold of what you got lessen first you got hold of something better."
— Rains' Rule of Wing Walking

In May of 1975 I was roped into an adventure that would be considered bizarre for any politician. Only members of the Senate and the Senate's Sergeant at Arms can be on the Senate floor when the Senate is in session. One Thursday, while we were in floor session, the Chief Sergeant at Arms approached and advised me that my Chief of Staff, Ross Pumfrey, was at the back of the room and wished to confer with me about something that was relatively urgent. After getting this information I arose and went to the back of the chambers in an area where the staff is allowed to speak to members. There Ross told me that a few weeks before some ladies with the Children's Home Society had approached him asking whether or not I would assist them in a major fund raising event.

I knew of the Children's Home Society because it was not only the world's largest adoption agency, but it was headquartered in Santa Barbara. I asked Ross in what way could I be of assistance. He said they wanted to know if I would ride in a bi-plane at an air show as they felt that my presence would allow them to draw greater attendance. In that I had ridden many times in bi-planes and had no particular concern based on what Ross told me, I said to check with my scheduling secretary and, if I had no conflict, that I would be willing to do it. I heard nothing further about the matter and it was the furthest thing from my mind until one day many weeks later when one of my secretaries, Marilyn Chapman, brought a note to me saying that Steve Lawrence of the Associated Press was on the line. I took the call and Steve asked, "Is this really true, Senator? Are you really going to be walking on top of a bi-plane?"

I said, "Steve, what in the world are you talking about?"

He said, "I have a press release from the Children's Home Society stating that you are going to participate in a fund raising event for them, and that you would do so by walking on top of a 1939 bi-plane piloted by a man named Joe Hughes."

I said, "Steve, I have no idea what you are talking about. You must be crazy." About that time I began to remember the conversation that I had with Ross several weeks before. In any event, I quickly said to Steve, "Steve, don't jump the gun - don't put anything out. There has been a mistake."

"I'm sorry, Senator, this went out over the wires about a half an hour ago."

About that time, Marilyn came back into my office and said, "Oh my Lord, you are not going to believe this. We are getting calls from all over the country, even some from overseas, wanting to know about this fundraising event in which you are going to participate."

I quickly went into Ross's office and found him with his hands over his face. Taking his hands down, he picked up a photograph showing a man upside down on the top of a pre-World War II bi-plane. The man's head was no more than six inches above Niagara Falls.

I said, "Is that what they expect me to do?"

"I'm afraid it is. Please forgive me. It's not at all what I thought, and I just saw this photograph within the last hour." Anyway, by this time sure enough the entire national press corp., electronic media as well as print media, was on top of the story and I was at a loss with respect to what to do.

I also thought that, given the photograph I was shown, I probably could not physically participate in this fashion because of the airplane accident in which I had been involved many years before. As mentioned earlier, I had blown out my entire right and left eardrums and had off and on ear problems after the incident with Bill Dulla at the Santa Paula airport. However, when I returned that weekend to Ventura County and checked with my ENT specialist, Dr. Clinton LaGrange, he informed me, at least based on what I told him about the flight, that I actually could participate. But he strongly urged that I not do so because of the danger to my heart. That caught me by surprise so I asked him why in the world it would affect my heart?

He related that there would be tremendous strain and stress on the heart and although I was still relatively young and in pretty good shape he didn't think that it was a very wise thing to do. I pretty much dismissed that as anything to be concerned about because I was, indeed, very healthy and in good shape for the most part. In any event, I was pretty well hooked in by this time because of all the publicity surrounding the event.

Before the event was held I did speak by telephone on one occasion to Joe Hughes, the pilot of the 1939 German bi-plane on which I would be standing. He gave me a lot of confidence because he sounded as though he knew what he was doing. I also had his background checked out and learned that he was world famous and had been an aerobatic pilot for a long time. Therefore, I decided to go forward.

Nevertheless, I did not actually meet Hughes until the day of the air show. At that time, accompanied by quite a few members of my staff, we went to the airfield in question and I for the first time saw the airplane on which I would be standing. I was very surprised to see that there really wasn't much to hold me on. The plane had been rigged up for a professional wing walker/acrobat who stood only 5 feet 4 inches high. At six feet, I was considerably taller than the man who ordinarily would do the routine.

There was a back brace but, again, it was designed specifically for the 5 foot 4 inch professional wing walker. The back support was really just there in order to keep me from being blown over backward. There were two small foot straps but they didn't cover the feet, only a slight portion of the toes so that an inch or so of the boot or shoe could be inserted. Then two guy wires came up from the top of the top wing of the airplane. They were the critical components.

The idea was to hold tightly onto the two wires at all times. Hughes told me what would happen. He warned me that I would not be able to last the entire fifteen minutes of the ordinary routine, but that at any time all I had to do was signal and he would bring me down. It was his estimate that if I was up for two, three, or four minutes it would be sufficient. He seemed certain that I would not be able to do the entire routine. That was the last thing he should have said to me. Anytime someone says that to me, I'm determined to finish the job.

I did realize that we were going to initially go up to about 1,000 feet and then make a very steep dive toward the runway. As we approached the runway, Hughes informed me he would do the first maneuver, rolling the plane upside down and then bringing it back around on the other side, then going back up and beginning to do loops when he got to about 500 feet. Thereafter we would be doing more rolls and loops and most of the routine would include cutting out the engine for dramatic purposes as smoke came out the back. Then starting up the engine again, doing dives that were not quite as close to the runway and pulling out in a rather precipitous manner on each occasion.

In any event, once I had a pretty good idea of what we were going to do, I climbed up onto the top wing and inserted my toes into the braces, and attached my hands very tightly to the guy wires. Hughes started the engine, and off we went.

As we taxied down the runway I rather felt self-assured and confident. It was a beautiful clear day—warm sun, blue sky—and the wind, though relatively brisk, felt good on my face. As we began to climb, I had a strong feeling of exhilaration at being airborne. At the same time, the humorous side of the entire adventure began to pop into my mind. I'd like to say that I pictured myself as Jonathan Livingston's seagull in search of freedom, but I actually felt more like Snoopy in search of the Red Baron.

After a rather slow climb to the designated altitude, approximately 1,000 feet, we abruptly started a 150 mph dive. At this point, it suddenly crossed my mind that I really ought to be lying in the sun on some isolated beach. The "G-Force" of the descent was much stronger than I had anticipated. I could feel it pulling at my face, helmet and goggles. During the dive, I became conscious of feeling fright for the first time during the flight. I didn't realize it, but I was experiencing ground rush. It wasn't like we were headed toward the runway, but rather that the runway was coming up toward us.

I actually thought we were going to crash, but about 50 feet above the ground Hughes began the first of numerous rolls of the aircraft. However, as we went into the first roll and as I was turned upside down on top of the wing I thought that my head was going to hit the runway. But then we went all the way around 360 degrees and headed up again. When we got to about 500 feet, Hughes went into his first loop and then cut out the engine, giving a dramatic effect, and then started it up again.

After that, it was simply a kaleidoscope of colors: the green of the grass and trees, the gray of the runway, the blue of the sky and the white of the clouds. Things moved so quickly that I really didn't have time to think of fear, joy, exhilaration, or anything else. I simply held on for dear life, determined to finish the entire routine—and I did!

As I think back, the most enjoyable part of the entire ride was, in fact, the interval when I was flying upside down. It was a totally sensory experience, as I grasped the wires as tightly as I could. It was from this experience that I developed the "Rains' Rule of Wing-Walking"—"Never leave hold of what you got lessen first you got hold of something better." As I said, there was no time to think, no way of putting all that was flashing past me into any sequence or perspective. It was simply a breathtaking mélange of colors and shapes—imagery more than detail.

However, when we began our descent and when the aircraft hit the runway, having been in the air for approximately fifteen minutes, I knew the ride to be almost over. At that time I became conscious for the first time of my heart. It was pounding unlike any time in my life, either before or after. It felt like it was going to pound right out of my skin. I then began to realize what Dr. LaGrange had referred to, and that things had moved so quickly in the air I had not been aware of it. My heart had probably been pounding like that the entire time I was in the air.

However, politician that I was, by the time we had taxied to a halt, with TV cameras, radio and TV mikes, and print media all around the plane, I was as calm as could be, or so I pretended. I answered all questions that were asked, and there were many. I described the joyful moments of the ride without at any time telling of the gut wrenching fear I had experienced on the first dive. I think I actually expressed the way in which I had experienced those same mixed feelings of relief and disappointment that one feels upon completing a ride on a giant roller coaster—a really giant roller coaster.

Everyone, I suppose, has a fantasy of from time to time doing something adventurous, exciting and different. As a self-admitted adrenaline junkie, I have had a lifetime of such experiences. But not often does an opportunity like this present itself. I certainly have no regrets over the experience but rather pleasant memories, and if it was of help to the Children's Home Society, it was definitely worthwhile.

There is a postscript to this story, however. Not long after my breathtaking ride, I witnessed a horrible accident on television. Jim Browning, Chief Consultant to the Senate Committee on Political Reform lived quite close to me when we were in session in Sacramento. Each evening before the Committee met he would come to my house or I would go to his to review the staff analyses of bills to be heard in Committee the following day.

On one such evening, I went to his place and we were lying on the floor looking through the bills and the analyses of the bills to be heard the following day. In the background, the TV was on very low. I heard the announcement that a world famous

wing walker had been decapitated earlier that day at the Reno National Air show …
"Stay tuned for the 11:00 news."

Curious about the headline, I sat up to watch. What I saw horrified me. The same airplane, piloted by the same man, Joe Hughes, doing the same routine I had done, was participating at the Reno National Air show earlier that day. The only difference was that the person on top of the wing was the professional who was ordinarily there. As Joe went into the initial dive—the one that had given me fright—and began his roll, apparently a downdraft hit the plane and the person on top of the wing, a very good and long-time friend of Joe's, was in fact decapitated.

To this day, people present at the Reno National Airfield when this tragedy occurred remember and talk about the incident. Joe Hughes gave up flying that day although I did read a few years ago that after almost thirty years of not flying he had taken it up again. In any event, I realized that what I had done, given the trust that approximately one million people had placed in me as their representative, had been an irresponsible act on my part. I was fortunate in that the press did not pick up on the fact that the horrible accident, again national news, was the same stunt involving the same plane and the same pilot in which I had participated just a short time before, and I certainly didn't mention it.

17

"Climbing" toward the Summit

If I once performed as the "Red Baron," then surely I could walk again—whatever others said.

"I'm going to walk," I told the physical therapist who came to the house three times a week to massage my legs, help me work on fine motor skills, and test my sensation with pin pricks during my recovery from the aneurysm.

"Not now, you're not," she said. "If the day ever does come that God blesses you to be able to stand and maybe even take a few steps, you're going to do it only after the doctors say so. You're not going to do it one minute sooner and you mustn't even try. I have instructions to reinforce the Doctor's orders about this."

"What a bunch of shit," I thought. The doctors had instructed her to tell me not to try to walk.

"You're at an advanced age," the doctors had said to me before leaving the hospital. "And more people die of broken bones at your age than anything else. If you do manage to stand on your own—and that's highly unlikely—you're going to fall. You'll break some bones, and you'll be right back in the hospital. We'll be dealing with yet more complications."

I appreciated the work that the therapist was doing on my behalf and the concern extended to me by my doctors. But they could not follow me where I was going. And the words "advanced age" frosted me to no end. My Lord, I was barely sixty and before my aneurysm and stroke I had been as strong and physical as the twenty and thirty-year-olds that often I hiked, climbed, biked and participated in sports with. That's where I was once again going and they just didn't get it—or maybe they did.

So I tried to walk when I was at home by myself because no one else was willing to help or let me try.

Just days after arriving home, I had been able to use the left side of my body to get a foot down to the floor. When I tried to get the other foot down, I crumbled. But I felt I had won! I had thought to myself, "Next time I'll do better."

The next day after that first attempt I tried to walk again. I was losing patience with therapy so I decided, "I'm going to do better. Yesterday, I learned some things to do and some things to be careful about and I will build from there."

I knew that I had to carefully watch the bed stand since my head had scraped the corner during my fall on my initial attempt. Although the bed stand was a source of potential danger, I had learned how to use it to provide assistance.

Within a day or two of trying to become ambulatory, I was able to do better. I managed to get both feet on the floor. Then again I crumbled.

"Victory again," I thought.

From the ground where I sat, I pulled myself up. It wasn't easy. In fact, it was damn hard. From one of my favorite poems, "Invictus," I kept saying to myself "I am the master of my fate; I am the captain of my soul".

I struggled to pull myself up. I reached over to the side slat of the bed, and using my left hand and every ounce of strength that I had, managed to push my body up to the top of the bed.

Once there, I balanced myself against the bed, and with one hand on the bed stand (I had refused a walker for fear I would learn to rely on it), I tried to take a step and fell yet again.

"That's okay," I thought. "I'm making headway."

I tried again. This time, I did it. I took two steps—and then promptly fell. But I had taken steps—two of them!

Each day, I made more progress. Soon, I was able to take two steps while steadying myself against the bed stand. The next goal that I set for myself was to take two steps while holding onto nothing. A few days later, I did so.

Not long after, I crossed the room. I was wobbly and tentative as hell, but I had covered about fifteen feet from the bedside to the wall. The "terrain" of the bedroom was flat and the "altitude" was low, but I might as well have been climbing a mountain. I felt like I had summited.

When you reach high altitudes while mountaineering, the air thins out so much that it's painful to keep going. It's hard to breathe and easy to stop. But whenever I had encountered that situation while climbing mountains I would say to myself, "All I have to do is take one more step. Now, another. Now, another." With that mentality, pretty soon I had climbed a mountain.

That was how I crossed the bedroom of my home in Carmichael during my recovery, too. One step; now another. One step more; and yet another. I made it to the wall in the most awkward, unsteady fashion—stepping with my left foot, then dragging my right leg to follow as the script played in my head. "One step; now another."

Pretty soon, I had crossed the bedroom. Yes, my steps were wobbly because I lacked equilibrium and balance, but I had achieved my first goal. Less than twenty days had passed since my release from the hospital, and I had walked.

18

George Moscone

"Dream as if you'll live forever, live as if you'll die today."
— James Dean

There had been several people who had left indelible impressions on me during my early years in elective office. One was certainly George Moscone. Although I had met him on several prior occasions, it was not until early 1974 that I became well acquainted with George. He had entered the California Gubernatorial race but eventually withdrew due to the name recognition of Jerry Brown and the vast sums of campaign money that Jerry's father, former Governor Pat Brown, was raising for Jerry.

As soon as I arrived in Sacramento, George befriended me. It turned out that we had an amazing number of interests in common and they extended well beyond politics. Most of all George loved sports trivia and we had constant trivia challenges—even when we were just passing each other in the hall. In short, George and I quickly bonded.

When George later declared his candidacy for Mayor of San Francisco, we held a fundraiser for him in Santa Barbara. For the fundraiser George was flown by one of his supporters from San Francisco down to Santa Barbara in a beautiful twin engine private plane. After the fundraiser was over and about 11:30 or 12:00 that night, I took him back to the small, but picturesque and quaint Santa Barbara airport where George was to be picked up. The airport was closed for the night as there were no more flights scheduled until the following day.

The pickup plane was late in arriving and when it did, it was a single engine prop job. George told the pilot that he didn't trust single engine planes and that they needed to bring in a twin engine plane. Now well after midnight, the pilot called San Francisco to see if a twin engine plane was available at that hour and, if so, if a trip to Santa Barbara was feasible that late in the evening. One was located we were told, but it would be several hours before it could be flown to Santa Barbara 400 miles to the south of San Francisco. I asked George if he wanted me to take him to a nearby hotel or motel. It was a typically beautiful Santa Barbara night. The stars were out and the temperature was mild. George asked, "Got a blanket in the car?"

"As a matter of fact, I do."

"Until the plane arrives, let's just lay out here and talk sports trivia and politics," George's two favorite subjects. Mine, too.

So, removing our coats and ties, we laid down and stretched out on the grass. We began to talk politics. George said: "Omer, you've just been elected Chairman of the Senate Majority Caucus, the number three position in the Senate and you're only thirty-five years old. I'm told you're the youngest person to hold that position in the history of the state. If you play your cards right, the options available to you are endless. You can become President Pro Tem when Mills steps down or is deposed. Phil (Congressman Phil Burton) has been doing polling in Lagomarsino's Congressional District and he tells me the seat is yours anytime you want it, although I think that would be a step down for you from your present position. Then there is state-wide office, though that's tough unless you're prepared to raise millions and millions of dollars to buy name recognition in the Los Angeles/Orange County and Bay Area media markets.

"Whatever your long term goals, let me give you some unsolicited advice. First, you need to slow down and try not to alienate those whose help you may need in the future. The word has gotten around that you threatened to turn in one of the most powerful lobbyists in the state. You know who I'm talking about. The members of the Third House feel they have to walk on tiptoes around you. Of equal importance, the legislative proposals that you push the hardest, campaign finance and reapportionment reform are an anathema to most of our colleagues. They are also miffed that you authored the bill to repeal the legislative pension program and you voted against their salary increases. Your pension repeal bill and salary increase vote has really pissed off Jim Mills. Look, Omer, from a public policy standpoint, you're absolutely right on most of these matters but when you talk about taking away from the fellows the ability to draw their own district lines and their ability to raise special interest money, you are threatening the advantages each has as an incumbent. Why don't you back off a little and take your time with these issues?"

"George, I don't have a lot of time. When I first ran, I promised to serve only three terms, including the abbreviated term. Although no one else seems to remember that commitment, I do. With that in mind, I am going to do all I can in the relatively short period of time I have to represent my district and those groups who lack the ability to spread around vast sums of money—senior citizens, children, minorities, women, and most of the environmental groups. I'm not stupid. I know my priorities will often clash with members of the Third House. I also know that most incumbents are wedded to the way in which they are able raise vast sums of money by doing the bidding of their favorite interests. You and I both know that it's gotten to the point that the Third House lavishes money not so much on whether or not one is a Democrat or a Republican, but rather on whether or not one is an incumbent. They realize that, to an ever increasing degree, incumbents are overwhelmingly reelected. More than anything else, this is because of gerrymandering of the districts. Let's face it, when redrawing lines is done by the very people who will be affected, there is an inherent conflict of interest that simply shouldn't exist.

"And George, it's going to get worse. Ken Maddy and I have become good friends. Ken recently got me an invitation to visit the Rose Institute at Claremont College. What I saw was scary. Rose has been retained by the Republican Party to put on computer the profiles of every single voter in the state. They can then tailor campaign mailers and hit pieces house by house, voter by voter. More worrisome though is that the primary thrust of the Rose work has to do with reapportionment. They're preparing reapportionment maps by cherry picking voters even at the expense of slicing up cities, counties and other communities of interest. The proposed districts I saw had the most dragon-like features imaginable, all designed to maximize Republican advantage and to protect each Republican incumbent. Admittedly, Phil Burton and the Waxman-Berman people are master political cartographers, but their skills are made antiquated by these new technologies.

"That is pretty scary, Omer. The Reeps already have some major nut-cakes serving right with us in the Senate, especially the neo-Nazi and his colleague, the book throwing, toupee topped, elevator shoe wearing John's from Orange County. How does one area elect so many weirdos?"

"That may be a bit unfair, George. Let's face it: we've got some pretty squirrely people on our side of the aisle too, and some of them come from the same area. Moreover, in my opinion, some of the finest people I've thus far served with are Republicans. Maybe I don't always agree with them, but how would you find better representatives and finer people than Peter Behr, Ken Maddy, Jim Nielsen or, in the other house, Frank Lanterman? Anyway, don't get me wrong—once Phil and the others understand these technical advances, they will catch up in a hurry. But from the standpoint of good government and public policy, this is bad shit. We will get to the point as a country where virtually every incumbent is entrenched and virtually immune from a successful challenge. Incumbents on both the left and right will be increasingly partisan, polarized, and extreme because their reelections will simply depend on appealing to the most extreme elements of their respective parties—those who more often than not vote in primaries."

"I see your point, but tell me what happens to your district, Omer, if you don't intend to seek reelection in 1982? Can any other Democrat possibly carry it?"

"Probably not—not as it's presently configured. We have done some polling. So has Phil (Burton) because I've shared my thoughts with him. I'm pretty safe now and, if I did seek reelection it's unlikely I will have a significant challenge and maybe not any at all. However, Gary Hart, the Assemblyman from Santa Barbara has only a 10-15% chance of carrying the district as it's currently configured, according to Phil. I think that's about right. For a variety of reasons, I'm not particularly fond of Gary, but he is a good vote on the issues. It's hypocritical of me, but if the current way of reapportioning the state and congressional districts remains in effect, my staff and I have figured out a way to give Gary, or another Democrat, a fighting chance. We would do this by chopping off the most southerly and the most northerly parts of the current district, as they are far and away the most conservative areas. We would then pick up the lost population by snaking the district down the coast taking in the Malibu area and then curve it around to grab the Warner Center and Studio City areas in Los Angeles County. Believe me, as I told Phil, I'm not going to be so sanctimonious and holier-than-thou that I'm just going to give the district back to another "do-nothing" or Neanderthal like Charles Teague. I may not like the current rules, but I will play by whatever rules are then in effect.

"Anyway, enough about me. I still haven't heard, George, why you are prepared to relinquish your position as Majority Leader of the California Senate. You talk of my options. My God, anytime you want to, you can become Pro Tem. Although we both know that to be a thankless job, it could launch you into the Governor's Office and, after that, maybe even the Presidency."

"I've certainly thought about that, Omer. You probably have, too. I would only trade my present position for three others in American life: President, Governor of California, and Mayor of San Francisco. Many have questioned my decision, but that's because they weren't raised in San Francisco. Those of us who were adore it and realize that it's unique among American—indeed—world cities. To be sure, it's a tough city to govern, but that just makes it that much greater a challenge. It's hard to explain my decision to someone who hasn't actually lived in San Francisco. Anyway, what do I have to lose? Worst case scenario: As a member of the California Senate, I'm one of the forty most powerful people establishing policy for the fifth largest economy in the world. The way I see it, I win whatever happens."

George continued, "OK, enough talk about politics—let's talk some sports…Sihugo Greene and Tom Gola. Where did they play and when?"

"Hey my friend, I'm offended that you would lob me such a soft pitch. Sihugo Green, 1954-1956, Duquesne University. Tom Gola, 1953-1955, LaSalle University. Let's play hardball. Give me the starting line-up of the 1948 Cleveland Indians."

"Jeez, Omer, 1948? Cleveland? OK, here goes, but I'm coming back to you with something equally hard."

And so a truly fun and memorable conversation continued for a couple more hours until the backup plane arrived in the wee hours of the morning. That was an unforgettable evening.

George was subsequently elected Mayor of San Francisco and he loved the job. Tragedy thereafter happened and it hit me like a hammer on the head. The notice of that tragedy arrived in a very unusual way. I had been invited to give an address at the annual American Association of Retired Persons (AARP) convention in Washington DC. While I was at the podium giving my talk, someone walked onto the stage and placed a note in front of me. I glanced down and looked at the note. The cryptic message was shocking and simply read: "The Mayor has been assassinated."

Glancing down at the note, my initial thought was that it must be one of the Mayor's in my own district, but which one of the eighteen elected mayors? Santa Barbara, Ventura, Oxnard, Santa Maria? Which? Who? I wrapped up my comments as quickly as possible and rushed from the stage only to learn with shock that the assassination was that of my dear friend, George Moscone, the Mayor of San Francisco. It was a particularly deep hurt, not just for me but for hundreds and hundreds if not thousands of others, all of whom had been close to George. His death, along with that of Supervisor Harvey Milk, was a senseless act of violence that stunned the entire nation. The outpouring of grief was incredible. George probably had as many close friends as anyone I've ever known. His death was a great loss not just to me, but to his city, and to the nation.

19

Jimmy Carter

"America did not invent human rights.
In a very real sense human rights invented America."
— Jimmy Carter

In February, 1975, Charles Manatt, the Democratic National Committee Chair came to Sacramento and spoke to me privately about a dark horse Presidential candidate who was setting up an impressive and, in his opinion, unprecedented organizational team. He had written two books, "Jimmy Who?" and "Why Not The Best?" This candidate had built an impressive organization in Iowa, New Hampshire, and other early primary and caucus states. His name was Jimmy Carter, and I was initially introduced to him by Manatt over the phone.

Later in 1975, I got to know Carter in person. When he came to Sacramento, I took him around and introduced him to the Democratic leaders in the State Capitol. Eventually in April, 1976, I was appointed by Carter to be his California State Chair and his Western States Co-Chair for his Presidential campaign. That involved helping to organize the thirteen western states. In making the appointment, the Carter campaign issued a press release, stating that "Senator Rains' outstanding record makes him a major ally in the Carter for President Campaign. He is one of the most distinguished public officials in Western America and will be taking on this important responsibility towards making Jimmy Carter our next President." In my opinion, I certainly didn't deserve those accolades, but by this time Carter and I had gotten to know each other fairly well and I had become quite impressed by his candor, work ethic and intelligence. Therefore, I was honored to accept the appointment.

Why was it that I, still a relatively new legislator, was chosen for this role over others? Was I the most powerful Democrat? No. Was I the highest ranking Democrat? No. Was I the most distinguished Democrat? No. The answer to all of these questions was unequivocally no. But I was becoming quite visible, my loyalty was unswerving to those with whom I could identify, and it didn't concern me that assuming responsibilities for the Carter campaign might rankle Governor Brown, who was also considering a run for the Presidency.

Being Co-Chair of Carter's western states campaign involved me getting to know him on a very personal basis. I found him, to an ever increasing degree, to have one of the most extraordinary intellects of anyone I had ever met in public service. His background was that of a nuclear physicist. I liked the fact that he was running a grassroots campaign, and I began to think that although he was a long shot, this dark horse could possibly win.

In advance of the Carter press release, I told Governor Brown of my intention to become involved with the Carter campaign. Since he was thinking of running for President, he tried to discourage me. I am not sure he ever forgave me for supporting Carter. In fact, I know that he didn't.

When Carter campaigned in the west, I generally travelled with him and with other members of the campaign team. During the general election campaign against Gerald Ford, it began to appear that the small state (from the standpoint of votes in the Electoral College) of Hawaii was to be more important than originally thought. As state after state was placed by pollsters in the electoral column of either Carter or Ford, Hawaii was a toss-up and thus became potentially pivotal. I was to make several trips there, traveling from island to island, going to Luau's and fundraisers and attending other political events. I found the Democratic Party in the state of Hawaii to be much more organized and disciplined than the disorganized party apparatus in California. President Gerald Ford early on had been expected to carry the state by a large margin because of Hawaii's large military presence (which traditionally votes Republican). Since Carter couldn't find time in his schedule to make a visit to Hawaii (nor could Ford) he sent his sister Ruth Carter Stapleton, as well as his wife, Rosalynn, and his son, Chip Carter, out to join me from time to time. They would each stay for a few days, and they were very helpful.

With only three electoral votes, Hawaii was looking more and more important. So, when the California Legislature went into recess in late September, I spent most of October and early November in Hawaii island-hopping. It was the most enjoyable campaigning I ever did. What a blast!

We ended up carrying Hawaii by a mere 2,000 votes and Carter won by about the same margin in the state of Ohio. These two states would prove to be the winning edge for Carter. If Carter had lost those two states, Ford would have been elected in the Electoral College even though Carter carried the national vote by a substantial majority. So what happened in the 2000 Bush-Gore campaign when the candidate who lost the national vote prevailed in the Electoral College almost happened twenty-four years earlier.

An especially memorable anecdote occurred in California early in the campaign. On a campaign swing in the western part of the country one day, we travelled on the campaign plane to several cities. At one point we were on the campaign bus when we were involved in a minor automobile accident. This delayed us for the rest of the day and it was very late when we got to our final stop that day. Everyone was very tired and prepared for bed when a group of Latino leaders demanded that they have a meeting with Carter that very night to air their grievances, no matter how late it was. When members of the campaign team balked because the candidate had already gone to bed, the threat was made that a news conference would be held the next morning and a further veiled threat was made that a switch of their support might go to Ford.

Several of us went round and round about what to do until finally the decision was made to awaken Carter. When I knocked on his door it was well after midnight and he was asleep. When he came to the door and I told him what had happened, he said, "I'll get dressed and come downstairs to meet with them."

While I was in his room I noticed a Bible on the nightstand—and it was in Spanish. Later, curious, I asked him about it. He told me, "I'm just a peanut farmer from Georgia, but when I was in the United States Navy I acquired a facility for language and I like to keep up on it so I often read in Spanish." This impressed me greatly. It might not other people, but for me it suggested an extraordinarily disciplined and intelligent man.

I know that the Carter Administration had and has many critics, but whatever one thinks of his administration, Carter has certainly demonstrated the kind of man he is since leaving office. He epitomizes how a former President ought to conduct himself. Most other Presidents, after leaving office, have made millions of dollars giving speeches, but Carter has chosen to dedicate the rest of his life to humanitarian causes (such as building homes for those in need), as well as doing all he can to bring justice and democracy to parts of the world where those conditions are lacking. His endeavors give more honor to the office of the Presidency than can ever be bestowed by simply enriching oneself.

In any event, after Carter's victory in November I was invited to the inauguration. I took Diana as well as some friends from all over the country including my dear friends from Hawaii, Ken and Mona Wong. Washington is cold and sometimes snowy in January and unfortunately Ken slipped and fell on the Capitol's icy steps breaking his leg. We got him to the hospital and he spent the rest of his stay on the east coast on crutches.

As for me, I had some tough decisions to make. As a person who strongly helped to elect the President, I was in line for a federal job in Washington if I wanted it. However, the only position that really appealed to me was that of Secretary of the Interior. While it was rumored that Governor Cecil Andrus of Idaho was Carter's choice to be Secretary of the Interior, I had a realistic chance of becoming Under Secretary of the Interior. But, in the end, I decided against applying for a Washington job for a couple of reasons. Probably first and foremost was that California politicians who took federal jobs historically had a very difficult time later trying to return to state politics. In addition, I had gained a position of power in California that allowed me to affect public policy not just in California but throughout the nation since California policies usually are later adopted by other states.

One day while in my office in the Capitol my receptionist, Marilyn Chapman, came in about something or the other and commented while there that she had just received two crank calls from someone pretending to be Jimmy Carter.

I asked, "Are you sure it really isn't the President?"

"The President of the United States does not place his own calls."

"Well, out of an abundance of caution, if the person calls again, go ahead and put him through."

Only a few minutes after Marilyn left my office she buzzed me and said, "The crank is calling again."

"Put it through."

I answered the phone. It was the President.

"Hi Omer. This is Jimmy." He began to laugh. "Do you know your secretary hung up on me twice?"

Marilyn never lived that down. Needless to say, after that call, the President was on the shortlist of callers that were to always be put through to me.

The others on that list were Diana Waldie (not yet my wife, but we were co-habiting), my parents, my children, Bill Kehoe, and John Reaves. Other than Diana, far and away the most frequent caller of these was John Reaves. After John suffered a serious but non-fatal heart attack, he retired and married one of the nurses he had met while in the hospital. A very intelligent and hardworking fellow, John quickly became bored sitting around. So he began investing fairly heavily in stocks, bonds, and commodities. He would call me every ten days or so to discuss his thoughts about a particular stock or industry. Invariably, as he had researched the companies or sectors before he called, he knew far more about them than did I. Nevertheless, it was fun and sometimes at night I would chart the advances or declines of one of his proposed investments and call him back with my thoughts. It was a good way to maintain the close relationship I had with John. One that was maintained right up until the time of his death.

Camp David, The Accords and Israel

Whether one approves or disapproves of the Carter presidency in general, his peace initiative at Camp David turned out to be historic. Some historians believe that we might actually have achieved lasting peace in the Mideast had Carter been reelected in 1980. Maybe yes; maybe no. To be sure, at the time there was a tremendous amount of trust between Carter and Menachem Begin of Israel and between Carter and Anwar Sadat of Egypt. This trust evaporated with the succession of administrations in each involved country, the United States, Israel, and Egypt. Nevertheless, the peace forged at Camp David has lasted between Israel and Egypt. I believe, along with many others, that Carter has not received the full credit he deserved for his peace efforts even though much later than ought to have been the case he was the recipient of the Nobel Peace Prize.

An administrative weakness of Carter's, just the opposite of Ronald Reagan, was that Carter involved himself in far too much minutia. He wanted to be involved in everything that was going on and wanted to be sure he understood everything that his administration was involved with. This simply isn't possible for the President of the United States. He simply must, to a very considerable degree, delegate most responsibilities to Cabinet Secretaries and others in whom he has placed trust by virtue of their appointments.

Two other things that probably spelled doom for the Carter administration were, for the most part, beyond the ability of the President to control. One was the incredible inflation that took place during the mid to late 70s, in large measure due to the actions of OPEC. The other, of course, was the taking of American hostages in Tehran, Iran, shortly before the Presidential elections of 1980.

In all fairness, notwithstanding the shortcomings of the Carter administration, I do fondly remember an administration that emphasized human rights around the world, that brokered a lasting peace between Israel and Egypt, that signed the SALT II Arms-Control Treaty with the Soviet Union, and that normalized diplomatic relations with China.

I also remember a President who repeatedly warned the American public of the dangers of our unrelenting and ever expanding dependence on foreign oil and of the need to begin aggressively to harness and develop alternative sources of "green" energy. Tragically, Carter was ridiculed and spoofed for these convictions by big oil and their allies. Now, of course, the chickens have come home to roost.

On a more personal note, I remember fondly the relationship I developed with both Jimmy and Rosalyn Carter and with just about every other member of the Carter family before, during, and after Jimmy Carter's administration. A number of events, some of which I have already chronicled, including dining and dancing in the White House, traveling with the President during the campaigns of 1976 and 1980, flying on Air Force One, being present for the signing of the Camp David Accords and, most of all, some personal moments that I shared with the President are truly treasured memories.

It was because of my closeness to Carter that I was invited to attend the signing of the Camp David Accords in Washington, DC. I was able to take Diana along. That night, after all documents were signed, we had a magnificent state dinner under tents on the White House lawn. The invited guests included major delegations from both Israel and Egypt. I had by this time gotten to know both Menachem Begin and Anwar Sadat, along with their respective wives, though not all that well. Sadat had struck me as a particularly impressive person, both in speech and demeanor.

The dinner that night was quite well organized. It was a lovely state dinner with multiple courses. An equal number of Americans, Israelis, and Egyptians were at each table. During dinner, a conversation ensued that I have never forgotten. I was seated directly across from the equivalent of the Chairman of the Joint Chiefs of Staff of Egypt.

He was an admirer of his President, Anwar Sadat. Nevertheless, because of his knowledge of feelings within Egypt and even the military over which he served as Commander, there came a point when he looked me in the eye and said, "Today my President has signed his death warrant—and he knows it…" The way he said it, and the steely look in his eyes, sent chills down my back. But the same gentleman wrote on the cover of my invitation: "We have signed a peace treaty where both nations have won." Today, over thirty years later, the treaty—unique in the Mideast—holds.

Sadat, of course, was later assassinated because of the actions he took in signing the Camp David Accords. Having studied the matter extensively, I do believe that Sadat probably did know that he might be signing his own death warrant. However, it is also my belief that he felt so strongly that it was necessary to reach an agreement—hopefully a lasting agreement—with Israel that he was prepared to accept the risk of a fate that although not necessarily inevitable, was likely. As a result, I have always held Sadat in the highest esteem possible, and believe he was one of the more courageous of statesmen in modern history.

As a result of getting to know Menachem Begin and other Israeli delegates at the Camp David Accords, in November of 1979, I was invited by the State of Israel to visit the country with a small delegation of elected officials from the United States. Diana was again able to accompany me. The purpose was to further familiarize ourselves with Israel, its history, culture, and geopolitical position.

It was an extraordinary trip. I picked up some ribbing from my colleagues when Diana and I were put up in the Presidential Suite in the King David Hotel overlooking the ancient Walled City of Jerusalem. I suspect that President Carter had something to do with that. Anyway, Jerusalem was full of wonders. It took us from the Wailing Wall to the Dome of the Rock. It was eerie to walk the streets of Jerusalem on stones on which Jesus himself might have treaded.

We traveled to every niche and corner of the country. It became readily clear just how small Israel is. And the implications of things we only read about and see on TV became abundantly clear. A good example is the Golan Heights on Israel's border with Syria. We often read about the Golan Heights, but to see it is to understand why the Golan Heights are so crucial to the defense of Israel.

Though the Golan Heights are not very high at all, no more than what I would call a relatively high bluff, if occupied by the Syrians they could rain artillery down on nearby

Israeli villages. On the other hand, if occupied by the Israelis, the road at the top runs straight through to the Syrian capital of Damascus. If the Israelis control the Heights, and they do, they have an open door to invade their historic enemy's capital no more than an hour's drive away. This is why to this day the Golan Heights are pretty much off the negotiating table.

Our contingent was also taken north far above the Litani river and fairly deep within Lebanon to meet with leaders of the "free" Lebanese army. One couldn't help but notice that the soldiers carried Israeli weapons, wore uniforms supplied by the Israeli's, and were paid by Israel. Almost every country involved in the Lebanese civil war had mercenary forces. I have since observed this practice in many parts of the world.

20
The Third Term

"The more things change, the more they remain the same."
— Anonymous

On April 3, 1977 at the age of thirty-six I married my second wife, Diana. She was twenty-six and quite lovely. We were married in the Chambers of the California Senate, the only time in the state's history when this was allowed. Seating in the Senate Chamber limited attendance to forty seats, one for each member of the Senate. The following weekend in Santa Barbara there was a huge reception for us with several hundred people in attendance.

For some time before our marriage, Diana was living with me in Sacramento and studying for her Master's Degree in Environmental Science at the University of California at Davis, about twelve miles west of Sacramento. After that, she began a PhD program and while still studying got a job in the Solar Division of the State Energy Commission.

Later that year during the legislative summer recess, Diana and I and my kids, Kelly and Mark, took a three week RV trip up the coast of California, Oregon and Washington and then over to the city of Victoria on Vancouver Island in British Columbia. From there we crossed over to the city of Vancouver and travelled up the Yellowknife Highway and eventually across the Canadian Rockies into Alberta Province north of Banff, and then South to Lake Louise and Jasper National Park. Eventually, we went further south to Calgary, site of the Calgary Stampede, home of the largest rodeo in the world. We spent a week in Calgary as guests of the Calgary Stampede and we had a great time.

After leaving office, I was later to return to Calgary often as a guest lecturer at the University of Calgary. One of those occasions was in 1988. That was the year the Winter Olympics were held in Calgary. While I was in Calgary for my lecture, work was being completed for the various Olympic venues. Then and there I had a unique experience. I was able to take a bobsled run with a Canadian bobsled team. Fantastic speed!!! A few weeks thereafter the Olympics started. I was able to be there on February 13th and 14th to watch the opening ceremonies and some of the competition that followed, but I had to return to Sacramento and then San Diego on the 15th.

By the end of our RV trip and after discussions with Diana, I was certain that I would seek a third term to the Senate. The reality was that I was seemingly very popular in my district, and certainly a household name throughout the central coast of California. My once quite vulnerable district (for me as a Democrat) was now a "safe district." Nevertheless, the Republicans still considered it a Republican District so I was to be their number one target of the three they felt they had a shot to win in 1978 (the other two they did win). In this campaign however, unlike the first two campaigns, I was able to do some professional polling and it showed that I was likely to win and probably in a landslide.

The Republican candidate was a wealthy businessman from Santa Barbara, E.G. "Wally" Wallenbrock. Wally had "the look." He was distinguished with a kind of Walter Cronkite type of dignified appearance but when he opened his mouth, he was in trouble. His rhetoric was dull, shallow, and uninformed. He did not at all have a significant grasp of the issues.

The Republicans thought, somewhat naively, that because Wallenbrock was the wealthy owner of a bottling company he would be an ideal candidate, especially seeing that the Bottle Bill which I authored year after year was such a hot topic with many organized groups lobbying in opposition to its passage.

As for me, I had an internal battle to decide whether, as in my first and second campaigns, I could afford to continue my policy of not taking corporate money or special interest contributions. One of my biggest shortcomings as a campaigner was that I was always a lousy fundraiser. I absolutely hated asking anyone for money. Yet, fundraising is essential to winning for most politicians, especially in a large and diverse district. So against my own convictions, I did accept some select special interest contributions during this third campaign. I probably would have won even if I had not made this decision, but I took the easy way out.

In addition, my old friend, Charlton Heston, helped me with fundraising and in October of 1978 he did a big fundraiser for me in the Santa Barbara area. Heston's image, of course, is that of the NRA champion. He is known for the iconic NRA photo of him holding a rifle in his hand and saying in effect that in order for him to give up his rifle it would have to be pried out of his "cold dead hands." So his image was that of a leading conservative but here he was helping me, a progressive Democrat. The truth is, Heston had a lot of depth and was quite progressive on most issues. Having marched with Martin Luther King Jr., he was especially dedicated to the advancement of human and civil rights. He was a very thoughtful and deep thinker and, in some heart to heart conversations with me at his Coldwater Canyon home, he relayed to me his sincere belief that the American people required weapons as an edge against tyranny. In one of those conversations we discussed the dangers of a military coup in the United States as depicted in a movie starring Burt Lancaster and George C. Scott. I believe it was called "Seven Days in May."

Although his arguments concerning a citizen's absolute right to bear arms of any kind did not persuade me as I thought that his position was far too extreme on this issue, it certainly did give me cause to stop and think about the issue once again. Chuck was a very bright man and the discussions we had from time to time tended to cover the political spectrum, not just gun control. Those discussions were always at a very high level. From a practical standpoint, Heston's blessing did me a world of good with the right-wing fringe in my district, most of which was in northern Santa Barbara County.

During the latter part of this campaign, I contracted mononucleosis and lost my voice which, for a politician, is like a hunter losing his bullets, so I fell back on my old formula of walking precincts ten to twelve hours a day since I had enough voice to generally deliver only one—maximum two—short speeches a day. Nevertheless, on November 7, the voters of the district went to the polls and I did in fact win in a landslide, getting more votes than any Democrat running for any office in the history of the Central Coast Area of California. In December, 1978 I was sworn in for my third term in the California Senate.

Back to business after being again sworn in, there were an unusual number of district projects that required immediate attention. One was the improvement of a state highway that was notoriously dangerous. That was Highway 126, which ran from Ventura to a place called Castaic Junction where 126 intersected with Interstate 5. The road was too curvy, too narrow, and had too many blind spots resulting in an inordinately high number of fatalities. In my opinion, it was the most dangerous road in the state. In politics, as in other aspects as life, often it's "the squeakiest wheel that gets the grease."

It took many years of tenacious fighting but eventually I got the 126 project considered, then prioritized, and finally funded. It was a major undertaking, but it did make the road a much safer one to this day.

On the energy front, OPEC was again in the news threatening oil price increases. Governor Brown jumped on the bandwagon at the behest of the energy industry (utilities, oil, and nuclear) and began to push hard for a liquefied natural gas (LNG) facility in California. It was a big issue at the time and high on the Governor's agenda. The sites under consideration were Oxnard, Long Beach, and Point Conception near the Diablo Canyon Nuclear power plant and not far from Vandenberg Air Force Base. Both Oxnard and Point Conception were in my district and I was vehemently opposed to either site. Liquefied natural gas is a highly flammable and dangerous product and an explosion could be catastrophic. I argued that if a serious accident happened in Long Beach or Oxnard it could potentially cause 100,000 casualties. For proof, I cited an LNG catastrophe in Japan involving liquefied natural gas. The danger of putting a facility near the nuclear plant at Diablo Canyon was to me also rather obvious. I was facing stiff opposition because huge amounts of money were being channeled into the coffers of the Governor and various legislators in key positions.

Led by Governor Brown, the fight went on for years. I was Vice-Chair of the Energy and Public Utilities Committee, the key Committee the proposal would come before and eventually a group of us on that Committee were appointed to study the issue. Certain members of this Committee travelled to Japan to further study the situation. I learned a lot. Properly suited up, I even went down several hundred feet to a temperature over one hundred degrees below zero to see how they solidified the gas. Solidification was necessary for purposes of shipping. After arrival at the plant site the gas would be thawed until liquefied and then pumped into pipes for distribution to final destinations. After this study in Japan, I came to understand even more how potentially dangerous all of this could be.

The LNG debate had heated up and the debate was really raging. This was a real hot potato for me. The US Department of Energy had spent millions of dollars on siting studies and they concluded that the less populated Point Conception area would be the safest among the three sites under consideration even though it was perilously close to Diablo Canyon. I thought this was insane, especially after what I had learned on my trip to Japan. Beyond the safety issue, I also had a lot of questions relating to the economics of the project. The sponsors of the project were also beginning to get cold feet and eventually we were able to defeat the proposal—but it had been a hard fought battle and, I had alienated a lot of powerful interests.

Before the various entities actually conceded defeat, the Senate Energy and Utilities Committee took another trip to Alaska. We landed in Anchorage and from there went up to the North Slope to inspect the pumping facilities near the Beaufort Sea above the Arctic Circle. As it was October, we spent a typical day for that time of year in twenty-four-hour darkness and were introduced to the oil company's underground cities. These were truly amazing and, though underground, were cities in every other sense of the word, right down to movie theaters. The employees were treated to "rest and recreation in the Lower 48" (generally Seattle) every two weeks to recharge their batteries before returning to work in this harrowing environment.

Our group travelled all the way down the Alaska pipeline to its terminal at Valdez. It was no junket but a solid five days of fact finding. One of the conclusions that I came to was that the oil operations were indeed affecting wildlife. The migratory patterns of the moose and other populations changed when they encountered the pipeline. I had heard the oil industry make claims that because the area around the pipe was warmer, the animals actually sought it out. But there was nothing to substantiate that claim. In addition, one has to factor into the equation the possibility of another oil spill disaster like the Exxon Valdez tragedy that was later to dump millions of gallons of oil into the water and which irreparably damaged wildlife and marine and shellfish populations, not to mention the billions of dollars in cleanup costs eventually absorbed in part at public expense. It took over ten years to again see clean water. In the meantime the economy in the region had suffered billions of dollars of damage.

About this time and feeling the need for a sanctuary, I bought a five and a half acre ranch near the north end of Folsom Lake about thirty miles northeast of Sacramento. The property, which we called the "Rest and Be Thankful Ranch," was located on Whiskey Bar Road, a name left over from Gold Rush days.

On the ranch we had horses, Nubian goats, dogs, and cats. Time spent working on the ranch was therapeutic and part of my escape mechanism. Sanctuary was as much a necessity as a luxury in those days. One time, Diana and I were having dinner in a very small secluded out of the way restaurant hundreds of miles to the north near the Oregon border, far from the Capitol and over 500 miles from my district. We had stopped to have an intimate dinner, but when I was recognized we found ourselves at dinner with a group of people. So much for a romantic weekend away from the hubbub of political life.

Despite all too infrequent diversions, my focus— as always— remained squarely on politics and my job. Today, when I look back at the state of politics in the late 70s and early 80s vis-à-vis our current situation, I see all too many similarities. Take terrorism. Terrorism is not a phenomenon of the new century. Certainly, it is a greater concern since 9/11 than before. However, there were numerous hijackings (often called "Skyjackings") well over thirty years ago and it was considered a big problem. Ed Davis, LA Police Chief at the time and later a colleague of mine in the Senate, when talking about terrorists who had made an attempt at a skyjacking at LAX famously said, "We ought to hang them at the airport."

There are also many parallels with environmental issues, especially those involving energy. Back in the 70s, elected officials all over the land were receiving sound, often brilliant demonstrations on solar, wind, biomass conversion as well as developing ocean technologies. We observed exciting proposals such as hydrogen automobiles, visual telephones, and many other advancements that were then and there developed technologies—not pie in the sky theories. So why haven't these technologies spread far and wide and been developed during the intervening years? Primarily because the willingness by all too many politicians to be controlled by powerful lobbyists and the financial support they receive from the already entrenched industries. Time and again throughout my life I have been reminded that in politics "the more things change, the more they remain the same."

During all of this time, I continued to carry an incredibly heavy legislative load. One item on which I worked yearly was the "Bottle Bill." There was a tremendous groundswell developing at the grassroots level statewide in favor of the legislation, especially as people became more and more educated on the issue. I was speaking throughout California on college campuses, to conservation groups, business groups, and doing numerous press conferences and radio interviews. Favorable press coverage was developing almost daily. Cartoonists were even providing help, not just in California, but elsewhere in the country including the St. Louis Post Dispatch, The Louisville Courier Journal, and in other urban papers on a national basis.

This increased public awareness created near panic in the interests that were affected. They brought in heavy guns from all over the land. Heavyweight lobbyists from throughout the country converged on Sacramento. Why? A fact of life in America is that if a bill affecting a lifestyle—in this case the throw-away ethic—becomes law in California, the rest of the country follows. Things often happen first in California and then work their way east. The bill's opponents wanted to kill it in the Golden State before it lit out across the rest of America. With almost 15% of the population and given the Interstate Commerce Clause of the US Constitution, to manufacture a deposit container in California would basically require the manufacturers to make the same bottle throughout the land.

Meanwhile, things were changing for me on a personal level. Having now created a relatively safe seat for me personally, I finally had the opportunity to accept some invitations I had previously turned down. An example was the Academy Awards to which I had been invited each and every year since I had first been elected. It is a fact of life that in California the political industry and the entertainment industry are incestuously intertwined. So, after many years of saying no to the invitation, I accepted the invitation of Lou Wasserman, the President of the Motion Picture Academy of Arts and Sciences. Diana and I were put up in the Beverly Hills Hotel. I dug out my tuxedo and Diana wore an elegant gown. When we emerged with the Wasserman's from our limousine and stepped onto the red carpet, a cheering, screaming section of women startled us. Assuming they must be screaming for me since Lou was quite elderly by this time, I puffed out my chest. Then I realized they were looking beyond me. I looked over my shoulder and saw Warren Beatty emerging from the next limo. Oh well, so much for my second in the Hollywood limelight. That was also the year that John Wayne made his last public appearance (he was fighting cancer) and he was awarded by the Academy with a Lifetime Achievement Award.

21

Turkey and Greece

"Never Stop Exploring"
— North Face

A more serious diversion also occurred that year. My dear friend, Ken Wong, who was now living in Hawaii, introduced me to a friend of his, Jimmy Yao. Jimmy and other members of his family had fled China in 1949 when the communists came to power. Jimmy seemed to have a never-ending supply of money. Although his much younger wife was President of a bank in Honolulu, that did not seem to be the source of Jimmy's money. When asked, Jimmy said that the source of his money was ownership of various Coca-Cola franchises in Asia. Early on I accepted this as fact—and it may have been. However, as the years went by, I did become suspicious that Jimmy might have received his funding from the CIA. That suspicion arose because Jimmy frequently made trips to Washington, DC. And, when not in DC, he did the gaming circle of the world from Las Vegas to Freeport to London to Paris to Macau, and so on and so forth. Jimmy was drawn to the gambling Meccas, and he dropped lots of money wherever he went. He would also be out of commission and unable to contact from time to time for undisclosed reasons.

However, I did not have any of these suspicions when I first met Jimmy in early 1979. Wong and Yao had requested on several occasions that I accompany them on a business trip to Turkey by way of London. Although I said no several times because of a conflict with legislative responsibilities, in early April during the Legislature's spring recess, I agreed to travel with them to London.

The problem was that Turkey, which had never defaulted on a bank loan since the Atatürk Revolution in 1927, was now in serious default. So an international consortium of banks led by Bank of America and Bank of Sumitomo was trying to negotiate a solution to what had become a fairly major financial crisis involving several hundred million dollars.

Wong and Yao had been asked to represent the banks or to get someone not identified with any of the banks to represent them in negotiations with the Turkish government. The Turkish government was rather unstable at the time.

Before leaving for London, I went to San Francisco and met with A.W. "Tom" Clausen, President of The Bank of America and later President of the World Bank. Clausen gave me the background information and told me that in London I would meet with Samuel Armacost (later President of the Bank of America) who would provide me with additional information.

Unfortunately, when it was time to go, Ken Wong had come down with an illness that would not allow him to travel so it was to be just Jimmy Yao and me. In London we met with Armacost who, at the time, oversaw Bank of America's European and Mideast operations. He provided us with the fascinating background surrounding the Turkish loan. It was a real eye opener.

During a series of meetings in London and afterwards in Turkey, I learned that most of the historic enemies in the Mideast had no problem working financial deals together so long as it was done in a clandestine manner. I learned that, when it came to business, countries that were traditional adversaries like Greece and Turkey, Israel, and certain oil-producing Arab states, as well as Turkey and Arab countries, were all working together on certain types of transactions. For example, Greek ships were sometimes used to transport Kuwaiti oil, utilizing Israeli middlemen and financiers, with cargo being used as collateral for Turkey in order to borrow money from major institutional lenders. It was very complex and I'm not sure I ever got the full story. In fact, I'm sure I didn't. However as the years went by and I later became more and more involved in international finance matters, I came to realize that these kinds of deals are pretty much par for the course.

However, before leaving London for Turkey, another problem arose. It turned out that Turkey had not long before recognized the People's Republic of China and Jimmy Yao was carrying a Taiwanese passport. As a result, he would be barred from entering the country, so I went on to Turkey alone.

Before I landed in Istanbul, and unbeknownst to me, as it literally occurred as I was in the air, martial law had been declared in Turkey due to terrorist activity. When my plane landed in Istanbul, my fellow passengers and I were surprised to see the Istanbul airport full of tanks, gun emplacements, and moving contingents of troops. Deplaning, I was met by the manager in Turkey for the Bank of Sumitomo. He accompanied me with a military escort across the tarmac where we boarded a domestic flight from Istanbul to Ankara, the capital of Turkey.

The Ankara airport was quite a long distance outside the capital city. When we landed at the Ankara airport, we were escorted to a waiting car for the trip into the city. Two other Sumitomo employees were in the car. The driver, though Japanese, spoke pretty good Turkish. They all spoke English, as well.

As we drove along, it quickly became apparent that Ankara is in a rather mountainous section of the country. From the front passenger seat, I was talking to the two gentlemen in the backseat when we rounded a bend in the road and came to an abrupt stop. A tank was idling in the road ahead of us and Turkish soldiers were conducting a search operation of every vehicle. It was a bit tense as we watched two armed soldiers approach. One was a Turkish officer with his braids and ribbons clearly on display. The other appeared to be a very young soldier. He was carrying a machine gun. When our driver with his window down began talking to the officer, I leaned over to hear what was being said, even though I didn't understand a word of it. Then I felt a gun barrel pressed to my temple. As I tried to move upright, this clown (young soldier) pressed the barrel tighter against my head. Rather than feel fear, I felt a hot rage building. Prudence would have suggested that I have some fear but I didn't. I was too full of rage. If I could have killed the S.O.B. I probably would have done so but I had the presence of mind not to make any precipitous move.

The driver tried to explain to the officer that I was a guest of the Turkish Government here on important business but seemingly he couldn't have cared less. They searched every single item in my suitcase, but finally we were allowed to pass. On the way, evidence of the fuel crisis caused by the OPEC cartel's embargo was everywhere. I thought it was bad in the United States. In Turkey I saw cars lined up for gas in lines that were literally miles long.

Over the next several days I had a number of meetings with various Turkish government officials, trying to get from them a timetable by which the country would begin to repay its international debt. When I left negotiations were ongoing, but a foundation for continuing discussions had been laid. Eventually compromises were worked out, and I felt that my own responsibilities had been successfully completed. The Turkish government had been very hospitable and they were quite careful to make sure that I boarded my plane in Istanbul for London in a safe manner.

So my first venture into the world of high finance had been beyond intriguing, it was an unforgettable experience. It had involved international chaos, danger, intrigue, and more. And once again I realized that I had possibly stared death in the face.

"Alexander the Great"

"There is nothing impossible to him who will try."
— Alexander the Great

A pleasant summer interlude from the Bottle Bill and other political wars was a trip to Greece during the summer recess of 1980. I was invited along with a group comprised primarily of Greek-American politicians to visit Greece from July 27 – August 8. I was invited because I had extensively studied the Minoan and Mycenaean civilizations, as well as the Classical Age of Greece, and had spoken on Greek history several times over the years. Our group travelled all over Greece and I was fascinated by it all, so much so that in future years I would go back numerous times taking groups and continuing to speak on Greek history and Greece in general.

During our visit to Greece, I first met Dr. Stephen Miller of the University of California. Dr. Miller was heading up an international archaeological team excavating the historic site of Nemea, second in importance only to Olympia insofar as ancient athletic competition was concerned. I got involved and remained involved for many years as first the track was excavated, then the baths and tunnels leading to the competition field, and finally reconstruction of the Temple of Zeus was commenced.

Near the end of our trip and having returned to Athens, a startling announcement was made. An historic archaeological discovery had been made near the city of Pella in the north of Greece, not far from Thessalonica. Initial reports were that they had uncovered the tomb of Alexander the Great. It later turned out to be that of his father, Philip of Macedonia. But a later world tour of artifacts discovered would still be called the Exhibit of "Alexander the Great."

Because the Greek government knew of my intense interest in archeology and anthropology, the government flew me to Thessalonica and took me by military jeep to the site of the discovery. It was completely cordoned off by the military and a tall fence surrounded the opening to the site. Everyone was excited by the discovery. Archeologists from all over the world were clamoring to get in, but for now were being kept out.

However, the Government allowed me accompanied by a guide to go into the tomb—what a privilege! For any person, even those not into archaeology, it would have been a moving and surreal experience. Everything about it: the aura, the smell, the history that seeped in from ages past. It was absolutely fascinating! Greek archeologists had started the excavation of the unusually well preserved site, untouched by human hands for over two thousand years. To see the artifacts and antiquities as they had been placed there almost twenty five hundred years ago was truly a privilege. I was honored to be able to view the site in its original state.

On a more humorous note, on our very last day in Greece, I told my friend, Angelo, that I wanted to buy a gold necklace for my wife. He said, "I will take you to a place very early tomorrow morning, about 5:00 am. We will be there ahead of the crowds and be back in plenty of time for you to catch your flight." I agreed.

In the wee hours of the morning, we made the hour and a half car ride to the building where he said I could buy gold very inexpensively. He said that he had made arrangements with the owner for him to be there quite early to allow us entry. Because of the time of day, there was no one on the streets. Arriving at the building, we began to walk up the stairs inside the building when I heard an ungodly amount of screaming and banging. I looked around and found where the racket was coming from. It was from an elevator. The door was shaking like someone on the other side was possessed.

I called out, "Who is in there?"

A voice answered, "Is that you Rains? Is that you?"

It sounded like one of our group, a huge ex-FBI guy named Lou Papan who was a legislative colleague of mine of Greek ancestry. He again started screaming incoherently. I called back, "What are you doing in there?"

His hysterical voice cried, "I came to buy a necklace. Get me out of here. I'm dying! It's incredibly hot!"

I called through the door, "Calm down, Lou."

"Get me out of here! Get me out of here!"

"OK, we'll get somebody. Just calm down."

We began pressing buttons and trying every way we could to open the door. I even mashed my hand trying to work the door open but no luck. My friend, Angelo, said, "I will go for help," and off he went.

When Angelo returned, he reported, "Nobody's up yet. I woke up a fireman but he said we would have to wait while he got some people."

Meanwhile Papan was screaming and shouting. He called out, "Don't they know that I'm the Chairman of the Joint Rules Committee?"

Hearing this, I burst out laughing. The funny image of some Greek knowing or even caring one whit of Lou's exalted position in the California Legislature was one of the funniest incidents of my life. I guess to some degree we all live inside our own little world, often overlooking just how insignificant things that seem so "important" to us must seem to others, especially in a foreign land.

When the firemen finally did arrive and the door was opened to reveal Papan, he looked like a bear that had spent hours in a sauna. He was stripped down to his underwear and his huge body was glistening with sweat. There was another person with him cowering in the corner in an effort to avoid Papan's thrashing fists and elbows.

The event was so funny that it causes me to break out laughing whenever I reflect upon it all these many years later.

22

Pushing the Limits

It's *true, I thought, Alexander had it right. "There is nothing impossible to him who will try." So one day I woke up and said to myself, "Screw it. Today I'm going to walk down the stairs."*

I knew that I would have to hold onto the banister, but if I could get across the room, why couldn't I also get down the stairs?

The doctors would have had a fit if they knew what I was about to try. The physical therapist wouldn't have allowed it either, and I hadn't mentioned to her or to anyone else that I had already managed to traverse from my bed to the wall. The stairs, for their part, were an obstacle course just waiting to break some bones. So be it. It was just another challenge and I was ready to do it.

Like so many days during my early recovery, I was home alone. With my daughter Jessica at school (in her senior year in high school) and Diana out and about, I was determined to hasten my progress.

I suppose it would have been easier to lay in bed the rest of my life, but that would have been for me intolerable. The truth was that I was the only one who could drag my body back to health—and I knew it. It was up to me to find my way back, whatever the challenge.

So when I got to the far wall, I leaned against it for support as I dragged my sensation-less right leg along behind me. Before I knew it, I was standing at the top of the stairs. For the first time since I had been carried up to my room by the medics, I could see the ground floor below.

I gripped the banister with my left hand as tightly as I could, and then I went for it. First, left leg down one step, but awfully unsteady. Now, how to get the right leg to follow? The right leg still refused to follow my brain's signal to move. And it wasn't really possible to lift my right leg up using my hands since I needed my left one to hold onto the banister and my right arm and hand were as impaired as my leg.

Somehow I managed to balance myself against the banister with one arm and drag my right leg to the same level as the left one. I rested there with both feet on the same step until I felt secure, and then I proceeded down one more step with the same method. Slowly, I balanced and dragged my way down those stairs—one step at a time—until I made it to the bottom. The bottom!

I wasn't sure how I would get back up the stairs, but that was the furthest thing from my mind. A whole new world of possibilities was open to me: The kitchen fridge and its contents were now accessible. I could get to the front door, open it, and go outside to visit the world. From the ground floor, I also had access to a car, as our garage was located off of the kitchen and a car was parked there. Another one was parked right outside the front door beside which I was standing.

My success had emboldened me with a completely stupid idea. Taking a key hanging next to the door and using the same step–drag method that had helped me down the stairs, I opened the front door and dragged myself outside. I continued further until I reached the door of the car. There I rested while leaning on the door. After a moment or two, I opened the door of my burgundy colored Cadillac Concours and crouched down until I was able to clumsily ease myself inside. I fastened my seatbelt and reaching across my body turned on the ignition with my left hand. The car purred quietly, in perfect working order. The question was, could I get my broken body to drive it?

We lived in a gated community and the drive from our home to the front gate was unobstructed. I felt I could steer OK using just my left hand, but I had no feeling in my right foot. How could I use the accelerator? Maybe I could force it. I wouldn't know until I tried. I told myself that I'd try to make it to the post office only a few blocks away where my mail had been piling up in a P.O. Box.

So with my left foot on the brake, I released the emergency brake. My right foot was on the floor hump with the inside edge of the foot barely touching the accelerator. The moment of truth had arrived.

I lifted my left foot off of the brake and my right foot slid down onto the accelerator. The car lurched—indeed jumped—forward and I steered toward the gated exit of our community. But I could not feel in any way the extent to which my right leg was pushing down on the accelerator and I knew I had to try to stop. Frantically, I used my left hand to pull my right leg off of the accelerator and place it on the brake. In fact, I forced both of my feet down onto the brake pedal and managed to stop the car.

Oh shit, I thought. I've pushed too far—too fast.

I felt thankful that I was still within the gated area.

I've got to get myself out of this car, I thought.

Then I started laughing, probably for the first time since I had been struck down. How dumb this would look to most people, a person lifting up his leg with his hand in order to drive.

"I just can't do this yet," I again thought. But I was pleased with what I had accomplished and I knew that I would try again—soon.

Putting the car in reverse and using only my left foot, I managed to awkwardly back the car to the front of the house so it was out of the way of other vehicles.

Then I just sat there quietly for a rather long time, thinking. I had gone down the stairs, out the front door, stumbled to the car, gotten in, turned on the engine, and driven a short distance.

"I'm on my way back; I'm getting there," I thought. "I'm coming back to life. I just have to push harder."

23

Decision to Run for Attorney General

"It is only in our decisions that we are important."
— John Paul Sartre

During the last year of my third term, sitting in what for me had seemingly become a safe seat in the Senate, I began pondering more and more my future. I had declared during my first election campaign that I would not serve more than three terms. I don't think anybody else remembered that. But I did. I could seek reelection and probably be convincingly reelected? Perhaps even unopposed. Should I run for Congress? I had a broad coalition and I probably could have won the Congressional seat. But why? I had become a major player in California politics, but in Washington I would be but one out of four hundred and thirty five votes in the House of Representatives and given the seniority system that is honored in DC it could take twenty years to even become a Committee Chair. Should I run for Attorney General of California? That had a lot of appeal because in California many former Attorney's General made it to the Governor's office. Examples are Earl Warren, Pat Brown, George Deukmejian, and recently Jerry Brown. Or, still young, should I just look for a new challenge outside of elective office and change direction completely, as I tend to do every ten to twelve years or so?

I went round and round and even briefly considered lobbying but that was far and away the least appealing of the options I had in front of me. I just couldn't see myself as a member of the Third House; no matter how well it paid, waiting around for some Senator, Assemblyman, or Congressman to fit me into his or her schedule. The whole idea of lobbying was somewhat distasteful and rather quickly was disregarded. For a while I was ambivalent about the future of my career, but I was trying to keep all of my options open for a while.

Not that I spent all of my time contemplating the future. To the contrary, I was still working extremely hard and concentrating on the issues with which we were as legislators daily confronted. Obviously, however, at that point in time, one of those issues was that of reapportionment. In fact, no issue is more important to any legislator. As Chairman of the Elections and Reapportionment Committee I was meeting with the Census Bureau and involved in drafting legislation and working with then-Congressman Phil Burton who was himself working with congressional colleagues to try to delineate lines for California's various Congressional districts. Burton, representing the San Francisco area, was the most powerful member of the California Congressional delegation and in some ways, though not Speaker of the House, was the most powerful man in Congress. When he died Nancy Pelosi was elected to the seat formerly held by Burton.

Phil Burton, though working at that time without the computer operation The Rose Institute provided the Republicans, was still a master political cartographer. He was coming up with strange and bizarre lines, and bringing them to my attention as it is the State Legislature that draws the boundaries for both federal and state districts. The United States Supreme Court had set down some rough guidelines. But, of course, like everything the court does, legislators throughout the country were pushing the envelope to see just how far the court would go in upholding their own opinions. We were supposed to adhere to communities of interest. But Burton was adamant. He was determined to carve up the districts so it benefited those that he and his colleagues wanted to protect and, at the same time, pick up extra seats being created in California as a result of population growth. He also wanted to create a district specifically for me, but I told him more than once that I didn't want to "suck hind tit" in DC for a couple of decades until seniority was obtained. Such language was the best way to talk to Phil. Phil and his younger brother, John (also a member of Congress and later President Pro Tem of the California Senate), were both known for their colorful language. But both, hard-nosed as can be, were also known as straight-shooters.

My outspoken opposition to gerrymandering of districts was very unpopular with my colleagues, both Republican and Democratic, but especially my Democratic colleagues as we were the party in the majority and here I was, the Chairman of the Reapportionment Committee, introducing bills designed to take the power to do this out of our own hands.

I introduced the bill to establish an independent Reapportionment Commission every year and it was defeated every year. However, it came superficially close one year as it came within one vote of passing the Senate. But deep down I knew it would never get passed short of a vote by the people. Although I got twenty votes (needing twenty-one) that one year, had I ever gotten to twenty-one, one of the recorded aye votes would have switched his vote from aye to nay. Politicians protect their own turf.

As I continued to ponder my next career move, Diana told me that she wanted to start her own business. She was still writing her doctoral thesis, but she wanted to go into a new business and she asked me to fund it. She was working with a good friend from Santa Barbara on something novel. It was a computerized legislative bill tracking system designed to track the thousands of bills annually introduced in the California Legislature. Whereas it usually took weeks for a bill to be manually tracked and analyzed, her system could produce all the essential information including amendments, supporters, opponents, everything there was to know about the bill on a daily basis. The company was called Capitol Information Management, Inc. (CIM) and was based in Sacramento. I initially invested or raised $225,000 of seed money and she got the person with whom she was working in Santa Barbara to invest $25,000.

It was bad timing for me, and certainly a bad business decision. I wish I could say it's the only bad business decision I have ever made. But I hated to turn her down as it had a lot to do with her own self-esteem so I said, "Go for it. If the business makes money, it's yours to keep." Even though the business was exciting for her at first, it turned out to be an ongoing drain on my personal resources and eventually the company was a business failure. Actually, the business probably would have succeeded but for the fact that the McClatchy Corporation, one of the great media empires in the country, began to replicate the work of CIM and, probably in violation of anti-trust laws, engaged in predatory pricing that caused the ultimate failure of CIM. CIM was ultimately "sold" at a huge loss to Electronic Data Systems (EDS) owned by Ross Perot. Diana and I went to Plano, Texas, just outside of Dallas to personally meet with Perot to finalize the terms and conditions of the transactions.

The one upside is that EDS did provide Diana with a good paying, solid job opportunity in its Sacramento based office. Meanwhile, I was working just as hard as ever on my legislative and constituent responsibilities. I never let up. In fact, I was wearing myself out and going as always with little sleep.

By this time, I had pretty much made a decision to run for Attorney General of California. Nevertheless, I really was not laying a proper foundation for that campaign, and fundraising was at the bottom of my list of priorities. This seemed to baffle most of my colleagues in that they felt, correctly, that in order to run a statewide campaign in California money was almost always the determining factor. Therefore, I repeatedly received advice that I should be skipping sessions and concentrating solely on fundraising throughout the year before the election. But I could not in good conscience do this.

In the Legislature, every year the Bottle Bill would heat up and my staff and I were always working hard on it. Ross Pumfrey was probably putting in about 80% of his time on it. His job was to help mobilize public opinion in favor of the bill's passage. I was getting a lot of visibility and publicity all over the state and our campaign was widely and quite favorably publicized. There were articles in newspapers and magazines, including editorials, radio and TV spots. Our efforts were powerful and the word was spreading far beyond California.

Actually, Vermont had passed the first Bottle Bill and its author came out to California to testify to its efficacy. But Vermont is so tiny that its experience could hardly affect the game as it was playing out in California. Everyone knew that if the bill passed in California, it wouldn't be long before the idea would spread throughout the country. That is why the special interests were so fearful and so determined to defeat the bill.

Therefore, it wasn't surprising that the opponents were throwing record amounts of money into their efforts to kill the measure. At first, many of my colleagues saw this as a "money bill" as their campaign coffers overflowed with contributions. But as the efforts gained statewide attention they began to resent the media attention their no votes brought. Also, due to the statewide and even national publicity, eventually there were huge volumes of phone calls and letters from their respective constituents in support of the bill, further putting law makers on the spot—something they did not appreciate.

As the end of 1981 approached, I realized that it was decision time. The more I thought about it, the office of Attorney General of California did appeal to me more than other options. It wasn't a job that just involved criminal law, but all aspects of law including civil appeals, white collar crime, and environmental law. It involved daily policy decisions as it represented all the agencies of the State of California and this also was of interest to me. I was, am and always will be a policy wonk. The Attorney General in California is second in power and influence only to the Governor and, as previously pointed out, has often been a stepping stone to the Governor's office.

As I began to informally and discreetly discuss this with some of my colleagues, one of them said to me, "I don't believe for a second you are truly considering a race for Attorney General. This must be a rumor to simply throw the Republicans off guard."

I said, "Why do you say that?"

"Well, there's no way that you could continue to be here on a daily basis working your butt off and doing research on various matters if you're running for statewide office—you'd be off fundraising full time. You know that when you run statewide in California, the one who raises the most money invariably wins unless you've inherited a famous name. So I can't believe for a second that you're running."

As I came to learn the hard way, what he said was and is basically and unfortunately true.

24

The Campaign for Attorney General

"Money is the mother's milk of politics."
— Jesse ("Big Daddy") Unruh

As word got around that I would indeed run for the office of Attorney General, momentum began to develop on my side and a lot of fine people and organizations advised me that they were prepared to endorse my candidacy. It appeared that I would have a clear path to the Democratic nomination and with the Republicans not having a particularly strong candidate seeking the job that year, the likelihood was that I would be the next Attorney General. I garnered the endorsement of most of the elected Democrats in California including most members of the Democratic Congressional Delegation.

I also lined up endorsements from just about every police organization in the state. In fact, every major law enforcement agency in the state endorsed my candidacy. They included, among others the Peace Officers Research Association of California (PORAC); The Marshalls Association of California; The Association of Special Agents, Attorney General's Office; The Latino Peace Officers Association; The California Sheriff's Association; The California State Police; and many others.

The most surprising "endorsement" came in a rather interesting manner. The former Police Chief of Los Angeles and Republican Candidate for Governor, Senator Ed Davis walked into my office one day and handed me a sealed envelope. In doing so, Ed said, "Omer, the contents of this envelope will not make my Republican colleagues happy with me, but it's the right thing to do. Use it as you see fit."

After Ed left the office, I opened the envelope and found the following language typed neatly on a piece of paper: "Our Committee (the Senate Judiciary Committee), under the direction and leadership of the Chairman, Omer Rains, has maintained impeccable standards designed not only to provide legislation which protects law abiding citizens but also to meet the safeguards of our state and federal constitutions." It was signed, "Senator Ed Davis, former LA Police Chief and Vice-Chairman, Senate Judiciary Committee."

During a later press conference attended by both Ed and I, Ed was to comment: "During the past legislative year more bills aimed at protecting citizens from criminal conduct passed the Legislature than during any year in recent California history. Our Chairman, Senator Rains, led that effort and in view of the state's diminishing resources, this was not an easy accomplishment." Needless to say, statements of this sort from one of the best known and most respected Republican leaders in the state were rather extraordinary and took great courage on the part of Senator Davis. I do think the endorsement of Ed Davis was fairly astonishing given the nature of partisan politics. It would be similar to Bill Clinton endorsing John McCain for President.

But I was soon to learn that name identification trumps endorsements in California with its massive and spread out population. Early on it appeared that my chances of winning were better than 50/50. For a campaign manager, I approached a fellow called Jack Mayesh. Jack knew what it took to run a statewide campaign as he had done it before. Moreover, I liked him and I thought we would work well together. But he offered the same advice other experienced managers offered and that I wasn't prone to follow. Not because it wasn't good advice, but because it just wasn't me. As I said before, money is key in a statewide campaign in California, especially if the candidate does not come from the major metropolitan areas of Los Angeles, San Francisco, or San Diego. And as I have also said many times before, I am simply a poor fundraiser.

So I set about campaigning but I was doing it my own way. Sure, I was focused, but I was running the type of grassroots campaign I had done in the past meeting with myriad groups, accepting every speaking engagement that I could possibly fit into my schedule while not interfering with legislative responsibilities, and continuing to author important legislation. Mayesh, with a lot of statewide management savvy, also signed up Governor Brown as a client that year in Brown's race for the United States Senate. Therefore, although he told me every time we talked to simply focus on raising money and nothing else, I found that I could not do that unless I was prepared to drop my other responsibilities—something I was not prepared to do. Jack also repeatedly informed me of something I already knew and that was that the effective way to win any election is to raise so much money before announcing for office that potential opponents are discouraged from running. For this reason, many election races are over before they ever start. My failure to effectively raise sufficient funds became fatal in the long run insofar as my candidacy for Attorney General was concerned.

Nevertheless, my candidacy and endorsements did discourage all others with but one exception. That exception and the person who turned out to be my only opponent was John Van de Kamp, scion of a hugely wealthy L.A. family. John was the District Attorney of Los Angeles County and almost forty percent of the state's population was covered by Los Angeles media. His family name was everywhere in California on bakeries, food companies, just everywhere one can imagine.

I genuinely liked Van de Kamp, then and now, but he had flaws that I thought would make him vulnerable. Although a very nice person, he was painfully shy and sometimes, when he was in a room full of strangers, he would go over in the corner like a wallflower and say nothing. Furthermore, as the Los Angeles District Attorney, some of his plea bargain deals were very controversial. One was the "Hillside Strangler" case. He sanctioned an unpopular plea deal for the defendant, Angelo Buono. Another case involved a man named Ron Settles who had been gunned down by police officers in Los Angeles. Van de Kamp did not prosecute the police officers, a very controversial decision, especially in the minority communities. In other matters, he had been reluctant to speak out. A glaring example was the parole hearing of Sirhan Sirhan, the convicted assassin of Robert F. Kennedy. Only later did Van de Kamp offer a timid response. Another was a child murder case in the Modesto area involving a person named William Fain. Fain's parole hearing raised so much public consternation that people were enraged that Van de Kamp refused to even meet with members of the victim's family.

As indicated, my campaign manager, Jack Mayesh had also accepted the assignment of running Jerry Brown's campaign for the United States Senate. And, as it turned out, that consumed virtually all of Jack's time. He was always in Los Angeles and most of the time I was in Sacramento. He did help me cut a few TV commercials but beyond that he simply offered advice that I should be doing nothing other than raising money—lots of it.

In March, the California Democratic Council (CDC) had an endorsement convention. The CDC has become more or less irrelevant over the years but back then it was still important. These were hardcore Democrats. They had never in their history endorsed a candidate for Attorney General. Other candidates tried to get the endorsement but always fell short. I went all out to get it, but I fell one vote short of the two-thirds vote necessary.

I was, however, poised to pick up an important endorsement from the American Federation of Labor and Congress of Industrial Organizations (AFL-CIO) in California. Jack Henning, a good guy, headed the union movement in California. He had assured me for over a year that if I ran for Attorney General I would get the AFL-CIO endorsement. On March 31, they had their convention. Jack was taken aback by the opposition to my candidacy by some really powerful parts of the labor movement in California. It was all because of my authorship of the Bottle Bill, which would allegedly displace some union workers. I didn't agree, but many labor leaders felt that way and as a result I lost the endorsement.

Approximately three months before the election, the Los Angeles Times came out with what in politics we call a "beauty poll." This was long before people had begun to focus on any of the statewide elections. In short it wasn't anything other than a name recognition snapshot and, predictably, it showed that Van de Kamp had a lead over me. It wouldn't have bothered me one whit but for one significant reason. It did have the effect of drying up a lot of campaign funds that might otherwise have come my way. It also caused some of my endorsements to turn soft.

At the same time, back in the Legislature, I didn't let up for a single minute. I carried a package of bills involving child abuse, as well as major legislation including crimes against the elderly. In addition, I continued to thoroughly prepare for and chair the many committees for which I served as Chair.

The Bottle Bill battle continued, and I remained front and center on the firing line. I provided the initial money to start a new organization called "Californians Against Waste," which was to coordinate a statewide campaign against waste. We began to circulate an initiative for the June 1982 primary ballot. It was important to me, to my campaign for Attorney General, and to the success of the initiative itself. We began to hold press conferences, and met with editorial boards of the major newspapers in the state, most all of which to the best of my knowledge endorsed the initiative.

As the election day neared, it was clear that there would be other significant items on the ballot at the same time as the Bottle Bill. In fact, there were so many items requiring TV time, unless one had their money to buy early, it would be impossible to even get TV time. One of the items on the ballot involved the "Peripheral Canal," a proposed canal around San Francisco Bay to take fresh water from the northern Sierra Nevada mountains south to the urban areas of Southern California. There is no issue more complex or convoluted in California than the politics of water. As Mark Twain once said: "Whiskey is to drink and water is to fight over." Water interests, including the Metropolitan Water District of Southern California and many others, were going to be involved in the fight. Also involved would be agri-business interests, environmental groups, and virtually every other faction in the state. All major interests were involved, all spending a lot of money on media and thus taking up media space. At the same time and on the same ballot was an initiative supporting a state lottery. Again both proponents (mainly Native American groups) and opponents (mainly Nevada-based gaming interests) were prepared to dump millions and millions of dollars into the campaign.

These controversial and expensive campaigns augured well for the Bottle Bill. Why? Because the message of our opponents would be lost in the avalanche of commercials that would go on nonstop for weeks and weeks before the June election date. However, once again "Murphy's Law" was to rear its head. Several weeks before the election, I met with the new Chairman of Californians Against Waste (CAW). I had not met him before, and I was shocked when he told me that he was removing the initiative from the June ballot and having it placed on the November ballot. I was stunned, stunned, stunned! He said that he could more efficiently organize the campaign by the fall ballot. I told him that the fall ballot would be devoid of other major issues and the opposition would bury the Bottle Bill with misleading and distorted commercials. He said his mind was made up.

He was very young and initially I just attributed his truly stupid decision to political naivety, but I was later told that he was working with the Van de Kamp campaign. Whether or not that is true, and I suspect it is, the decision caused the Bottle Bill initiative to lose in a close election in November, whereas with the visibility my campaign would have given the matter, I'm convinced it would have passed in June.

Nevertheless, momentum remained on the side of the Bottle Bill and soon after the initiative defeat, the bill did pass in the Legislature though in a substantially weakened form. Nevertheless, not having the Bottle Bill on the ballot cost me heavily in my campaign for Attorney General in that it was not an issue in June. Therefore, the newspapers who heavily supported the effort did not give it (or me as the author) coverage at that time and the student communities and environmental groups and others who worked so hard in favor of the bill just sat out the election in June.

So when election day did finally come, I lost the race to Van de Kamp. Everything had gone wrong: (1) I hadn't raised enough money, and that was my fault; (2) the early LA Times beauty poll dried up money that I think otherwise would have naturally flowed to me; (3) I lost the AFL-CIO endorsement because of some union opposition to the Bottle Bill; and (4) the Bottle Bill was inexplicably (at the time) jerked from the ballot at the last minute. Nevertheless, the race for Attorney General was the closest of all the primary races on election night and I had carried the vast majority of California's fifty-eight counties. However, I was slaughtered in the Los Angeles media market where my opponent's name recognition was virtually 100% and mine was low due to the inability to buy time for TV advertising in the incredibly expensive L.A. marketplace.

In retrospect, I know that I would have won that race had I chased money instead of issues, so I have always taken personal responsibility for the loss. It all came down to TV coverage and name recognition. So this time I could not and did not pull off the miracle of my election to the Senate. But at least I had remained true to my core beliefs and fought hard for the causes in which I so strongly believed.

25

Reflections on Public Service

"I've learned that people will forget what you said, people will forget what you did, but people will never forget how you made them feel."
— Maya Angelou

As the sun set on my political career I reflected, wondering, searching the corners of my conscience and my heart to see if I had any regrets. It didn't take long to come to the conclusion that I didn't regret one second that I ever spent in public service. It was truly a privilege to serve my district and the people of California. I was secure in the knowledge that anyone who ever examined my legislative record would come away convinced that I had left an imprint on the lives of every single Californian that very few people of my generation would ever have the opportunity to do. While my primary legislative interest was on the environment, civil and human rights, and political reform I had been very active in other areas as well.

As the Legislature's representative on the California Law Revision Commission, I had carried a series of bills that struck from the books innumerable outdated laws, and as the Legislature's representative on the State Judicial Council I had taken action over strong opposition of the insurance industry to aid aggrieved parties and consumers by authoring landmark legislation allowing for the payment of pre-judgment interest on court judgments for the first time in Californian history.

My efforts in the area of criminal law produced in 1981-82 what has been referred to as "the most comprehensive anti-crime package in California history" and this was accomplished without, in my opinion, sacrificing the vigilant protection of constitutional guarantees for which I had always actively stood and fought.

In the area of child molestation and child abuse, I authored a bill that specified that if a social worker, teacher, doctor, or police officer observed evidence of child abuse, it would be incumbent on him or her to report it to the appropriate authorities. Every group affected said, "Great idea, but it shouldn't apply to us." Some, especially doctors, resisted strongly not wanting either the responsibility or the potential liability since there were sanctions for those who failed to report abuse. I will never forget the headlines in a major California daily a year after this bill went into effect. It read something like "Child Abuse in California Increases Tenfold in Last Year." Obviously child abuse had not increased—it was simply being reported!

In the area of children's rights, I had also authored legislation to ensure that all school children are immunized against measles, polio, diphtheria, whooping cough, and tetanus—five dreaded childhood diseases that some families could not afford to provide their children.

To provide part-time work for persons unable to work full-time, I authored legislation to establish California's first "Part-time Employment Act." In addition, to help prevent a healthcare breakdown, I carried legislation during a special session in 1975 designed to curtail skyrocketing malpractice insurance rates which had placed California's healthcare services in serious jeopardy.

I fought with vigilance for more fiscal responsibility at all levels of government, not just in the aftermath of the passage of Prop 13, but throughout my legislative career. Sensitive to the needs of California's business community and as Chairman of the Select Committee on Government Regulation I acted to identify and cure regulatory abuses. In addition, I authored laws streamlining the state's cumbersome permit process, in addition to starting California down the road to "zero-based" budgeting and establishing timetables for periodic review of state agencies (encompassing the "Sunset" concept to eliminate programs whose existence could no longer be justified). Vigilant adherence to zero-based budgeting and sunset provisions for all new legislation are absolute imperatives if anyone is serious about halting the growth of government, either at the federal or state levels.

To further the creation of a more healthy business climate in the state of California, I jointly authored the "Holmdahl-Rains-Lockyer Economic Development Act" which consolidated the economic planning functions of several state agencies into one Department of Economic and Business Development, and established an "Office of State Tourism."

In the area of political reform, and as Chairman of the Senate Committee on Elections and Reapportionment and of the Select Committee on Political Reform, throughout my legislative career I vigorously fought for the principles of full disclosure and open government and authored far reaching legislation that has minimized false endorsements in political campaigns and banned the fraudulent solicitation of campaign funds. Another of my measures created a Code of Fair Campaign Practices to which candidates running for public office would subscribe. Admittedly, however, the latter bill has been of limited success since in order to secure the votes to gain passage, it was necessary to make the act voluntary. Guess how many candidates choose to subscribe?

One of the projects during this period that did not come to fruition while I was still a member of the Senate was my strong push for a state college in Ventura County. Governor Brown was against the idea because he didn't believe it was needed given the proximity of the University of California, Santa Barbara to the north and California State College at Northridge in LA County to the south. But from my point of view, Ventura was the only heavy population center that did not have a State College or University Campus in or near it in the state. Moreover, the infrastructure was already in place by way of use of the truly beautiful grounds with structures still in good condition at the then recently closed and vacated Camarillo State Hospital. After Governor Brown left office, the college gained approval and was named Channel Islands State College.

I pressed and gained funding for restoration and renovation of the historic Presidio in the City of Santa Barbara. The Presidio is a monument to the history of this beautiful and famous city.

Having been steeped in the civil rights movement and as Chairperson of the Joint Committee on Legal Equality, the only Legislative Committee in the United States established to address legal inequality between the sexes, I authored and developed a comprehensive package of sixty-eight bills to allow the cause of women's rights to successfully advance in California from one of discussion to one of action and to bring California's codes into compliance with the "Equal Rights Amendment."

However, I am sure that I am best remembered for my constant fights to preserve, protect, and enhance California's precious and unique environment. In this regard, one matter on which I worked long and hard and hand-in-hand with Congressman Phil Burton of San Francisco was the sponsorship of a bill to create an expanded Redwoods National Park in Northern California. Burton carried the bill at the federal level and I carried necessary enabling legislation at the state level. The bills passed in both DC and Sacramento. This National Park, with its phenomenal trees covering thousands of square miles was open to the public in the late 1970s and will remain a national treasure for all time.

Similarly, I worked with certain members of California's Congressional Delegation to establish the Channel Islands National Park comprised of five Islands (offshore in the Santa Barbara Channel and within my District) stretching from Point Conception in the north and running south to Anacapa Island off the coast of Ventura. Concurrently, I labored successfully to have the Park Headquarters located at the Ventura Port.

The California deserts are unique, too. There is certain plant life found in that environment that is to be found nowhere else in the world. People were digging up and pirating many of California's exotic and native plants, especially rare members of the cacti family and selling them on the open market. They were showing up all over the world. Many of them ended up overseas in Japanese gardens. Not only was it denuding the desert of much of its native growth, but it was removing important parts of the desert's ecosystem. I authored legislation to put a stop to that.

I hate the possibility of destruction of any aspect of nature. Nature has always been my cathedral. This was especially true when it came to protection of California's beaches. To this end I authored the Oil Spill Liability Act, which specifically sanctioned oil companies if they spilled oil in our oceans and caused damage to our beaches. In addition, I authored legislation to purchase beach property for public use and an act of legislation to prevent strip mining in California's national and state forests.

As Vice-chairman of the Senate Energy and Utilities Committee, as a member of the Senate Natural Resources Committee and as the Gubernatorial Appointee to the State Geothermal Resources Taskforce and the SolarCAL Council I authored pioneering legislation encouraging the development and use of alternative energy sources such as solar, geothermal, co-generation, wind, bio-mass conversion, and developing ocean technologies.

I also authored legislation to ban plastic "six-pack" holders, a petroleum bi-product that is not biodegradable, and which ensnares in a death grip birds, fish, and other wildlife. Unfortunately, after my retirement from the Senate, this legislation was repealed through efforts of those whose opposition I had originally managed to overcome.

I also oversaw establishment of an interconnecting network of hiking, biking, and equestrian trails between state parks, California missions and state and federal historic sites which is unique throughout the United States. The state of California subsequently named one of these trails after me: "The Omer Rains Bike Trail" which runs through some beautiful country offering panoramic vistas connecting various state beach parks from south of the Santa Clara River to north of the Ventura River—now finally ending up in the city of Ojai, nearly twenty miles in length.

A close friend of mine, Mark Dubois, had in the mid-70s started an organization called "Friends of the River." The organization tried to prevent construction of a dam on the Stanislaus River southeast of Sacramento in the Sierra Nevada Mountains. Eventually the issue was placed on the ballot where it lost in a statewide election by a narrow margin. However, that effort led to the passage of the Wild and Scenic Rivers Act, which I co-authored and strongly supported in concert with the bill's principal author, Senator Peter Behr. This act emboldened similar measures in other states and in other countries too. This was a classic case where although the battle may have been lost, the war in large measure was won. As for Mark, he was to go on and eventually become International Chair of Earth Day as we entered the new millennium in the year 2000.

The measure for which I am probably best known is the California Bottle Bill. Each year, with the reserved number of Senate Bill 4, I introduced the legislation. This was my annual bill to encourage the return of reusable and recyclable beverage containers. Passage of the bill in its purest form was designed to save enormous amounts of energy wasted in the manufacture of over 60 billion "throw-away" bottles and cans each year. Obviously, it would also have reduced litter and, in addition, would have saved consumers money with each purchase. According to an article that appeared in Reader's Digest, the opposition to my bill was described as "the most powerful and well-organized in the entire country." It added, "This lobby plays hard and it plays for keeps." Nevertheless, some years I got the bill to the Senate floor and some years it remained "bottled up" in Committee. Because of the size of the California marketplace, the Container Deposit Legislation that was eventually enacted became in effect a national law. I do not necessarily deserve the accolade, but I'm proud to sometimes be introduced as the "Father of the Bottle Bill."

26

Letter to a Son

"The only people who never fail are those who never try."
— Omer Rains

Having lost the race for Attorney General, I penned the following letter to my son as the date of his graduation from high school approached.

"You are now eighteen, and I want you to know how very proud I am of you as tomorrow's high school graduation approaches. But how did the weeks, the months, and the years move so swiftly by? The memories of your birth are as yesterday, and the various milestones in your short lifespan all seem as though they just happened. It is truly hard to believe that you have already reached adulthood…

Having said that, I want to talk a bit about myself and, in so doing, hopefully impart to you not just a better understanding of me, but also lessons which may help guide you as you continue down the roadway of life.

I haven't forgotten, for example, that you asked me the night I lost the race for Attorney General why I had given up a safe seat in the Senate to engage in what was obviously an uphill fight against a better financed, better known opponent. I remember telling you that I felt good about the challenge I had accepted, even though I had lost, and that I thought that every person must from time to time face defeat in order to proceed into the future with humility and with renewed vigor. The fact is that as someone once said: "Although most people can see, few have vision." Sometimes it's not until one steps back (even if involuntarily) away from something in which he has been totally immersed, that one can again speak with the vision that any true leader must from time to time have. It's akin to the proverbial not being able "to see the forest because of the trees."

My loss in the Attorney General's race is, for illustrative purposes, good to dwell on for a moment, because I suspect that to most people it is the one great stumble I have made around the track of professional life. But I do not look upon it that way. Remember that as you go through life, the only people who never fail are those who never try. The fact of the matter is that I, at that particular time in my life, simply needed a new challenge. From time to time in your life you will find that you, as well, need new challenges. I also had come to realize the extraordinary sacrifices I had made in order to engage in public service. Although I am very proud of my accomplishments in public life, I realize how unfair public service can often be to one's family and I certainly feel deeply how much I missed in not having more time to spend with you as you grew to adulthood. But as one travels the road of life, one often comes to forks in the road, and for better or worse one must decide from time to time which fork to take (with apologies to Robert Frost). You will often encounter such choices as well.

In my case, by choosing public service I know that I had an opportunity to serve which few shall ever have. Being but one of forty members of the Senate representing the interests of over thirty million people allowed me to set my imprimatur on the history of California and to some extent the nation in a way that would otherwise have been impossible. I worked hard and I left the Legislature with a clear conscience. I represented well my constituency during a trying period in our political history, especially in the aftermath of Watergate, Vietnam, and other traumatic national experiences. I tell you this because as you travel the road of life, if you get from one spot to another and feel good about the route you have traveled, that will give you a sense of enormous gratification, and it will make the road taken (however much in need of wear) a great adventure.

Also when I left the Legislature, I truly did not know what the future portended. But I did know that there were new horizons to view, new mountains to climb, new challenges to face, and I have begun to view those horizons, to climb those mountains and to face those challenges — without regret. In other words try always to look forward with optimism and hope and without bitterness over past losses, defeats or failures, for surely you as everyone else will from time to time have losses, defeats and failures, whatever you seek to accomplish in life.

In addition, I want you never to stand in awe of any other person, for I assure you that you are his/her equal. I have had the opportunity to know so many of the "greats" of the world — John F., Robert, and Teddy Kennedy; Martin Luther King, Jr.; Menachem Begin; Anwar Sadat; Margaret Thatcher; Tony Blair; Prince Charles; Mother Teresa; Gerald Ford; Richard Nixon; Jimmy Carter; Ronald Reagan; Muhammad Ali; Larry Holmes; both Sugar Ray's (Robinson and Leonard); Larry Bird; Kareem Abdul Jabbar; Bill Russell; Magic Johnson; Willis Reed; Joe Montana; Steve Garvey; Ozzie Smith; Reggie Jackson; Evel Knievel; Mario Andretti; Arnold Palmer; Charlton Heston; Johnny Cash; Bo Derek; Elvis Presley; Steve McQueen; Sammy Davis Jr.; Ella Fitzgerald; John Denver; John Malone; Bob Magness; Leonard Tow; etc. The list could go on and on and on. It would, to be sure, include virtually every politician about whom you have read or heard during the course of your life, and an extraordinary number of entertainers and sports heroes, as well as so-called "captains of industry" and "beautiful people," whom we individually and collectively tend to worship in our society.

The importance of this is not that I have met and gotten to know such people, but rather that I have learned from such acquaintances that although many, indeed most, of these people are very nice, they are also very ordinary. I cannot really tell you what separates the so-called "great" or famous people of the world from anyone else you meet in daily travels —it may be a matter of inheritance, or timing, or luck, or hard work— who knows. But what I can tell you is that what separates these people from anyone else is really very small, very miniscule or very slight and almost impossible to discern, much less to describe.

Don't get me wrong. There are many great people (Anwar Sadat, for example, truly stands out in my mind as a man of extraordinary vision and courage, one who was prepared to make the ultimate sacrifice for what he believed to be correct; and who in modern history has been more inspirational than Nelson Mandela; and who has been more admired — except by a few Chinese government officials— than his Holiness, the Dalai Lama). But the point I am trying to make is that most who inhabit this earth are really not that different from their neighbors. We all have strengths and we all have weaknesses, and we all put our pants on one leg at a time. You should never, therefore, be afraid to challenge another for fear that he is smarter than you, or richer than you, or more athletic than you, or in any way better than you. If called for, make your challenge and if in so doing you fail, that's okay so long as you have given your best.

Perhaps that person who best summed up what I have been trying to say to you in this letter was Theodore Roosevelt. Roosevelt so well articulated on several occasions the importance of trying, of doing one's best even when on occasion that means failure. I have looked up a few of my favorite Theodore Roosevelt quotes, and I would like to share them with you:

'Far better it is to dare mighty things, to win glorious triumphs, even though checkered by failure, than to take rank with those poor spirits who neither enjoy much nor suffer much, because they live in the gray twilight that knows neither victory nor defeat.'

'It is not the critic who counts; not the man who points out how the strong man stumbled or where the doer of the deed could have done better. The credit belongs to the man who is actually in the arena; whose face is marred by dust, sweat, and blood; who strives valiantly, who errs and comes short again and again ... because there is no effort without error and shortcoming.'

'It is the man who actually strives to do the deeds who knows the great enthusiasm; the great devotions; who spends himself in a worthy cause; who at the best knows in the end the triumph of high achievement ... and who at the worst, if he fails, at least fails while daring greatly, so that his place shall never be with those cold and timid souls who know neither victory nor defeat.'

In short I started this letter by saying how proud I am of you, and that I am. You shall achieve great things, and I pray that you shall also enjoy great happiness. But I am fully cognizant of the fact that your achievements and happiness will not come easily, because it does not come easily for anyone. It must be worked at. From time to time you will stumble and, indeed, you may fall, as from time to time I have stumbled and fallen. But there is an old Scottish ballad that goes something like this: "I am hurt, but I am not slain. I shall lay me down to rest a little and then get up to fight again." Whenever you stumble or fall, just get up, pull yourself together, dust yourself off and continue forward—continue forward, always forward, and never backwards—throughout life. Do this, and your journey will be a glorious one.

Your proud and loving father."

1941 Photo – On Lap of Great-Grandfather (age 95)

Harvest Time, circa 1944 (Omer & Older Brother, Roy)

Official Senate Photo

Honorary Banquet with Diana

The "Red Baron" in midst of a roll

Best Wishes
to Omer Rains

Jimmy Carter

Greeting President Carter in the White House

Discussion on Air Force One with the President

To Omer Rains
With best wishes,

Ronald Reagan

President Reagan – A Friend for over 25 Years, in and out of the White House

Announcing Relocation of the KINGS from Kansas City to Sacramento

Mountaineering

Typical Whitewater

Laying Foundation Stone at Ullon Gram, first READ Project in India

With Women's Committee in Kingdom of Mustang, Nepal

Expedition Landing by Zodiac in Antarctica

Gifts & Playtime in Bolivian Orphanage

Grandchildren with New Friends Near Site of Proposed Orphanage in Nicaragua

Spartacus

Family (Children & Grandchildren)

27

Return to Private Life

"We have met the enemy and he is us."
— Pogo Possum

Deferring to Diana's wishes, I agreed to stay in the Sacramento area until she completed her PhD and until her mother passed on. As it turned out we remained in Sacramento for the duration of our marriage more than twenty years after I retired from public office. To this day, having now lived on two continents and on both coasts of America, the central coast of California is still the best place I ever lived. When people ask, as they frequently do, what is your home town, I still generally say Ventura because it is the city with which I most closely identify.

———————

From a professional standpoint, when I left office, I had numerous offers from both lobbying organizations and law firms. I had no interest whatever in lobbying and eventually accepted an offer from a national law firm to be a senior partner in that firm. The firm, Farrow, Schildhause & Wilson, focused primarily on First Amendment and anti-trust work, especially in the telecommunications field. We had offices in Oakland, California, Washington, DC, and Los Angeles and when I accepted the offer from the firm, we opened a Sacramento office. At the same time, the firm's name was changed to Farrow, Schildhause, Wilson, & Rains (later Farrow, Schildhause, & Rains).

I rented space in the Senate Office Building, a historic building directly across the street from the Capitol and optioned additional space next door for expansion. I then began to hire other attorneys and staff. We threw a huge party to kick off the new office and close to a thousand people attended.

About this time, I also accepted an invitation to join the Board of Directors of the Robert Maynard Hutchins Center for the Study of Democratic Institutions, an internationally renowned think tank that was headquartered in Santa Barbara. It was a very intellectual and academic think tank—a prestigious organization with which I was proud to be affiliated.

As for the new law firm, I jumped right into things by working on a major case in the state of Michigan. It turned out to be a landmark case in the cable television industry. It arose out of Marquette, Michigan. Marquette sits in the Iron Range Mountains on the shore of Lake Superior. If you don't have cable TV in Marquette, you don't get TV reception. None! No other signal could get through the mountains.

Right after the first of the year in 1983, I flew to Marquette which has a harsh climate in the winter time. The current franchise of Cox Cable Communications had come to an end and, in the bidding process that followed, the franchise had been awarded to a new franchisee by the City Council. Cox said, in effect, "No way. We are not leaving nor are we going to allow the existing cable infrastructure or cable equipment to be used. If we don't get the contract, we are going to tear everything down."

There is a state prison in the Marquette area and TV is about the only outlet for the inmates. People who don't understand prison life probably underestimate its importance. But when the TV screens went dark, the inmates rioted. It took the state militia to put the riot down. At the same time, people in the community were up in arms about the failure to get TV reception.

The City Council threw up their collective hands and said to Cox, "OK, you win. You can come back. We will take the franchise away from the other company and give it back to you."

It was at about this juncture that our law firm was retained, and we filed suit against various entities including the city and Cox Cable, doing business as Iron Range Cable Television. We alleged all sorts of violations, both constitutional and statutory. It was complex litigation in large measure based on anti-trust law because of Cox's determination to monopolize the market place. We took the position that they could compete but could not prevent another firm from also doing business in the area.

It was during this case that I learned something about my new firm. While the firm held itself out to be a trial firm, it was really an appellate firm, a brilliant and successful one I might add. But the only partner with any real trial experience turned out to be me. Harold Farrow always held himself out to be a trial attorney, and while he was in fact an extremely competent—even brilliant—appellate attorney, he was absolutely incompetent in front of a jury. As a result, all of a sudden, I was handling most all of the firms trial work throughout the country and ours was truly a national practice. In connection with the Marquette case alone, in a three month period I took depositions in more than twenty-five cities spread throughout the east and Midwest. I was on airplanes constantly and travelling almost nonstop. There were many delays because of bad weather and a lot of very bumpy flights.

But whatever the inconveniences, it was well worth it. I took some extraordinarily successful depositions, especially those of Bob White, President of Cox Cable (and later President of NBC), and David Van Valkenburg, formerly Vice-president of Cox and later its President.

At the end of a full week of depositions in Cox's Atlanta, Georgia headquarters, there was a complete capitulation by Cox. Not only did Cox relinquish its right to do business in Marquette, but it gave up all of its franchises in Michigan to our client. This was the only time in cable television history when an incumbent operator was forced by litigation to leave a city. The theory that we successfully developed was that the whole system of awarding cable television franchises did not allow for competition *in* the market place. That it was competition *for* the market place. Once a franchise was awarded by a city or county, in effect a monopoly was allowed to develop.

After the success we enjoyed in the Marquette case, our firm began launching a series of cases that truly changed the telecommunication industry forever. When cities and counties put out bids for contracts, basically they were saying to each bidding company: "We will give a monopoly to that company from which we can exact the most tribute." It was insidious on the part of both the governmental agencies and the companies involved. By awarding the "winning" company an exclusive franchise, it had the effect of prohibiting competition in the marketplace. That's why virtually every city in the country has but one cable TV operator.

One of the curses of this system is a concept that came to be known as "rent a citizen." When a cable company wanted to bid on an award, it would round up the most prominent people in town and tell them, "We are going to pay you money and give you a share of the franchise if we get it. All you have to do is see that the City Council votes our way." Some folks had a lot of influence with city council members because of friendship, family connections and, more times than not, financial contributions.

The so-called bidding process became, in fact, a "liar's contest." Each participant would come in and lie about what they would do and at what price, knowing full well that when they got the monopoly, the terms of the agreement would not effectively bind them. I remember C.K. McClatchy, the editor of The Sacramento Bee and a really good guy, asking me when the franchise was first awarded in Sacramento, "How can we complain? Look at this agreement. The winning company is going to give service throughout the entire community for only $2.00 a month and provide over one hundred channels."

My answer was, "C.K., you are a really smart guy, and you can't be that naive. Look, the company with the best connected citizen group has been awarded the contract and I guarantee you that very quickly, as there is no competition, the price for the most basic service will not be $2.00 a month but rather well in excess of $20.00 per month."

"What about the agreement?" He asked.

"It will be honored in the breach. Mark my word."

And sure enough that's exactly what happened. So we began to file lawsuits, not just in Sacramento but in cities throughout the land, resting basically both on anti-trust law and on the First Amendment of the United States Constitution. The First Amendment may be the most important provision of our constitution. Historically, every single communicator has had to fight for its First Amendment rights: Pamphleteers, newspapers, magazines, radio, and TV. Now cable TV had to do the same.

Using Sacramento as an example, the argument that we basically used in jurisdiction after jurisdiction was that the city of Sacramento should not have a right to say to a cable TV operator that it has to provide a weather channel. If that were the case, then it should be able to say to The Sacramento Bee newspaper that it had to provide a color weather page like USA Today. By the same token, the government does not have the right to say to a cable company that it has to provide a public access channel where people can come in and say what they want, any more than it can say to the local newspaper that it has to put aside a page or two for people to write whatever they want or to say to the TV operator that it has to provide channels in various foreign languages any more than it has the right to demand that the local newspaper print a portion of its paper in foreign languages. Those are simply editorial decisions—not decisions for government to make.

In short, while these might be good public policy decisions, we must not let the government dictate what can or cannot be printed or broadcast. That, I argued, is a violation of basic First Amendment rights. So using this approach, on behalf of various clients we brought a number of lawsuits around the country consistent with the theory we had originally advanced in the Marquette case. As a result, I was admitted to practice not just before all federal courts in California, but also before federal courts in the states of New York, Michigan, Missouri, Minnesota, and Ohio, as well as the United States Supreme Court.

By the end of 1983 we had filed so many of these cases that eventually we managed to get one of them before the United States Supreme Court where we prevailed in a 9-0 decision that changed the cable television industry forever. I am not saying that we busted up all of the monopolies. That would be like trying to stop the rain from falling. There are still such monopolies in many parts of the country. There are two main reasons for this. One is that so many of the existing cable companies got their monopolies before opinions allowing for competition in the market place came down. The other reason comes down to simple economics. It is very expensive and difficult to become a new player in any given market, especially when another company has been in business there for ten to twenty years or longer. It's difficult and expensive to come in after the fact when all of the lines and facilities are laid and to have to go to the extraordinary expense of digging up and laying new wires.

Nevertheless, going forward, the rules had been changed. Although most of the large cable television companies felt very threatened by the approach we were taking, some saw the handwriting on the wall and began to retain us to represent them. One was Telecommunications, Inc. (TCI), then the largest cable television operator in the United States. Bob Magness, a pioneer in cable TV was the principal shareholder. His CEO was Dr. John Malone, who then was and today remains, a corporate titan and financial giant in every respect of the word.

Malone, an absolutely brilliant businessman, wanted to take over Liberty Media Corporation in the Pacific Northwest, a company then headed by another of our clients, Carolyn Chambers. The problem was that the biggest franchise controlled by Liberty was the one in the city of Portland, Oregon. The City Council of Portland was not prepared to allow TCI to come in and take over the Liberty operation, so I flew to

Portland and spent considerable time there meeting and negotiating with City Council members in what was ultimately a successful campaign to allow the transfer to occur. The rest is history. Malone went on to take Liberty to bigger and better things and to diversify it in all kinds of ways as he used that company to become the linchpin of a whole new communications empire. In addition to his media empire, John was to eventually become the largest landowner in the US outside of the government itself.

28

Lake Tahoe: Back to Nature, Back to God

Before *I even arrived at Dr. Dozier's office one afternoon several months into my recovery, I had already made up my mind. I was going to return to Lake Tahoe—and soon.*

Truth be told, I had never been enthralled with Sacramento, of which Carmichael is but a suburb, albeit a nice one. There had only been two reasons I had ever lived in Sacramento: First, because the State Capitol was there and, as such, that is where my work as a State Senator had taken me. Second, because when I decided not to run for reelection and retire from electoral politics, Diana pleaded with me to remain in Sacramento for "a short while."

Did I want to remain in Sacramento when Diana asked me to? Definitely not. Were there countless other places where I would have preferred living? Of course. In my Senate District alone were communities where people anywhere would love to reside: Santa Barbara; Ventura; Ojai; the Santa Ynez Valley; to name but a few. But I was married and my wife wanted to stay put near her mother and father and the company that she was then running. I thought it only right under the circumstances to support her. The company was important to her, and I knew I could successfully practice law or engage in other business endeavors most anywhere. In my view, marriage was about compromise. So I agreed to stay, at least until Diana's ill mother passed on.

But many things had changed since I long ago agreed to stay in the Sacramento area at Diana's request. We were separated now and I had been renting a lake view home in Tahoe for several months before my aneurysm. The only reason I wasn't there now was because the doctors had forbidden me from returning to the Tahoe altitude while I was recovering.

Admittedly, living in Tahoe meant I'd be a couple of hours drive from my daughter, Jessica, and that was the one aspect of my life at the Lake that I did not like. To compensate, however, I made it an absolute priority to drive back and to see her often, being sure that I attended each and every school event and other outing. I also brought Jessica back to Tahoe with me as often as she could be away from school, especially on weekends and during school breaks.

In Tahoe, I had built a new life for myself—made wonderful friends and spent every free moment I had in nature or hiking with my dog, Spartacus, or engaging in sports activities with friends. Tahoe had become home and I was as anxious as I could be to get back there and away from the toxic environment that I felt Diana had intentionally caused to develop in Carmichael.

I told Dr. Dozier as he entered the appointment room, "I'd like to return…to Tahoe."

"Omer," he responded, "The progress you've made defies any medical explanation. I and others who have followed your case are baffled at how well you are doing. From a medical standpoint we simply can't explain it. Nevertheless, I don't think you should go to an altitude as high as that of Lake Tahoe."

I explained to Dr. Dozier that I had lived at that altitude for many months before the aneurysm—my body knew how to handle it. And I reminded him that over the years I'd climbed many times higher on various climbing expeditions all over the world.

"But not after your brain aneurysm and stroke, Omer," he replied. "I just don't think you should do it—at least, not yet."

I listened to Dr. Dozier's opinion. I respected and valued it. But I had always written my own rules and followed my own dictates. Hell, had I followed the doctor's admonitions, I wouldn't even have been in Dr. Dozier's office that day. I would have been confined to bed in my home in Carmichael.

"I can handle it," I said. "I want to do it and if I am going to come all the way back I need a different environment."

"I've come to know what a stubborn cuss you are, Omer. I strongly advise against it, and I think you're making a big mistake. But if you decide to go against my advice, it is absolutely critical that you have someone drive you."

Dr. Dozier knew me well enough by then to know that I would make my own decision and that didn't mean I didn't respect his advice, because I did. So if Dr. Dozier had driven a silver stake through my heart or had said it was guaranteed that I would die, I would not have tried to return to Tahoe at that time in my recovery. But Dr. Dozier had left the door cracked for me, and I was planning to walk through it.

"It is absolutely critical that you have someone drive you," Dr. Dozier said.

I told a white lie in response. "Of course," I said. "I understand."

A day or two later, I said a temporary goodbye to Jessica, and within hours of that goodbye I proceeded to climb into the driver's seat of my car and began my journey back to Tahoe.

I did not need to pack anything for the trip because Tahoe is where I had been living pretty much full-time before the aneurysm. Presumably, all of the things I had left were still there. In the trunk lay the same box of important papers I had put there the night before my aneurysm, as I had been scheduled to see my accountant the next day. There was also a suitcase, filled with clothes for the trip on which I was about to embark when I suffered the aneurysm and stroke.

Finally, I was ready to leave the Central Valley of California and return to the fresh mountain air of the Sierra's. As I drove out of the Sacramento area ever so carefully, slowly, cautiously—I felt no need to say goodbye. Assuming I made it to Tahoe as planned, I would not miss the valley smog that sometimes got so thick that you could not see the car just a few feet in front of you, or the heat of the summer days, or the traffic congestion that had resulted from Sacramento becoming one of the twenty largest urban areas in the country.

I would get to Tahoe without problems, I told myself, as I drove east on I-80. If I stayed focused and kept attentive, if I was sure to drive no more than the speed limit, if I stayed in the right lane the whole way, I could return safely to Spartacus, my friends at the Lake, and to the beautiful and spiritual view of the Lake that my home there provided.

Coming from Sacramento, I approached the Sierra Nevada Mountains from the west side where the ascent is gradual—unlike the steep, escarped east side of the mountain range. As a result, I knew that my body would gradually acclimatize as I drove along. That was one of the reasons I was confident that my body could safely handle the drive, even when Dr. Dozier was advising me not to make it.

It was probably the slowest and most carefully set pace I'd ever driven on an interstate highway, but I was being especially cautious. Traveling east on Interstate 80, it was pretty much a straight shot to the town of Truckee near Donner Summit. Turning off I-80 at Truckee, I came to a stop sign on a road I'd driven countless times. But the stop sign shouldn't have been there. And the road didn't go straight toward the Lake as it should have. Suddenly, everything looked all wrong. I was totally disoriented.

"Oh, Jesus," I thought. "Something isn't right."

I had been on this road so many times, but now I was completely confused. Had I made a mistake trying to return to the Lake too soon? I did not know what to do or where to go, so I just sat there. And sat there, and sat there.

Cars piled up behind me—maybe twenty or more of them. Horns started honking.

"Damn, maybe I shouldn't have come up here," I thought. "Maybe Dr. Dozier was right."

Suddenly, a man on foot approached on the driver's side of my car. I lowered the window, letting in the cold but fresh mountain air.

"What's wrong, friend?" he asked. "Is there a problem with your car?"

"I'm just confused," I explained. "The road doesn't look right and I know it well."

"How long since you've been up here?" he asked.

"Several months," I said. And then he saved me.

"Oh, they've changed this road so you are able to go around Truckee now," he said.

I exhaled. The road was supposed to look different—it was different.

"What are you looking for?" he continued.

"Highway 267 towards Kings Beach and the north shore of Lake Tahoe," I said.

"Just turn right at this stop sign and you'll be headed straight toward Kings Beach on 267," he said.

I thanked the man and turned right. A short distance further on I saw the 267 sign, the road became familiar, and I breathed a big sigh of relief.

"Oh, Lord, thank you," I thought. My mind hadn't failed me after all. Roadwork had simply changed the landscape.

As I drove slowly and carefully along 267, I felt the tension ease from my shoulders. I was on my way back again, inching ever closer to the life from which I had been severed on the night of my aneurysm and stroke.

As I traveled southeast on 267, the road rose higher and higher until I came to Brockway Summit where the road crests at 7200 feet. Below me, I looked down upon Lake Tahoe stretched out magnificently, as brilliantly blue as any lake in the world, its ripples gently rolling to the sandy shore. The mountains surrounding the Lake were covered with picture perfect snow, The green pine and fir trees glistened with snowflakes and the clouds which floated by above were as white as the snow below; the sky as blue as the lake below. God never painted a more beautiful picture. My chest swelled. I was at peace for the first time since I had been unexpectedly struck down so many months before. Why I had been so blessed, I didn't know, but I was suddenly overwhelmed with confidence that everything was going to be all right. Nature can do that to a soul.

29

The Sacramento Kings and the NBA

"Winners never quit and quitters never win."
— Vince Lombardi

In March 1983, Greg "Dutch" Van Dusen came to my office. Van Dusen represented a couple of fellows in Sacramento who were interested in buying a National Basketball Association, a Major League Baseball, or a National Football League franchise. They had heard that I had good contacts in the sports world and wondered if I might be able to help. I was retained and my first trip was to New York City to find out if there were any NBA franchises for sale. Two were: The Indiana Pacers and the Kansas City Kings. This wasn't public information, but it was disclosed to me in meetings held with Larry O'Brien, then the outgoing Commissioner of the NBA, and later with David Stern, the incoming Commissioner. My focus soon became that of the Kansas City Kings because the price for the Indianapolis franchise was well beyond my client's reach. In Kansas City, I negotiated the terms and conditions and, along with Bob Margolin, counsel for the Kings, drafted the documents with respect to the acquisition. The purchase occurred in late April 1983.

In 1984, several of us associated with the acquisition including the principals, Gregg Lukenbill and Joe Benvenuti, began working with the other NBA franchise owners as we needed their approval in order to move the Kings to Sacramento. Visits were also made to the San Francisco Bay area to meet with the owners of the Golden State Warriors as they were trying to prevent the relocation of the Kings. The Warriors had reason to be concerned. Sacramento is one of the largest media markets in the country, with about

2.2 million people within a forty-five-mile radius and the Warriors considered this part of its own media market. Needless to say, there was a lot of money at stake.

In June of 1984, I went to Salt Lake City for the annual NBA owner's meeting. Our arguments to justify the relocation of the Kings were strengthened by virtue of the fact that the attendance in Kansas City was abysmal. The Kings were playing half their games in Kansas City and the other half in Omaha and were not drawing crowds in either place. Of course, one reason for the poor attendance was the persistent rumors that the Kings would be leaving Kansas City for Sacramento.

Ultimately, over objections from the Golden State Warriors, we received NBA approval to relocate the franchise to Sacramento for the 1985 season. A press conference in Sacramento to announce the Kings' relocation was a major event in the sports world at the time. On October 25, the Kings played their first game in ARCO Arena. Typical corporate name, right? Not exactly at that time. These days, yes, as the practice of naming sports complexes after commercial interests is now commonplace but back then it was not. The Kings were the first major sports franchise to sell the name of their arena to a corporate sponsor. ARCO paid a heavy sum for that privilege and soon thereafter teams in most all professional sports followed suit.

Of course not everybody involved in the ownership of sports franchises is necessarily a fan. Not by a long shot. A prime example of this is Joe Benvenuti, a very savvy real estate tycoon who was the principal money man behind the Kings acquisition. After the contract signing in Kansas City we went down to the court at Kemper Arena in Kansas City. Joe picked up a basketball and asked, "How do you throw this?" Believe it or not, he wasn't kidding. Joe, who stands about five feet five inches tall, proceeded to underhand the ball about two feet above his head. When the laughter subsided he said, "Well, I've never seen anyone throw one of these because I've never before watched a game." And now he was the principal owner of a professional basketball team. To Joe it was simply a business decision. And a very good one.

The initial ARCO Arena was constructed as a temporary one to provide the team a place to play while a permanent structure was being built. The first thing I did was select four seats directly behind the Kings bench so that I could literally lean over and be involved in the discussions taking place at courtside. Loved those seats! When the permanent structure was finished a few years later, the press table was stretched out between the player's bench and the first row and, although the seats were as good as any in the arena, I didn't have the opportunity to listen in on discussions at courtside as once had been the case. However, I was to keep those seats for over twenty years before I was to relinquish them due to my later relocation from the Sacramento area.

Having the Kings as a client was fascinating. I was drafting the contracts for all of the Kings' players and coaches and getting to know each of them, as well as their agents, both on and off of the court. I also represented a number of the players, so long as there was no conflict of interest, in small civil matters that arose from time to time. For example, one player was named in a paternity suit and another had a number of relatively serious traffic violations. Fairly standard stuff, but I was glad to help out when I could.

In mid-June 1985, we had the first year of the lottery system where the weakest team in the league got to pick first and a container full of ping pong balls was used to dish out the selections. It was a system where the team with the worst record at the end of the year had the most ping pong balls. Commissioner David Stern, having replaced Larry O'Brien, would pick the balls after rolling them around in a circular basket.

We ended up that year with the sixth pick. I was in the room when General Manager Joe Axelson was getting ready to make the Kings selection. It had come down to two players. One was a center out of the University of Arkansas named Joe Kleine. We had a major weakness at center and Joe felt we had to draft for the position. The fellow passed over was out of Louisiana Tech named Karl Malone. As history reflects, Axelson decided on Kleine. Unfortunately, the word quickly got around the league that "people were always throwing the ball to Kleine in the wrong place. His hands." Nice guy, but he had the worst hands I ever saw. Malone, of course, turned out to be arguably the best power forward in NBA history.

While the Kings weren't necessarily my most important client, they were by far my most fun client. Though I was in effect part of the Kings' organization, my interest in basketball predated my work with the Kings. I had always loved the Boston Celtics going back to the days of Bob Cousy and Bill Sharman, and I was certainly a fan when Bill Russell made the Celtics the team that came to dominate the league for better than a decade.

In late 1986, we discreetly reached out to Russell to see if he might have an interest in becoming the Kings' coach. In 1987 these discussions became serious and I entered into negotiations with Russell's agent, which culminated in April of that year. As it appeared that we had reached agreement on virtually all terms and conditions by April 27th, Russell surreptitiously flew into Sacramento. We had a room reserved at a hotel at the Sacramento Airport. Russell and I holed up there together for most of the day. His agent was up in Seattle and we were on the phone with him and faxing documents back and forth all day long trying to finalize matters. Russell and I were talking throughout this time, mostly about sports nostalgia and trivia as he left all of the business talk up to his agent. No doubt about it, Russell was one of the greatest players of all time. I took an immediate liking to him. He had this big grin and, as he laid around most of the afternoon with his shirt off in the hotel room, I could tell that he was still in great shape. We used to joke that our center, Joe Kleine, was as good as Bill Russell. Of course, Russell was in his fifties at the time. In any event that evening the contract was signed and a press conference was scheduled shortly thereafter.

Unfortunately, I must confess I lost a lot of respect for Russell during his tenure as coach of the Kings. He was seldom at the workouts and rarely in his office. He had a great passion for golf and was on the links most of the time. He didn't seem to take his job as seriously as he should have. He only coached the Kings for two years. Like so many great players, regardless of sport, Russell expected his players to be as great as he was without much coaching. We were playing the Los Angeles Lakers during one game and they scored almost thirty straight points to start the game. It was just brutal. Yet Russell would not call a time out or allow any player to call a time out. He wanted them to be embarrassed.

We signed Willis Reed as Assistant Coach that year—a heck of a nice guy. I admire him to this day. Reed, of course, is also a Hall of Famer. Russell and Reed, both physical giants, would stand up during most of the games. Because of their respective heights, it was difficult for me at floor level to see over them. As a result, I eventually moved my seats up three rows so that I had a good line of sight at all times. That didn't matter very much because by this time we were in the new arena and my first row of seats would no longer allow me to be, in effect, part of the huddle.

———————

Needless to say the Kings were an important client of mine and what happened during the breakup of the Farrow, Schildhause, & Rains law firm was also depressing. The Kings had always been slow payers. They would pay only after lots of work had been done and that was always OK with me because I always knew I would get paid. At one point the team owed me about $100,000. My partner, Harold Farrow, who was in debt to the IRS, sued the Kings alleging that he and I were partners (true) and had been when all billings had occurred (again true). As a partner I intervened on behalf of the Kings and filed a cross complaint in federal court against Farrow. The court ruled in favor of the IRS saying that since both Farrow and I were general partners of the firm, any firm asset belonging to one general partner could be used to satisfy the debt of the other partner. I lost the $100,000 plus.

Eventually there were several other lawsuits in which Farrow became embroiled, one of which was an action I brought against him in which I was ultimately the prevailing party.

30

The Sherman Anti-Trust Act

"The good you do today, people will often forget tomorrow. Do good anyway."
– Mother Teresa

The Sherman Anti-Trust Act, advocated by Teddy Roosevelt and enacted during his administration, is designed to prevent monopolies from forming. It is, in my opinion, the Magna Carta of economic freedom in America. Because I was becoming rather well known for anti-trust work, a man named Larry Wolford came to see me in Sacramento. He was the President of a company called American Computech, doing business as West Coast Medical Specialties. Computech had entered the kidney dialysis business in the San Diego area.

National Medical Care (NMC) and its subsidiary, Bio Medical Applications (BMA) were both subsidiaries of WR Grace & Co. BMA had a virtual monopoly in the national dialysis market as it had dialysis treatment facilities throughout the country. BMA had achieved this status by paying doctors under the table to make sure the doctors always sent their patients to BMA clinics. In the San Diego area, BMA was trying to drive Computech out of business, again getting the paid off doctors (nephrologists) to go to the hospital directors and get them to break any contract they had with Computech and to sign only with BMA. Wolford said, "They (BMA) are about to drive us into bankruptcy."

I agreed to represent Computech and filed an anti-trust case against NMC and BMA as well as against a number of prominent San Diego doctors who were complicit. We alleged every anti-trust violation under the sun. As it turned out the case was destined to go on for years and eventually, after a six month jury trial in federal court in San Diego, a several million dollar jury verdict was rendered in favor of my clients. It was the first such suit of this nature ever successfully prosecuted either against NMC or BMA.

This case had really been uphill from day one. Nevertheless, as I learned just how outrageous and unlawful the actions of NMC and BMA had been, the more determined I became. Their under the table payments to doctors had been going on for years and years, and they referred to their patients as "cash cows" because the federal government paid all the bills for any dialysis treatment provided. Millions of dollars had changed hands in order to get the doctors to refer all their patients to BMA facilities, no matter how good or how bad they were—and most were quite bad. Their unethical approach to the care and treatment of seriously ill patients was in my mind was almost criminal.

Unfortunately, the greed of my own clients and my own ignorance was to leave a bitter taste in my mouth. To begin with, I was reluctant to undertake representation of American Computech in the first place because it was not only going to be a very difficult case but it promised to be a very long jury trial in federal court in San Diego, 500 miles from my home. But my brother knew Larry Wolford and his partner, Dennis Fox, and asked me to represent them. So I did.

As the trial actually got underway several years later, Computech did go ahead and file for bankruptcy protection. Before this happened, Wolford and Fox had pleaded with me to change our financial agreement from an hourly rate to a contingency rate. Again, given the uphill fight ahead of me I did not want to do this but ultimately I agreed. They then went ahead and filed for bankruptcy. Being ignorant of bankruptcy law, I didn't realize that it was requisite that I go into court and get our contract approved by the bankruptcy court. That being the case, in the aftermath of our trial victory, the bankruptcy attorney my clients had retained sent me a letter saying that since my contract had never been approved by the bankruptcy court, Computech was under no obligation to pay attorney fees. This was more than modestly disturbing since the fee that I was to receive was in the millions of dollars. I went to a bankruptcy attorney to see if what I was being told was true and found out that it was. Meanwhile NMC and BMA filed an appeal from the jury verdict and, under threat of losing everything, we agreed to accept compensation at approximately twenty five percent of what we had coming to us.

But the greed of my clients rose up to bite them in their respective asses. Their sanctimonious bankruptcy attorney embezzled over $5 million of the money I had won for them which had been placed, at the attorney's suggestion, in his law firm trust account. The attorney wound up going to prison, but neither my greedy clients nor I got what was coming to us. This was in fact a startling example of human greed at its worst. As a result, everyone lost. Wolford and Fox could have retired for life or, alternatively, built a truly large company. Their crooked bankruptcy attorney wouldn't have ended up in prison, and I wouldn't have been denied what I had labored years to achieve for them.

31

Ross Perot

"Politics is The Art of Compromise."
— Walter Lippman

On the home front, another unpleasant reality was that my wife's business, CIM, was failing. The major reason for this was unfair competition. A very large and powerful national corporation had purchased a small startup firm in the same business as CIM. It was called Legitech. The corporation, which had newspapers in several large cities in the country, came into the office of CIM under the false pretense of a news organization doing a story on the company. Diana, though very bright, was still sufficiently naive from a business standpoint that she didn't get suspicious when multiple "reporters" spent an entire week with her. They exhaustively went through the CIM operation, including its sophisticated technology and its sales techniques. When I later asked Diana about it, she said, "They were the nicest people so I wanted to be as helpful as possible." I told her that a news story doesn't take a whole week and several people unless it's a story with the significance of something like Watergate. But it was too late.

So Legitech began to engage in predatory pricing. When bids went out they not only would underbid, but did so even if it was going to suffer a financial loss. The parent company had such deep pockets that they could suffer a deep loss until they drove the competitors out of business. CIM couldn't compete under such unlawful circumstances. Likewise, CIM could not possibly bring a suit against the parent corporation. It would have buried us in paper and it would have cost well over a million dollars in attorney fees to prosecute. It would also have been a drawn out affair no doubt lasting several years. Large corporations do this to crush competitors all the time. Even though it violates anti-trust laws, most of the time it is a successful tactic because of the expense a victimized company incurs in prosecuting such an action.

For a long time, I kept pouring money into the company to keep it propped up. Finally, an approach was made to Ross Perot's Electronic Data Systems (EDS). EDS did substantial business with the State of California and had an office in Folsom on the outskirts of Sacramento. Meetings were initiated with EDS to see if it might be interested in purchasing CIM. Eventually Diana and I travelled to the EDS headquarters in Plano, Texas for meetings with Ross Perot, corporate counsel and various other members of Perot's staff.

Perot's office was adorned with western sculpture and bronze work, primarily that of Frederic Remington. Perot held himself out as a man of the west. I found Perot to be a very bright and gregarious guy. He was a salesman of the first order. At lunch time we all went to eat in the corporate cafeteria and I have to say there was nothing elitist about the guy during that day. At lunch, we got at the end of the lunch line and we sat at cafeteria tables with EDS employees. Perot was chatting with everyone and I could see that company morale was seemingly quite high. But I could also sense that Perot had a thin skin. When somebody would say something which he took the wrong way, he would bristle. This character trait would later become evident to the entire country. This was when he decided to run for President as an independent in 1992.

In my opinion, Perot's entrance in the 1992 Presidential race served a valuable purpose because it forced both Bill Clinton and George H. W. Bush to focus much more sharply on the key issues of the election. Otherwise, if given a chance, they would gladly have spent the entire campaign on peripheral issues.

However, politicians in a democracy have to compromise in order to accomplish anything. After all, politics is the art of compromise. I didn't see this ability in Perot. He had somewhat of an authoritarian personality and I did not believe he would make it in politics. He lacked the thick skin that a politician must have. Sure enough, he was to drop out of the Presidential race at one point in time because, as he put it, "The Republicans are going to embarrass my daughter at her wedding." I have no idea whether or not this was true but even if it was, I thought, "Welcome to politics." Although Perot was later to reenter the race, he had lost whatever momentum he had and eventually became but a footnote to history.

In any case, EDS did offer to buy CIM under terms that amounted to a giveaway of CIM. However, EDS did offer Diana a good job in its Folsom office. All that was in it for me was that the bleeding stopped — I lost my entire investment.

32

From Chaos to Order

Although I had been able to make the two-and-a-half hour drive from Carmichael to my home at Lake Tahoe, I was going to need help removing items from the car and taking them into the house. As a result, when I steered my car into the driveway at Tahoe, I was met by George and another local friend. They welcomed me back, then carried my suitcase and a box of papers and files into the house as I slowly followed behind, left-right-left-right, my left foot always leading, my right foot dragging behind.

Entering the house, I marveled at the Lake view through the picture window in the living room. It was uplifting, even more spiritual than I remembered it. I hobbled over to the couch and sat down just to take in the Lake and its marvelously beautiful natural surroundings.

My tranquil state was pleasantly interrupted when the front door opened and my dog, Spartacus, came charging in full-speed and full of vim, vigor, and excitement. He raced over to me and thrust his huge paws into my lap. He licked my face. He barked. I leaned into him and ran my hands down his soft, short Weimaraner coat.

Spartacus and I hadn't seen each other for months and he smothered me with licks and kisses, as if I were a ghost come back to life. I'm sure he thought that I was gone forever from his life.

But there I was! Alive and returning his kisses with hugs, pats, and embraces. Although all of my body parts didn't work quite right, it didn't matter to Spartacus. I was back! And I was with him!

Furthermore, my physical condition had not degraded during my ascent to Tahoe. As far as I could tell, my mobility and sensation were just as they had been when I left Carmichael *earlier that day. The neurologists' concerns about me returning to Tahoe were no doubt prudent, but I had been right. I had been ready to handle the altitude change.*

———————

One day my daughter Kelly called with some interesting news. She knew a doctor who, in turn, knew a renowned rehabilitation therapist in the Los Angeles area who might be able to help my advance on the road to recovery. Waleed Al-Oboudi was his name, and he specialized in working with stroke victims and with people who had suffered brain injuries. Although he did not generally take patients directly—instead spending his time training other physical therapists in his sought-after approach—Oboudi became interested in my case and said he would like to work with me. However, he would only be able to do so for one week because of previous commitments—and he would need authorization from my physicians.

I called Dr. Dozier to get his opinion on the safety of my traveling by air and to secure from him authorization to see Al-Oboudi. "It's a short flight from Reno to Los Angeles and the cabin is pressurized," he said. "Nonetheless, the cautious approach would be not to do it. But I know you're going to do it whatever I say, so if you feel you're up to it, go ahead. Omer, I just ask that you keep in touch with me by phone during the time you're in Southern California, starting with the moment your plane lands." I assured him that I would.

I had done fine on the drive to Tahoe and I felt that I could handle the plane ride as well. So I informed my new physical therapist's office at the Lake that I would be leaving for a week, and the receptionist there helped me make travel arrangements. George drove me from the Lake down to the Reno airport on the scheduled day and I boarded the plane for LAX. The flight was uneventful, and when I arrived in Los Angeles I was picked up by my good friend, Bill Raffin, whose office in Manhattan Beach was only a short distance from Al-Oboudi's office in Redondo Beach.

Al-Oboudi's facility, like a fun house for kids, was lined with mirrors and filled with colored balls, bands, low-to-the-floor trampolines, tubes, and tunnels. Though a child would have been at home there, much of the equipment was new to me, including the bosu, a rubber half-ball meant to create an unstable standing surface and thus to challenge one's ability to balance.

Al-Oboudi immediately started by asking me to step up onto the wobbly bosu surface. The flat surface of the bosu was face-down on the ground, which meant I'd have to step on the ball side, which was soft, unsteady rubber. Balance was still difficult for me when "walking" on regular or flat surfaces, so this would be a challenge. But wasn't that why I was there? To get better, I had to keep challenging myself and to have others challenge me.

As I stepped up onto the soft rounded half-ball, I pitched forward and then backward before falling off to the side. This happened time after time until I managed to attain some degree of balance while standing on the bosu. Even then it was like standing on the edge of a boat without any rails in choppy water.

As time passed, Waleed and I made small talk and got to know each other. He was a highly educated Iraqi-American with dark hair, olive skin, and a light accent. He had practiced physical, occupational, and rehabilitative therapy for many years in North America and Europe, and though we did not discuss it I suspect that he emigrated from Iraq around the time that Saddam Hussein's Baath party came to power.

As that first day progressed, Oboudi ran me through one exercise after another. Although these exercises would have been simple for me several months before, under the changed circumstances they were incredibly challenging.

Eventually, I was able to stand on the bosu, however unsteadily. Oboudi then began to toss balls to me while I stood there wavering back and forth on the unstable surface. He also had me stretch taut, relatively thick exercise bands with my weakened and still quasi-lifeless arm and hand and then navigate on all fours through tunnels. I tried to walk on a tube that twisted and turned beneath the weight of my body.

Whenever I attained some degree of stability in a given exercise, Oboudi would change things, always pushing me to the next level. He'd put light weights in my hand and ask me to do the same activity I'd finally managed to do without weight, or he'd have me transfer a skill to an increasingly uneven surface. There was constant emphasis on balance.

With each exercise, I could tell that I was growing steadier, stronger, and more confident. When I had arrived in Southern California to work with Oboudi, I had regained about half of my lost weight. Quite quickly during our work that week, I could sense my muscles and tone starting to come back.

"Muscle memory is an extraordinary thing," Oboudi explained. "You were in good shape for much of your life, Omer, and your muscle memory from that time will be of immense help during your recovery process. You are already beginning to gain weight and definition. I can see it. What we've got to do is really emphasize that. It can be done, but if you don't work hard to redevelop those muscles, they will be lost to you forever."

Thus, I learned from Oboudi that it's not just the brain that has memory—other parts of the body have memory, too. Before the aneurysm, my muscles were accustomed to a certain environment, and they strived to get back there again. With some help, I believed they could and would.

One day early on, Oboudi took me out onto a tennis court. He put a racquet in my right hand, and I did my best to grasp it. "Okay," Oboudi said as he walked to the other side of the net. "I'm going to throw a tennis ball underhanded over the net and show you approximately where it's going to go. Watch where it lands and how high it bounces." I did.

"Now, this time, when I throw it over the net, try to hit it back to me," he said. The first time I tried, I missed. "That's alright—that's what I expected," Oboudi said.

He continued to throw gentle underhanded tosses to me. On the third one, I softly and clumsily hit it back. "Okay, I want you to just keep hitting it right there," Oboudi said, and he continued to throw thirty or forty more balls to my new "sweet" spot.

"Wow, you're really doing well, Omer," Oboudi finally said. "But you want to know something? That's not life. Right now you know pretty much where the ball is going to land, how high the ball is going to bounce, and what you need to do to get the ball back to me. If we keep this up much longer, you will be slamming those balls back to me. You could probably do so while eating a ham sandwich. But that's not life—whether it's tennis, business, or personal relationships. Life isn't easy and it certainly isn't predictable. In fact, it's chaotic. So what we're going to do is come out here again tomorrow. But the ball is not always going to go to the same side of you. It may go over your head, drop in front of you, or land on the other side of you. You might swat and miss; you might fall down. But you must start the practice of reacting to the unexpected."

"By God, Oboudi is right—life is chaos," I thought. I could do the same thing over and over again but that was not going to help me a whole hell of a lot. I needed a body that once again could respond to uncertainty—a body that could handle not knowing what was coming next.

So Oboudi and I worked from nine to five each day that week, and with each and every task that we did, I would be forced to progress from certainty to chaos. That was life after all: messy, untidy, and uncertain. Although I had always known that, Oboudi's emphasis on it as an integral part of my therapy had a pronounced effect on everything I was thereafter to do during my road to recovery.

Without question, therein would lie one of the secrets to any long-term recovery I might make from my brain aneurysm and stroke. I had to train for chaos. I would have to push past every comfort zone and expose my body to uncertainty in order to trigger my muscle memory and rebuild my physical capacity. Before I could succeed, I had to face extreme vulnerability even if at the risk of falling and suffering injury.

By this stage of my life I was certainly no stranger to pushing beyond limits so I was primed and ready for Oboudi's wisdom. Just as I had been willing to fall out of bed when I first tried to walk, I would now go back to Tahoe and enlist my physical therapists and friends in putting me to the test of chaos in every activity in which I engaged. We would start one place and often end up at another altogether unexpected place. I would take my body to new places until they felt old and familiar again.

As we said goodbye, Oboudi shared these parting words with me: "Your recovery is now up to you, Omer. If you don't remain determined, whatever minor progress we've made this week, you will lose rather quickly. But if you remain determined, you will get there—I'm convinced of it."

To this day, I consider Waleed Al-Oboudi not just a friend, but an angel.

33
The Light of My Life

"Life is full of beauty. Notice it. Notice the bumble bee,
the small child, and the smiling faces."
— Ashley Smith

As always, life has its curveballs. One came on February 19, 1986. I was in Boston on business when I got a phone call from Diana.

"Are you sitting down?" she asked. Before I could reply she blurted out, "I'm pregnant."

Wow! Talk about a bolt from the blue. It was a complete shock. I was so surprised I didn't immediately respond. I was in my mid-forties and the first thing that came to my mind was would I even be alive when the child graduated from college? I just sat there trying to absorb the startling news—totally unexpected. Diana and I had previously discussed having children and had decided not to but Diana was still a young woman and I guess her biological clock told her it was now or never.

Early in the pregnancy the doctor called and said there was a problem, an abnormality on one of the chromosomes of the fetus. It was a disturbing turn of events and I feared the worst. We had tests. I held my breath until we discovered that Diana had the same abnormality. That allayed our concerns. The pregnancy went full term without any complications and on August 17, 1986 we had a beautiful baby whom we named Jessica Erin.

After Jessica was born, we would take her with us wherever we traveled, domestic or foreign. Sometimes we were camping; sometimes we were on luxury cruises, sometimes we were on adventure trips. I have never seen a child take to travel as much as Jessica. She absolutely loved it then, and still does.

As Jessica grew up she enjoyed opportunities that I never dreamed of and even had I dreamed of, could never have afforded during my own formative years. We gave her skiing lessons, tennis lessons, soccer lessons, rock climbing lessons, kayaking lessons, and more. Piano lessons were also provided but she didn't seem to really take to any of these. That surprised me only because most everybody in our family has enjoyed these types of activities when they had the opportunity to participate in them.

Jessica also was the first in the family to attend a private school. In fact every school she ever attended during pre-school, elementary school and high school was a private school. As part of this experience, she was able to take school trips to the Boston area, to the New York City area, and the Washington DC area. The school also took the students on annual trips to the Shakespearean Festivals in Ashland, Oregon. During her elementary school years she attended a school known as St. Michael's. I was extremely involved not only with Jessica, but with her class and with the entire school throughout the eight years she was at St. Michael's. I would frequently speak to her class on politics, history, personalities I've known, foreign affairs and travel. I loved the opportunity to be involved with Jessica's school and my presentations were always well received by the kids.

Starting about the fifth grade, in either September or October, I would take the class for a nature trek in the Sierra Nevada's. I gave them talks on mountaineering and showed them the types of equipment used in high climbing. It was a great opportunity to introduce many of these children to nature up close. I have since heard that for some of these children it started a lifelong relationship with nature.

In 1998, as soon as school was out, Jessica and I flew to Ireland. I had programmed for her a riding course at a noted equestrian facility south of Dublin in County Wicklow. After completing that course, she went directly into a program called Adventure Ireland. Adventure Ireland provided a cultural program as well as a number of sightseeing opportunities. The last part of Adventure Ireland was in the west of Ireland for rock-climbing, sea kayaking, and lots of other fun stuff. It was a great experience for her.

In 1999-2000 we were to take a trip to Antarctica. By this time, Jessica had visited all seven continents. She was only twelve years of age. It may be that at that point in time she was the youngest person in history to have actually set foot on all seven continents as not many young people had actually set foot on Antarctica before 2000.

When I first considered setting up an office in Geneva in addition to the one I maintained in Sacramento, I was worried about the time I might spend away from Jessica. I had spent far too much time in politics away from Kelly and Mark—not to speak of the incredible obstacles Judy placed in my way when I tried to see them—and I didn't want to have the same experience again.

As part of Jessica's private school experience, in 1999 between Jessica's seventh and eighth grades, a very wealthy Greek-American friend of mine, Angelo Tsakapoulous, and I planned a trip to take the entire class of students to Greece. Angelo, who came from Greece when he was young, was very well connected politically in Greece (as well as in America). He was on his second marriage and had a daughter in Jessica's class.

With Angelo's contacts in Greece, and our joint knowledge of Greek history, we felt that we could put together a rather amazing trip for the children. That we did. Many other parents went along on the trip and, as a result, we were able to keep everything under control quite well.

There were two loves in Jessica's life that remained constant. One was and is a love of traveling. I suspect this is something that she came by from me given my own insatiable wanderlust. In my case, it has been a lifelong quest for knowledge and new experiences. As I often say, "not all who wander are lost." In Jessica's case I think it is primarily just a way of life that she greatly enjoys. However, I'm not sure during her formative years that she actually realized just how unique her life experience was in this regard.

Her other great love that was a constant in her life, and remains so today, is a love of horses. Around age five we began to give her horse riding lessons. She turned out to be an apt student, and over the years became quite an accomplished equestrian. Eventually she was entering competitions all over California (and later Nevada as well), and often winning events in which she was entered—including California State Championships.

Jessica was also quite talented when it came to drawing, and she seemed to have creative writing ability as well. As we often had visitors coming from various parts of the world, Jessica also had the opportunity to become quite comfortable with different ethnicities, cultures, and nationalities. She had and has a joyful personality, a big heart, and people found her quite pleasant to be around.

Before my marriage to Diana began to unravel, Jessica and I were pretty much inseparable, especially on various trips, many of which she and I took together and many of which we took as an entire family. When I set up an office in Geneva, I also made sure that I returned for any event in which she participated whether it was a dance recital at school, a father/daughter prom, the annual Christmas program, her various equestrian events, and so on. Nevertheless, we were not together during that period on a daily basis and I missed her greatly. I am sure that she also resented my absence during this period and for some time our father/daughter relationship became more distant than had previously been the case. This broke my heart, and I suspect it did hers as well.

I think both Jessica and I were confused, neither quite understanding what was going on in our family life. To me, I was not only doing what I thought to be necessary to provide financial stability to the family but I was doing what I thought was best in an attempt to try to save the marriage. In retrospect, I probably was not doing the right thing in trying to give my wife complete freedom. Jessica, of course, was oblivious to what was going on behind the scenes and Diana and I always put on a good front in her presence.

Today, Jessica lives with me and we continue to take wonderful trips together as she nears completion of her college studies. Most recently, we took a trip to Scandinavia, the Baltic States, and Russia.

Two summers ago Jessica had an internship with the United Nations in New York City. Specifically, she did work for the Convention for the Elimination of Discrimination against Women (known by its acronym, CEDAW). She is and always has been a hard worker at those things that she enjoys and she acquitted herself well in this position. She was also able to sit in on most meetings at the United Nations other than those that were closed. This was a great experience that few people ever have.

The bottom line, however, is that Jessica is a treasure to me. She always has been, and she always will be the light of my life.

34

"The Rest and Be Thankful" and Fire

"The ache for home lives in us all, the safe place
where we can go as we are and not be questioned."
— Maya Angelou

The home in which we lived when Jessica was born was on a small ranch which we named "The Rest and Be Thankful." Notwithstanding my dislike of the Central Valley of California, the "Rest and Be Thankful" was a rather cool place to live. We had horseshoe pits, pinball machines, video games, a pool table, two ponds connected by a shallow stream, all on five and one-half acres of very beautiful property. In the pasture, we had five horses, among them a Tennessee Walker named Tennessee Mash, another named Kentucky Bourbon, and a very beautiful horse named Georgia Sunshine, one of the famous Adolfo Camarillo horses which I presented one year as a birthday gift to Diana. We also had two dogs, from time to time cats, and about ten really fun Nubian goats that just ignored the electric fence that I had placed around the pasture. It was effective in keeping the horses in—but not the goats!

My two older children, Kelly and Mark, were able to spend considerable time with us at the ranch over the years. They called it the "Work and Be Thankless" ranch. Kelly, four years older than Mark, graduated first from college. After Mark graduated from high school, he next entered the University of California, San Diego where he received his BS Degree. He was later to get his Master's Degree from the University of Washington and thereafter his PhD from the University of California, Davis. Today he is a tenured Professor of Hydrology and Geology at the University of South Florida in Tampa.

March 9, 1987 turned out to be one of the most traumatic days of my life. About 2:30 am, Diana and I were asleep in the master bedroom and Jessica was asleep in her bedroom across the hall from us at our "Rest and Be Thankful" ranch on Whiskey Bar Road. Suddenly, I was awakened by a strange sound. It was the smoke alarm. I jumped out of bed and ran down the hallway. I saw flames leaping up high from the lower level of our split level home. There was a huge fire. I went charging back down the hallway and scooped up our seven-month-old daughter, got my wife out of bed, gave the baby to Diana and told her to go out the sliding glass door and to rush up to the caretaker's house to call the fire department. I ran back to try to fight the fire. It was spreading rapidly, and I couldn't figure out why. Timbers began to crash all around me. The smoke was so thick I couldn't breathe. I finally stumbled out, coughing, and fell to my knees gasping for breath.

Quite a while later, the volunteer fire department engine and men arrived, and they did the very best that they could. However, we were in a remote location and by the time they arrived, the house was gone. Basically all we had left were the skivvies in which we had been sleeping. I realized that furniture, furnishings, clothes, etc., were just things, and things can always be replaced. However, what cannot be replaced are personal items such as diaries, important papers, photographs, etc. Everything was lost except for certain items I had in my office in downtown Sacramento. I did not even have a photograph of any of my children left. Moreover, a diary that I had kept for approximately fifteen years was gone. I had made copies of a lot of things, but lo and behold, stupid me, the copies were in the house as well.

The cause of the fire was rather bizarre. I had chopped wood and stacked it near a back door, I would bring it in as and when we needed it to build a fire. The night before the fire, we had a guest who smoked heavily. He knew we didn't allow smoking in the house. During dinner and the early evening he would go out and have a smoke. It's possible that in some way a butt or ashes landed in the sawdust next to the wood and began to smolder. Another possibility is that since Diana's parents were coming to dinner the following night, she cleaned out the fireplace. Perhaps it still had hot embers and it's possible that she put some of the hot embers outside.

We do know that the fire actually started outside near that wood pile. I hired an expert and the insurance company did as well to find out where the fire started. It definitely started near that pile of wood and burned from the outside in. When it entered the house, the fire found itself in a large library and game area lined with bookshelves six shelves high around the entire room. That room was also full of video tapes, scrapbooks and photographs. All of these are items that burn well. That's why when I got to the fire it was already blazing out of control.

The following day I was sitting outside on a stump, stunned, just gazing at the smoldering embers when an insurance agent showed up. He handed me a list of things I had to do for them and ourselves. That was the second part of the nightmare.

Our insurance company, State Farm, refused to admit we had the coverage that we did have. Our copy of the policy had been burned. State Farm provided us with a partial copy of the policy but one which omitted key portions. A big legal fight commenced. Just what you don't need at a time like that. Initially, I represented myself. I came to the realization that if an insurance company jacked me around like that, I could just imagine what they do to most people—people who do not have the legal training or background that I had. During discovery, I kept finding documents that they had hidden or on which they had redacted information. They had clearly engaged in bad faith and ultimately they knew that I knew it.

With evidence of bad faith in hand, I retained an attorney named Bill Shernoff in Claremont, California. Bill was a friend of mine and was the most renown insurance bad faith attorney in the country. He had tried some landmark cases and established new case law in many of these cases. Eventually, after a couple more years of being jacked around by the insurance company, they decided to settle the case for considerably more than I had originally demanded. This was a direct result of the bad faith in which State Farm had engaged.

I had purchased a home for Diana's parents close by in Rocklin the year before so we stayed with them for a week or so while looking for a place to rent. Thereafter, I purchased a home in Carmichael, a suburb of Sacramento. The home sat on bluffs overlooking the American River and a wildlife sanctuary. I decided to sell the land on which the Rest and Be Thankful had been situated. I think part of my decision had been emotional because of the artifacts, diaries, scrapbooks, photographs, family heirlooms, and other personal things we had lost.

In the aftermath of the fire, people would often say "I know exactly how you feel." In retrospect, I realized that unless they had gone through a similar experience, they really didn't. I remember an earlier time when over three hundred homes were lost to a fire in the Mission Oaks section of Santa Barbara. I remember my heart going out to those people as I first helicoptered over the fire and, after the fire was brought under control, as I walked amongst the remains of the fire. In speaking to those who had lost their homes, I deeply and truly thought that I could empathize with them, but after suffering my own fire, I realized that I really hadn't and in fact couldn't have entirely empathized with them. It's one of those things that actually has to happen to you, personally, to fully understand the extent of the loss and its impact on one's life.

However, the important thing was that both my wife and my daughter were alive and had not been physically harmed. That was a blessing and everything else was secondary.

As the years went by, our new home in Carmichael was often jokingly referred to as the "West Coast Branch of the United Nations." We hosted more visitors from various countries in the world than anyone I have known in my life. They came from the Isle of Man, Costa Rica, Pakistan, India, South Africa, Sudan, Lebanon, Israel, China, Gibraltar, Vietnam, the Philippines, Saudi Arabia, Bulgaria, Ukraine, Iraq, Nigeria, Ghana, Austria, Switzerland, England, France, Italy, and elsewhere in the world. There were also lots of visitors from various parts of the United States. Often our guests would stay overnight, though some came just for daily meetings or dinner. It was a very enriching environment, especially for Jessica who grew up in this environment.

Diana was intrigued with these foreign visitors and always involved herself in discussions about banking procedures, as she got to know many of them on a personal basis. This would become more relevant later in my life.

As for me, throughout those years, I continued to travel and seek new experiences in my ongoing quest for knowledge and adventure.

35

"The Troubles," Costa Rica, and Worms

"I will not die an unlived life."
— Dawna Markova

As a member of the Irish Forum, a group of Irish Americans interested in learning as much as could be learned about "the troubles" in Northern Ireland, I decided along with some of my colleagues to travel there. Some members of our contingent were from the Catholic tradition and some were from the Protestant tradition—a distinction that never signified any meaningful difference to me as both traditions pray to the same God.

Northern Ireland was then under martial law. Concrete barriers blocked almost every public and private building. The British military presence was everywhere, army patrols in the street and helicopter gunships hovering overhead. The people of Northern Ireland, amongst the friendliest on this planet, didn't congregate in parks, in front of their homes, or on street corners. Rather, they hustled about their business, closed faced and suspicious of everyone who might come from the other clan. In Belfast, because of IRA violence, the British searched every single car coming into the city. The Catholic and Protestant areas in the city were divided by an ugly wall erected by the British and army patrols were constant.

Being there to learn what was going on first hand, we met with Gerry Adams and Mark McGuiness of the Sinn Fein Political Party, the more extreme of the two major organizations representing the Catholic population. By the same token, we met and spoke with Ian Paisley and Peter Robinson of the Ulster Defense Council and also the leaders of the Democratic Unionist Party, the largest party representing the Protestant population. Then we met with John Hume, the leader of the Socialist Democrat and Labor Party. Hume was a practical man, winner of the Nobel Peace Prize, and known to take a more moderate approach than that of Sinn Fein. We further met with the British military command and finally with leaders of both the Republic of Ireland and the United Kingdom. This included Garret Fitzgerald, Prime Minister (known as the Taoiseach) of Ireland. On a subsequent trip, I was also to meet with Margaret Thatcher, Prime Minister of the United Kingdom, along with other members of the British Parliament. One had just recently been elected—his name was Tony Blair.

All in all, the trip was very intense. Very fascinating. We visited the prison that the British call The Maze or Longdesh as it was known to the Irish. That's where Bobby Sands and nine others had died as a result of a hunger strike that had garnered worldwide attention. Because of my work with the California prison system, and previous visits to all prisons in the United States that had suffered from inmate uprisings, I was extremely familiar with prison structure and was accustomed to seeing and evaluating inmates. The Maze was different from any correctional facility I had previously experienced. The prisoners in most American prisons look menacing, and you see rage in the eyes of many inmates. However, the prisoners in The Maze just seemed like ordinary guys. They simply considered themselves prisoners of war.

When the trip was over and others returned to the States, I did not immediately return. Rather, I rented a car and drove south into the Republic of Ireland. Ireland has twenty six counties and Northern Ireland, part of the UK, has six. I had an amazing feeling of relief, peace, and contentment after crossing the border into the peaceful Republic of Ireland. I guess I hadn't realized just how much tension and anxiety had built up during my stay in the north and now I could fully enjoy the stark and tranquil beauty of the Republic. I had never seen more rustic charm or greener fields.

I fell in love with Ireland and the Irish people on that trip. I am often asked what is my favorite place in the world. I can never answer that question because places are just too different to compare. However, in all candor, I must say that no people are more hospitable or friendly than the Irish. If there are more friendly people in the world, I haven't found them and that's after travelling north, south, east, and west throughout all regions of the world.

I wanted to go to a village called Renvyle in County Galway because I was told by a number of people that I really needed to meet a man called Leo Hallissey. He was purported to be a fascinating man, a schoolteacher, a scholar of Irish history, and an author. I enjoyed my time in the Connemara region of County Galway as I drove along and took in the sights of pastoral villages and of an ultra-green countryside. I had no idea where Leo Hallissey lived so when I arrived in Renvyle on the Atlantic seashore I went to the local pub and asked the pub master. He said "Leo lives around here somewhere but most of the time he hangs around Letterfrack where he teaches school." The fellow added that the Lady McCarthy who lives a few doors away from the pub might be able to help me. He directed me to a building with a red door down the street. The doors in Ireland are generally painted vibrant colors. So I went to the red door and knocked. I heard a clunking sound and a feeble voice calling out, "Please wait." A minute or two later the door opened. Here stood this elderly lady leaning on a walker. She was at least eighty-five, a handsome woman with beautiful silver hair and pink cheeks.

Before I could say anything, she said, "Come in, come in," as she turned her back, slowly making her way into the house. Entering a small living room, she said, "Sit down please. I will get us tea and crackers." I had not yet even identified myself. Finally I said, "Ma'am, can I help you?"

"No," she replied. "You just make yourself comfortable." Walking rather feebly without her walker, she soon returned with tea and crackers. I jumped up and took the tray from her. I then helped her sit down on a couch opposite me. Once settled, she put her hands on her knees and said, "Now young man, how can I help you?"

It was amazing to me that this elderly lady would eagerly invite a perfect stranger into her home and offer him hospitality and refreshments. I could never see this happening in America—or perhaps any other place else in the world.

Soon, a young boy who turned out to be one of her grandsons came in with his arms full of peat and started making her a fire in the fireplace and sure enough, the Lady McCarthy was able to tell me where I would find Leo Hallissey. She said he lived across the road from the ocean a few miles out of town. She said that his house was next to a bombed out castle-like fortification.

After appropriately thanking her, I left and drove in the direction she had told me to go. When I spotted the bombed out castle, I saw a house next door to it. A boy was walking into the yard carrying a hare on a stick. I introduced myself and said, "I am looking for Leo Hallissey. Does he live around here?" The boy introduced himself as Fiachra Hallissey, "Yes, he is my father. Please come in. He will be home in about half an hour. Meanwhile I will fix our dinner." I followed him in. He started skinning the hare and fixing dinner. He was about eleven years old.

In about a half hour, Leo Hallissey did arrive. He turned out to be a very intelligent man, extremely conversant with Irish history and nationalism—a truly fascinating fellow.

I had only intended to stay one night and Leo asked me if I would come and speak at his school the following day. I agreed. When I arrived, he had prepared his class and they did a little performance for me with an angelic-voiced boy singing accompanied by a flutist. I enjoyed my visit with the class so much that I ended up staying three days on that occasion and returned several times in future years.

Costa Rica

One of the prices I paid due to exploration and adventure came in the aftermath of a trip to Costa Rica in 1984. Costa Rica was beginning to establish itself as a country with a heightened sense of environmental consciousness. Among other things, it had declared two of its rivers wild and scenic. They were the first two rivers so declared south of the United States in the America's. A group of us decided to be the first to run those rivers. They were the Rio Reventazón and the Rio Pacuaré.

Diana and I flew to Costa Rica with a small group headed by a rafting friend of mine, Dave Everson. We also had along a young adventurous doctor named Charles Whitcomb, his wife, and another couple. Since at that time there wasn't a raft to be bought or rented anywhere in the area of these two rivers in Costa Rica, we took our own rafts. Logistically, this was a difficult trip since we had to carry our backpacks on the airplane, too.

We first ran the Reventazón. The area through which the Reventazón flows, like most of Costa Rica, is quite beautiful. However, the whitewater itself left much to be desired. As for the Pacuaré, it starts high in the Talamanca Mountains of Southern Costa Rica not far from the Panamanian border. The area through which the Pacuaré flows is very primitive. There are no roads, no electricity lines, nothing—at least not in 1984. This made it special.

Starting high, the Pacuaré flows down through heavy, dense rain forest and cloud forest all the way to the Caribbean. With but one exception, we saw no other humans during our entire trip on the Pacuaré. What we did see were multi-colored birds and all kinds of exotic wildlife, including the largest tarantulas I have ever seen. Because of the excessively and almost constant rain and plentiful sun, everything in the rain forest is king-sized from the insects, which range from butterflies with wings almost six inches long, to enormous and colorful birds. The latter includes the Quetzal found nowhere else in the world. We also saw translucent frogs where we were actually able to see through the skin and observe the skeleton of the frog.

In short, the Pacuaré was heavenly and I could run out of superlatives trying to describe the country through which the river flows. Suffice it to say that it was truly glorious. The ecosystems were so unique that they would enthrall a scientist and simply bedazzle an adventurer.

One day we came around a bend in the river and spotted a very primitive shelter not far from the bank made of branches and leaves. A family of indigenous people (Native Indians) was living a pre-Columbian lifestyle there. The man had a bow and arrow and darts for hunting. The male and the female and the children all wore loin cloths. They spoke neither Spanish nor English. The only way to communicate with them was with smiles and handshakes. They offered us a broth which everyone declined except me. Our doctor friend, Charlie, suggested that I not eat it but I did so out of respect. Much to my regret. At the time though, it just seemed like the polite thing to do. A short distance further down river we set up camp for the night. However, that night I literally thought I was going to die. My insides were in agony and I knew that I was suffering from some form of food poisoning. Charlie didn't have anything that could help me. I had to get what I had ingested out of my stomach but I couldn't disgorge it no matter how hard I tried. I suffered the awful pain of dry heaves for hours on end. This became serious. This went on the entire night. It is hard to describe the depth of my distress after hours of this going on non-stop.

Finally, exhausted after twelve hours of constant dry heaves, I suddenly disgorged a piece of pork. Disgusting, yes. But amazingly, within an hour I felt fine. Charlie thought it was salmonella but of course we couldn't be sure. It didn't really matter to me what it was. My relief to finally be rid of it was indescribable.

When the whitewater part of our trip was over, our small group of rafters split up. Some went back to the States. Diana and I, however, went over to Manuel Antonio National Park on the seashore near a small town called Quepos on Costa Rica's Pacific coast. There we found one of the most beautiful beaches to be found anywhere in the world. It was idyllic with arched coconut palms growing on the jungle fringe. Here rain and cloud forests meet the beach. An expansive sugar white sand beach stretches to the aqua green surf rolling in under white, frothy combers.

I had good friends from Ventura who had an exquisite home above the beach. They had purchased this in the late 60s or early 70s. They had actually asked me to join them but at the time I declined. They thereafter took as partners a Costa Rican family that became very powerful. It was the Carazo family and the patriarch rose to become President of Costa Rica. The President's son was an attorney in San Jose, the nation's capital. His wife was the curator of the National Museum, also in San Jose. It was at my friend's home that we stayed while we were at Manuel Antonio.

One morning we were hiking through the rain forest not far from the beach when I was hit on the head by something soft. I reached up and felt something mushy in my hair and beard. I looked up and saw a chattering white faced Capuchin monkey. It had defecated on my head, and now he was pointing and laughing about it! As were his friends who had gathered in the trees around us. Yes, these genetic cousins of mankind do laugh. Diana used my handkerchief to try to clean my hair and beard but it was difficult. She then checked me out more closely and gasped. "Oh my God. It's in your moustache too." So we headed for the beach, the closest water, where I did the best I could to wash everything off in the saltwater ocean. I can look back at this with a chuckle now. But it certainly was disconcertingly gross at the time.

When we returned to California in early January, my legs were covered with insect bites. Even with sleeping bags and mosquito nets for protection, the jungle floor along the Pacuaré had been alive with swarming insects, and more than a few of these pests got to me—big time. I assumed the bites would just go away after a while. Most of them did. However, a few did not. I went to see a doctor who in turn referred me to a dermatologist. The dermatologist gave me some topical ointments and sent me on my way. There was one particularly sore spot on the back of my calf. It was very red as well as being hard and swollen. Diana had a small red spot in much the same area.

In February I was driving to the airport early one morning to catch a flight to New York City when I was struck by pain in the back of my right calf so sharp that it caused me to jam my foot down on the accelerator. That pain passed, but it returned when I was on the airplane flying east. It occurred a third time while I was in a meeting in the World Trade Center in NYC.

When I returned to California from New York, I drove to our ranch house, arriving well after midnight. Diana was still up. She said, "When I took a hot bath tonight, I began squeezing that spot on my leg."

"Yes?"

She then picked up a jar on the nightstand next to her and showed me. "Look what came out."

"Lord!" There was a worm in the jar. "So now I know what is in my leg."

I swallowed hard knowing that many of our troops in Vietnam had died because worms had gotten into the body and eventually worked their way to the brain.

So I went back to the doctor with the worm in the jar and showed it to him. He said, "Well I don't know much about tropical diseases but I will send this off to the lab for analysis. In the meantime let's do some probing there in your leg."

I soon found myself lying on my stomach on a doctor's table. He gave me a local anaesthetic and said, "I'm going to make some X-shaped incisions in your leg. Here we go." After cutting, he began probing. Soon I heard the nurse who was assisting him gasp and I heard her say, "Oh my God, I am going to get sick." This was coming from a medical person whom I'm sure had seen almost everything! As it turns out, the doctor was pulling worm after worm out of my leg. I was there for some time.

What had apparently happened was that a pregnant worm had entered the leg, probably through a spider bite. There it had laid eggs which had hatched inside my calf. Although this is obviously not common in the United States, such tropical afflictions are apt to occur in the equatorial parts of the world at any time. I don't recall how many worms were pulled from my leg that day but there were a lot.

Worms, tarantulas, and other unusual fauna notwithstanding, I was in love with Costa Rica and thereafter took many trips to that beautiful country involving both business and pleasure. In 1990 I had occasion to mix the two.

———————

I had met an American biologist who was building an eco-tourist hotel near Cabrillo National Park called Rara Avis (which I believe means "Rare Bird" in Latin). Rara Avis sits in the most beautiful setting one could ever hope to see. Going in by tractor-drawn trailer, it took about four hours of boarding rivers and creeks to arrive.

The eco-tourist hotel sits right in the midst of an incredibly beautiful rain forest. There was fantastic wildlife and butterflies as big as crows. By this time, the world had become increasingly concerned about the cutting of trees in Central and South America as well as elsewhere in the world. However, it did not do much good to preach to local people about the worlds need for oxygen from their trees. Even though the potential for ecological disaster is quite real, at the local level understandably enough, the people are trying to feed their families and survive. Therefore the task was to demonstrate that there was an economic incentive for people to not cut the trees; that is to maintain the rainforest or the cloud forest or any forested area for the creation of oxygen. That's what had been done at Rara Avis—a small and primitive hotel with no electricity and no running water. It was an ideal setting for eco-tourists.

Only people who lived in the vicinity were employed. The people were also taught that to harvest certain tropical plants that had medicinal qualities could bring them more income than they would receive by having another cow on the land. Also, the butterflies in this region (which the natives call "moths") were the largest and most beautiful to be found anywhere in the world. Breeding programs were started and some of these butterflies were then sold, after mounting, at significant prices in Western Europe.

An American foundation had also built a canopy across the treetops. It is truly an educational experience to go above the trees and look down at the tops of them. Looking down one sees ecosystems that can never be seen from the ground level looking up. I was also fascinated by something else that was larger than I had seen anywhere else in the world. Although I had observed enormous colonies of ants in other places, especially Australia, what I saw at Rara Avis was almost unbelievable. Here in one of the hotel rooms—that's right, inside the hotel—the entire room was full of ants. There must have been hundreds of millions of them. The queen had gone in and vast armies of ants followed. Every single square foot of the room was jammed with ants. Clear to the ceiling.

36
China

"You are my new friend; when we next meet, you will be my old friend."
— Patriarch of a Chinese Family

In May 1989, I traveled on the first of what turned out to be many trips to China. I had been retained by a group that wanted me to explore on their behalf an investment that they were considering in a wood plant and a furniture factory in Liaoning Province, as well as to be on the lookout for other investment opportunities for them. Some members of the investment group accompanied me during the first part of the trip and for the second part I was traveling alone to go to some places in China I had always wanted to see.

Although we initially flew into Beijing, we quickly traveled east to the port city of Dalian where many of our meetings took place. Dalian was once part of Russia and, as a result, much of the architecture there is still Russian in style. Sitting on the Pacific Coast of China, Dalian is one of the largest of the country's industrial ports.

In Dalian I had meetings with numerous government officials both federal and provincial. One was with the Governor of Liaoning Province. He had just returned from a visit to Scandinavia. During a dinner meeting, he commented in a very discouraging way on how "socialistic" the governments were in Scandinavia. This was from a communist official in China in 1989! Although I knew the country was changing very fast, I had never anticipated such a comment from a government official.

Extraordinary changes have taken place in China over the last twenty years. Most assuredly, when I visited the country in 1989 it was as poor as a country could possibly be. The country one sees today with shining towers, high rise buildings, modern highways, high speed trains, and host to the Olympics is far removed from the country of China one generation ago. Even today, once one goes out of the large cities and into the countryside one sees poverty most everywhere.

I must say, however, that in mid-1989 people in China were talking very freely and being quite critical of the government. At the time, the change sweeping China was going pretty much unnoticed as most of the world's attention was riveted on the whirlwind changes taking places in the USSR. But I saw up close that China was the place where the greatest transformation, with far reaching ramifications for the world, was taking place.

Given events that were taking place, I do not for a moment think that the young people of Tiananmen Square anticipated the severe and oppressive reaction that was soon to take place. It was clear to me at the time of Tiananmen Square, and thereafter, that a major power struggle had taken place between the old guard that had ruled China for a long time and the technocrats who were trying to come to power. Once again, perhaps for the last time, the old guard won out. The events at Tiananmen Square took place not long after I returned to the States. Watching those events on television, I must say I was shocked and appalled. Again, I had not seen or heard anything that would have led me to believe that such an event would have taken place when it did.

While in China I was doing business with, among others, two brothers named Zhang Yibing and Zhang Yifan. In China, the last name comes first and the first name last. One of the brothers, Yibing, is now a citizen of the United States. The other, Yifan, is a resident of Hong Kong. Although we initially met in Dalian, Yibing and Yifan invited me to come to Shenyang, the capital of Liaoning Province, once my colleagues and I had concluded our business in Dalian. Both Yibing and Yifan were employed by the International Trade Corporation which was owned by the government.

Traveling alone from Dalian to Shenyang on the train, I discovered many of the shortcomings of China at that point in its history. The train was very old and incredibly crowded. Everyone was smoking and the windows could not be opened. And, of all things, I had diarrhea. This turned out to be one of the more embarrassing experiences of my life. Nobody on the train spoke English. I knew there had to be a bathroom car somewhere. So I am going from car to car, and it's a long train, worrying that I wouldn't make it.

Finally, I opened a door and entered a smoke-filled car crowded with Chinese men, most of them peeing in a hole in the floor. Clearly, that was the bathroom! I quickly pulled my pants down. I'm the only white guy in the train. Everyone is staring at me. I am squatting there over the hole and diarrhea is coming like crazy. Thank God it was going into the hole. Still, very embarrassing.

Shenyang, in the midst of coal country, was the most polluted city I've ever been in—anywhere in the world. Sewage effluent was being discharged directly into the waterways. Worse yet, you couldn't see more than five feet in front of you and soot was in every orifice—nose, mouth, ears and eyes. Everywhere. It was just awful. After a short time outside, clothing even turned black. I wasn't surprised to learn that life expectancy was approximately thirty-five.

When I asked provincial officials if they weren't at all concerned about the environment and the detrimental effects it had on the citizens, the answer I received was that, "We have a billion mouths to feed. Once we are able to do that, we will give thought to the *luxury* of environmental matters."

When I left Shenyang, I decided to do the touristy things. First I returned to Beijing to see the sights of that city and to visit the Great Wall of China and other famous sights in that part of the country.

As China is geographically a large country, it was necessary that I fly to the other venues that I wanted to visit. In order to do so, it was necessary to fly CAAC, China's only domestic airline at the time. Yibing told me that CAAC stood for either "China Airlines Always Canceled" or "Catch Another Air Carrier." I learned why. The planes were rickety and again as crowded as can be. In the smoke-filled airports people were constantly shoving and pushing and it had nothing to do with my ethnicity.

I flew first to Xian to see the famous Terracotta Warriors. Viewing the army of warriors is quite a sight. Xian is an amazing place for other reasons as well. On the outskirts of the modern city can be found some of the oldest developments of human civilizations including some that date back well over 12,000 years.

Another place I wanted to visit, because paintings of it are seen all over the world, is the city of Guilin in the south of China. The river that flows through that part of China eventually flows into the Yellow River before it flows into the China Sea. The mountains one sees around Guilin have been cut by rivers, wind and water erosion to create an amazing escarped landscape—often enshrouded in fog.

During my visit to Guilin, I had met a family by happenchance and I had dinner with them in their home the night before I left. As I was leaving the following day they gave me some presents. The old man who was the patriarch of the family said, "You are our new friend. When we next meet, you shall be our old friend." That meaningful saying has remained with me ever since and I often use it myself.

From Guilin I went to Shanghai, historically the commercial center of China. It was coming alive and hotel construction was every place I looked. It was, unlike most every other part of China, as vibrant as a city could possibly be.

The two brothers I had met first in Dalian and then later in Shenyang, Yibing and Yifan, remained in touch with me even after I returned Stateside. Even to this day I remain in touch with them. Interestingly enough they had been longtime dedicated communists. However, by the time I met them in 1989 they had each come to resent greatly what had happened to them, to their family, and to their country during the Cultural Revolution of Mao Tse Tung. Both Yibing and Yifan are very intelligent men. But when the Cultural Revolution broke out, embracing Mao's teachings, they left college and went into the fields to do hard manual labor because Mao said it would be a good thing. It had taken a huge chunk out of their lives, never to be regained.

Yibing was to eventually make his way to the United States where he was to start and run his own business. Today, he is a retired man, happily married with highly educated children making their own way in our country.

When I took this trip to China in 1989 there were lots of tourists and construction activity was everywhere in the big cities. When I returned the following January, one year later, I did not see another occidental face. All of the hotels and high-rises were boarded up. Everything had ground to a complete halt as a direct result of what happened on June 4, 1989. The horrible event at Tiananmen Square set China back for better than a year. Eventually though, because of the tremendous economic potential of China, the money began to flow again and of course continues to do so to this day. Although the actions of the government at Tiananmen Square was a temporary setback and caused the drying up of foreign investments and tourism, it did have the long term effect of strengthening the technocrats and ultimately leading to a change in Chinese policies.

I have made several subsequent trips to China and each time I have been more and more amazed at the changes taking place over a short period of time. The rapidity of change there may be unique in world history.

37

A Fisherman and the Albatross

"A wife lasts only for the length of your marriage,
but an ex-wife is there for the rest of your life."
— Jim Samuels

The year before the death of John Reaves, he called me about a problem that had developed in his life. John had some family history in Amador County, California, where his forefathers had come during the gold rush to try to make their fortune. He still had close ties to the old family homestead. He wanted to maintain the property and upon his death convey it to my son and his grandson, Mark, who had spent quite a bit of time with him over the years.

John's problem was that he had received notice from Amador County that, as a cost saving measure, it intended to stop maintaining and to block off the road that led to his property as well as that of others.

John and his second wife, Ann, drove up to our home and spent several days with us as they had done on other occasions over the years. Ann stayed with Diana and John and I made the first of many trips up to the area around Plymouth, California, the small town near where the old homestead was located. There, we started visiting various county officials, especially those on the County Board of Supervisors. Another attorney in my office and I began to research the law, even as the County was proceeding to file a lawsuit against all property owners involved. Everyone else gave in and acquiesced. We were the only ones to resist and on behalf of John I filed multiple causes of action against the County. We really hit them hard and with success in that John eventually got everything he wanted including, but not limited to, ongoing access to the family property.

Ironically, John and I had spent more and more time together as the years went by. I would stay with John and Ann whenever I went to Bakersfield to see my accountant, who also lived in Bakersfield. Sometimes I would go down just to see John and Ann at their invitation. I would always stay in their home, the home which I helped build. Whenever they came north, they would always visit with us in Sacramento, sometimes overnight. They made multiple trips to see us during 1990.

Although we had reached a complete agreement with the County of Amador and all documents had been drafted, we were still awaiting final approval by the Board of Supervisors of the agreement that had been reached. Throughout this time, John asked if I would be helpful with him in connection with some other items. I did ask him, "You know John, Judy is now married to an attorney named Fred. Fred's right there in Ventura closer to Bakersfield and Judy is right there as well." He knew what I was getting to, but he made it clear that he didn't want to deal with Fred. I never really asked him why but I got the impression that he either didn't like or didn't trust Fred. John made it clear, "I don't want Fred handling any of my matters. I don't want him to know anything about my business, and what you and I are doing is for you and me to know and not for Fred or for that matter Judy to know."

So, as always, I did whatever work he needed done although I never charged him as a client. I was doing legal work for him and anything else I could to be of help. So there were a lot of visits throughout March, April, and May of that year. Separate and apart from the lawsuit, John wanted to see a lot of people in the Amador County area. I think he had a premonition because we spent the better part of a week that spring visiting people he hadn't seen in close to fifty years. It was obviously very nostalgic for him. He wanted to look at some places around the county that he had not visited since his childhood. We also took the time to do further surveying and we put up some fences as well.

In late August and early September John and Ann came again to visit us in Sacramento. They were with us for about four days. When they left, they went back to Bakersfield and John lapsed into a coma. He never came out of it. Ultimately, the family decided to pull the plug because several physicians told them there would be no way for him to recover. In fact, he would just languish there for another day, maybe for another week, but it would be in a vegetative state. So John died at age seventy-one.

John had been a great outdoorsman, but he always had health problems. One leg was shorter than the other and as a result he had a bit of a strange walk. I believe his condition was congenital. He would often complain about pain he was having and then at an early age, in his fifties, he had a major heart attack. He was hospitalized in Southern California for a substantial period of time. His second wife, Ann, was a nurse and that's when and how they happened to meet.

After he recovered from his heart attack, John realized that life is short and bad things can happen unexpectedly. So, with him being a relatively wealthy man, he retired and with Ann spent much of the remainder of their lives together traveling, relaxing and enjoying life, which pleased me greatly.

There was a memorial service for John on September 6 of that year, and I took the train down to Bakersfield for the service. Afterwards there was a reception held at the family home. There were a lot of people that I hadn't seen for a long time, especially John's relatives. We were talking and trying to make the best we could out of a very somber and sad affair. Judy came up to me, took me aside, and glowered at me with daggers in her eyes. She said: "How dare you come here? You know I don't want you talking to any of my family members."

I shouldn't have been surprised at her attitude. I would think that she would say: "How gracious of you to come. Thank you very much." But not Judy. I knew why she didn't want me communicating with her family members. She didn't want them to know about her background and about how close John and I had remained over the years. I already knew, and John confirmed from time to time, that she hated our continuing friendship. He told me that on multiple occasions. More than once, according to John, he told her, "Judy, I've told you before, stay out of my life. You know Omer and I are good friends. We have been friends. We are friends. We will always be friends, and if you don't like it that's tough. You are not going to dictate to me, your father, who his friends are. You made a mistake in divorcing the guy. I've told you that several times. Let's not go over that again. You did it. It's over. It's history. That doesn't mean I divorced him." I know that was always under her skin. It still is to this very day.

In reply to Judy on the occasion of the memorial reception, I simply commented, "Judy, I'm surprised at your attitude. I'm here out of respect for your father. You know that John and I were very close right up until the end. You know that he was with me the last few days, right before he lapsed into the coma, and I'm just terribly disappointed at the attitude you're displaying. Relax, I'm not going to say anything bad about you."

To this day Judy continues to tell outrageous lies to people about how I divorced her, how I abandoned my family, and how I refused to pay child support. All lies. In part, I'm sure this was and is a defense mechanism to divert attention from the truth, but I suspect in part it also was and is a simple matter of jealousy for whatever success I have enjoyed in life. She has even gone so far as to write letters to newspaper reporters and editors, who from time to time have asked me whether or not Judy is mentally stable. I truly don't know. What I do know and what I have simply accepted is that Judy is a possessed person, at least when it comes to me. She is an albatross that I am destined to suffer wherever I go and however long I live.

38

Nelson Mandela & South Africa

"I am the master of my fate: I am the captain of my soul."
— William Ernest Henley ("Invictus")

By 1990, it had become increasingly evident that the practice of apartheid at long last was coming to an end in South Africa. In February of that year Nelson Mandela, whom I believe to be one of the greatest men of modern times, had been released from Robben Island after serving twenty-seven years there in prison. Moreover, the De Klerk administration had announced the abolition of apartheid and the movement toward true democracy. By that I mean democracy so that every individual in the country had one equal vote regardless of color or ethnicity. De Klerk did this, notwithstanding his awareness that the African National Congress (ANC) would no doubt win the election whenever it was held. When that occurred, there would be the first government dominated by black Africans in that nation's history.

Back when I was in the Senate and for years thereafter, I was deeply involved in getting impositions and sanctions imposed against the South African government due to its apartheid policy. The State of California, due to the urgings of many of us, had been the first to divest itself of any investment, including stockholdings, in companies doing business in South Africa. This action was followed by other States. CalPERS (the California Public Employees Retirement System) and STRS (the State Teachers Retirement System) were the largest public pension funds in the United States and possibly in the world. Therefore, actions of this nature had a direct and powerful affect on the South African economy.

Because I had been visible in this effort, I received an invitation in late 1990 from an entity that had been established to discuss the probability of a new South African constitution being drafted. I was invited to visit South Africa to discuss American democracy and our constitution. Also being invited were representatives from the United Kingdom and from a few other democratic countries. With the governmental commitment that apartheid was being abolished, I agreed to travel to South Africa to consult with people who would at some point in time be instrumental in establishing a new constitution for the country.

I spent the entire month of October 1990 in South Africa having meetings primarily, but not exclusively, in Johannesburg, Cape Town, Durban, and Pretoria with representatives of the ANC, the De Klerk government, and representatives of other political parties that would be involved in establishing a new Constitution for the country. Although I had not asked for any compensation, all of my expenses were being paid. While there, extensive discussions regarding the shape of a new constitution were held. These meetings were to serve as a prelude to the Constitutional Principles set forth in an interim Constitution adopted in 1993 and in the work ultimately done by the Constitutional Assembly the following year.

At the end of my trip I had a meeting with Nelson Mandela and others, including members of both the De Klerk administration and the ANC, with whom I had been working. I was asked if there wasn't something that I would like to see or do in South Africa before returning to the States.

I had already been doing a lot of traveling throughout South Africa during the month I had spent there. I had even been to Swaziland and Lesotho, small independent countries completely within South Africa itself. I had also spent an entire day walking around Soweto (South West Township) and yet another day in squatter encampments on the outskirts of Johannesburg. Although people were talking about the riots that had previously taken place and how dangerous it was for a white person to be there, I felt no danger whatsoever and walked about comfortably throughout those days even though I was usually the only white person on the street. In short, I simply did not feel any malice or hostility.

Having said that, however, I will say that I went to another place to the west of and on the outskirts of Cape Town called Crossroads. Crossroads was another squatter's camp where major riots had, with considerable loss of life, taken place a few years before. I told people in the Cape Town community that I was going out to Crossroads and with unanimity people advised me not to and they said that would be insane, warning me about the danger of the situation. But I rented a car and drove out there anyway. I simply wanted to be friendly and get out and see what it was like at Crossroads and mingle with the people.

However, I will confess that I was surprised. Unlike Soweto which was so often in the US press, I detected within Crossroads a place full of rage, anger. and hatred. The experience was not at all like that in Soweto. It had been my intention, as in Soweto, to get out of my car and walk around. Probably do some shopping and talk to people just as I had done in Soweto. I spent about fifteen to twenty minutes cruising the streets of Crossroads before deciding that I was sufficiently uncomfortable that I should return to Cape Town having not even gotten out of the car.

Other than that uncomfortable experience at Crossroads, I found South Africa to be a remarkably beautiful and diverse country. Cape Town is in one of the most striking natural settings of any city in the world. So when I was asked what I would like to do, I responded, "I've had the opportunity to see much of your country and it is incredibly beautiful. I also know you have a great national park called Krueger up in the northeast corner of the country. I am told by many that it is perhaps the finest of all the game reserves in Africa. I think you will find it cluttered with visitors once the apartheid system is completely abolished, just as visitors flood the wildlife reserves in Tanzania and Kenya. But I understand that there are some private game reserves adjacent to Krueger that don't have the restrictions that one encounters in Krueger and elsewhere in Africa. In fact, I am told in these private reserves it is possible to go off-road, day and night, unlike the reserves in Kenya and Tanzania. Apparently, you have the same type of restrictions in Krueger itself. I would love to visit one of these reserves."

They were happy to oblige and I was told that they would arrange everything for me—and they did. I flew up there from Johannesburg and I had a great experience. The private game reserve at which I stayed had within its borders virtually every species of animal life found in East Africa.

When I arrived, the Chief Ranger at the reserve assured me that I would be able to see the "Big Five," as well as scores of other animals in a relatively short period of time and in a wild and natural setting. The "Big Five" refers to the lion, the elephant, the spotted leopard, the water buffalo, and the rhinoceros. I would be there a full week and hoped that during that time I would in fact be able to see the Big Five. As it turned out

I saw all of them within hours after I arrived. I was to see much, much more during the ensuing days.

Our party consisted of a very well educated driver and guide of Afrikaner descent, a Zulu tracker, a young couple from the island of Guernsey, Dominic and Paula Clark, and myself. I was happy that the Clarks were with us because they had a video camera and they made a neat video tape, a copy of which they subsequently sent to me and which I still have. The Zulu tracker usually walked in front of our vehicle, an open Land Rover, no top but with a front windshield. He had the most incredible sense, the most incredible instincts, the most amazing eyes. He could see an animal miles away in rugged terrain. He would speak to our guide in the Zulu language and we would charge off in our Land Rover. As a private game reserve, we did not have to stay on any roads. In fact, we were seldom on the roads as we would go charging right through the brush, going over mountaintops and forging through creeks. In this way we were able to get really close to the animals.

We were able to get within five feet of a pride of majestic lions. We saw a spotted leopard take down a zebra and the strength of these animals, the jaws and the legs, is just amazing. Seeing it leap up into a tree onto a branch while holding its prey was remarkable. We would sit there and see this dramatic example of the food chain in action occurring right before our eyes. We could not only see it but we could hear it as the bones cracked. Bits and pieces of the animal that the leopard was feasting on would fall down below and the jackals and hyenas and other scavengers were all over the place. This was unusual because the spotted leopard is seldom seen and is the most difficult of the Big Five to spot. The spotted leopard is the most beautiful and majestic of all the African animals in my opinion.

One night, about 3:00 am and pitch black, we suddenly heard a lot of noise. The place where we stopped the Land Rover and turned off the engine was filled with dust. Soon we saw that hundreds and hundreds of water buffalo were surrounding us and stirring up all kinds of dust as they migrated from one place to another. We had no alternative but to stay where we were even though the buffalo were bumping the Land Rover, almost tipping us over. They were not attacking in any way. There were just so many and they were so crowded together that we were being jostled back and forth and, again, we were completely exposed inasmuch as there was no roof or top on the Land Rover. Thankfully we did not tip over and we managed to live through the dust, although I was congested for several days thereafter.

We were generally out at night as well as in the day. One reason is that there is an opportunity to see things at night that one cannot possibly see in the daylight. "Spotting" was also allowed. Our guide would sometimes turn on a powerful light when he saw eyes shining in the darkness. That would cause the animal to freeze. This also would allow us to get extremely close to some nocturnal animals that ordinarily are not at all seen in daylight hours.

The only time we encountered a dangerous situation was when one day we encountered a Bull elephant who charged the vehicle. We barely got away from him in time. We weren't sure what had made him angry, but clearly something had. All in all South Africa had been an unforgettable experience.

Before leaving the southern part of the African continent, I also took short excursions into Mozambique, Zimbabwe, and Botswana. These countries were all less developed than South Africa and I really, with one exception, did not spend enough time in them to do the countries justice. The one exception is that I did have an opportunity to do some whitewater rafting on the Zambezi River. I had hoped to also get over to Namibia, but was unable to do so on this trip.

Africa in general is a place for which I have very fond memories. Both before and after my trip in 1990 to South Africa, I travelled extensively in various other parts of the continent—both the Saharan region of the north and the Sub-Saharan region that covers most of Africa. Although political instability is found almost everywhere on the continent, the continent's natural beauty is unforgettable. The sunsets, especially those of East Africa, are some of the most beautiful to be found anywhere in the world. They are just as depicted in the movie "Out of Africa." They are purple and red and yellow and mixed colors, so beautiful that you just can't take your eyes away. I know that you aren't supposed to stare at the sun, but when it gets low enough…Well!

39

Recovering At North Shore

When *I left Waleed Al-Oboudi's facility, it was with a true sense of elation. I had made so much progress in a single week: Catching balls while standing on the wobbly bosu, slowly crawling over and through rubber tunnels, and even weakly hitting some tennis balls. Now I was more determined than ever to hasten my recovery.*

When I returned to Tahoe, that is just what I did. I enlisted my physical therapists at Incline Village to engage me in practices similar to those I had learned at Oboudi's clinic. In my "off" hours, friends would sometimes informally help me continue with my therapy. Recovery was pretty much a full-time job.

My friend Stu Fishman and his wife, Debra (a pilates instructor), were two of those who helped. One day, while I was standing on their bosu, I said: "Stu, I want you to throw a ball at me." He did, though quite easily. To his surprise, I was able to catch it and throw it back.

I then asked Stu to throw it high, low, and to the right side and the left side—all over the place. "I've got to catch it and toss it back to you without stopping or falling off, and I have to use my right hand as well as my left one," I said. "But don't tell me where it's coming. Also change the pace on me. Everything has to be unpredictable."

Another day, while Stu was lobbing balls at me as I balanced on the bosu, he said, "Okay, Omer, let's box." Stu isn't a youngster, but he's still muscular and as sturdy as a fire hydrant. At an earlier time in his life, he owned a gym in the LA area where he used to train boxers in the ring.

"Interesting," I said. "I don't know that I'm up to that but I'm certainly willing to try."

So Stu and I put on gloves and began to spar. "Let's improve your hand speed," he said. "Let's get you moving and see how we can also improve your leg work. Your left side is really doing well, but you still need a lot more work on your right arm and right leg—the side that was completely paralyzed."

When boxing with Stu, I started with limbs that were getting stronger, but still fairly useless and an awfully long way from where they once were. But again muscle memory began to play an important role. Before long, I was beginning to throw jabs, hooks, and uppercuts. Not with great authority, but my arms—both of them— were starting to move again.

At the same time, George and I would go out on the tennis courts where he was the tennis pro and he'd use the ball machine to shoot forehands and backhands at me. Then, with me hobbling and limping along, we'd play a game of singles or doubles. Obviously, he played down to my handicapped level. But, hell, he used to do that even before I was struck down.

One day, at Lake level and below the snow line, I climbed on my bicycle and George climbed on his. My balance was still not back to what it used to be but we found some dry pavement and it seemed like an okay place to start. I might have preferred to be biking off-road where I could be closer to nature, but I knew I had to start on a more stable surface first and, in any event, the weather wouldn't yet allow for biking off-road.

Was I a little unsteady? Lord, yes. Could I have fallen and injured myself? Certainly. But I had to keep pushing. One of the things that I had learned in my recovery was that doing activities—not refraining from them—was what would help me regain my strength, balance, equilibrium, and dexterity.

I knew that I had to crawl before I could walk, and once I could walk, it was time to try running. So I just kept pushing onto the next new thing until my body and limbs could complete the activity—maybe not perfectly but sufficiently well until yet another challenge could be tackled.

With all this daily effort to exercise and challenge my body—and a good deal of support from my friends and therapists—it wasn't long before I was back to a limited amount of biking, playing tennis, shooting hoops, and trekking: many of the activities I had enjoyed before my aneurysm and stroke. I was not doing those things at the level that I once had, but I was doing them, and I was getting stronger and stronger and more and more confident— maybe too much so.

It was spring by this point in my recovery, and I wanted to test myself at skiing before all the snow melted. I told George I wanted to ski; he said I shouldn't.

I said, "I've got to do it, George. If not now, when? If I don't try now, it'll be next Thanksgiving before we have snow again."

George reluctantly acquiesced. "Only if I go with you and stay with you the whole time," he said. "Because you're going to try things that you shouldn't—I know you too well."

The truth was that in all those months of recovery when the doctors' and therapists' advised me to slow down or not to do something, George rarely said "no" to me, knowing that I'd simply go and do it anyway—by myself if necessary. Instead, George followed me wherever I wanted to go and made sure I didn't kill myself in the process.

40

Lives of Quiet Desperation

"The mass of men lead lives of quiet desperation."
— Thoreau

Yes, I had spent a lifetime searching for new adventurous experiences pretty much as and when I decided to do them—often on my own—and often in the wilderness surrounded by the spectacle of nature. First in high school and later in college I had read of the thoughts and experiences of Thoreau during that period when he isolated himself at Walden Pond in Massachusetts for two years in the mid-19th century. In a well-known passage from "Walden," Thoreau stated his purpose.

"I went to the woods because I wished to live deliberately, to front only the essential facts of life, and see if I could learn what it had to teach, and not, when I came to die, discover that I had not lived. I did not wish to live what was not life, living is so dear. Nor did I wish to practice resignation..."

In the first essay which he entitled, "Economy," Thoreau commented that most men are slaves to their work and enslaved to those for whom they work. He concluded with his famous passage: *"The mass of men lead lives of quiet desperation."*

The reader of this book may legitimately wonder from time to time whether or not my elevator goes all of the way to the top, but whatever one thinks in that regard I don't believe anyone could conclude that I have led a life of "quiet desperation." With a passion for adventure, nature, archaeology, anthropology, and the simple acquisition of knowledge, my travels had already taken me to well over one hundred countries. My adventures, exploits and willingness to stretch my mental and physical limits had become relatively well known. They had included, among others: airplane wing walking; fire walking; Brahma bull riding; whitewater rafting; skydiving; paragliding; mountaineering; jungle exploration; bungee jumping; caving; hot air ballooning; steer wrestling; cobra dancing; glacier and rock climbing; and hang gliding. Space does not here allow for a robust explanation of the events surrounding each of these adventures, but they do evidence a restless mind wishing to explore one's own limits and to experience life at its base level.

At fifty-five years of age, I was as active as I had ever been, not only professionally but also insofar as my quest for adventure was concerned. Within a two week period in and around Las Vegas and elsewhere, as well as in areas in and around Moab and Zion and Bryce National Parks in Utah and various other parts of the Southwest, I did competitive skydiving, bungee jumping, some significant rock climbing, paragliding, and whitewater kayaking and rafting.

As an admitted adrenaline driven thrill seeker, I have always had a special passion for whitewater rafting. By age fifty-five, I had rafted over eighty rivers in North America, South America, Asia, Europe, and Africa. Paragliding was a new sport to me, but I also fell in love with it. Paragliding is quite different from parasailing where you are tethered either to a boat or to a car. In paragliding, you as a human being are riding the wind currents. A few years later I was to do considerably more paragliding outside of Geneva and also off the flank of Mont Blanc near Chamonix, France. I loved it. I soared like a bird. It involves literally running as fast as you can, which is not very fast at all due to the chute being dragged behind, on takeoff until the thermal currents lift you up. On the south side of the Sierra Nevada Mountains near Lake Tahoe and above the communities of Minden, Gardnerville and Genoa you can take off from the high Sierra's and if you catch the wind currents right, it's literally possible for someone with far greater experience than I to stay up for hours at a time right along the escarped eastern side of the Sierra's.

I'm sure it's because of the nature of my personality that I have been drawn to people such as Steve McQueen and Evel Knievel. I first met Evel in early 1986. He was from Butte, Montana and was making a living by showing up at functions around the country. In doing so he pretty much lived and travelled out of a very nice RV. Of course, he also stayed in hotels when he traveled. We first met in Sacramento at a party held by a mutual friend and we hit it off pretty quickly. We decided to have breakfast together the next morning at the Hilton where he was staying with the idea of getting to know one another better. It turned out that we had much in common.

Evel had become famous by performing one motorcycle stunt after another, each more spectacular than the last until he became a legend. One of his problems, however, was that he had attained most of his fame in the late 60s and early 70s and was now beginning to fade in the public memory and imagination. We did a few things together, but nothing that involved motorcycle riding. Nevertheless, we managed to stay in touch with each other over the years and we were able to coordinate our schedules when I was traveling in the States in order to meet in other places as well.

One of the things that most people don't know about Evel is that he was a very talented artist. Most of his artwork represented landscape scenes, mostly of the American West and of Native American Indians. Evidently, he had started painting around the age of eight. Some of his paintings have now been sold for high prices. I bought some of his paintings, and he gave me a few more. I am sorry to say that the originals were all lost in the fire of 1987. However, hearing about the fire, Evel sent me prints of all of the originals I had. I gave one to my son, one to my nephew and had the others framed and they were hung in various parts of the home in Carmichael. Visitors were always intrigued when they saw paintings by Evel Kneivel as his daredevil fame had spread pretty much throughout the world.

Shortly after learning that Diana was pregnant and, not knowing whether the baby would be a boy or a girl, Evel painted Bambi in a snow covered forest for the yet to be born baby. He gave it to me midway through Diana's pregnancy with the inscription "To Baby Rains from your Daddy's friend" and signed it Evel Knievel.

Evel came to Sacramento several times in subsequent years to testify before legislative committees on matters concerning safety precautions for those who ride motorcycles. On those and on other occasions, Evel and I would get together and share stories. As for motorcycles, I had always shied away because I had a number of friends killed or maimed riding motorcycles. They are just too unforgiving in the event of an accident. Although I have done a lot of things in my life which others would consider dangerous, I usually did them with prudence and, for the most part, with experience behind me.

When Evel's son, Robbie, began to acquire some of the same kind of fame that Evel had attained, Evel's own fame and recognition was somewhat resurrected. This was a great psychological boost for him as his name was again frequently in the papers and on TV and radio. Partly as a result of this, he got his life pretty well straightened out before he died. I was happy for him.

41

Being Alive at 55

"I get called an adrenaline junkie every other minute and I'm just fine with that."
— Steve Irwin

As a result of my lifestyle, one day at fifty-five years of age I received a telephone call from Larry Udell. Larry was and is a longtime friend as well as an occasional business acquaintance. Larry called to see if I would give the keynote speech at a convention which he was chairing. Those attending, according to Larry, would be business executives primarily in their 50s and 60s. He said that most of them were half dead because they thought they were. He added: "Omer, knowing the things you do, I sometimes think you're crazy. On the other hand I've always admired you for what you do. So now I want to ask a favor. I would like you to give this keynote speech and I have a topic all picked out." Being accustomed to public speaking, I said, "Well, what's the topic?"

Larry said, "Knowing you as I do, I know that you are now fifty-five years old. Therefore, the topic I want you to speak on is "Being Alive at 55" with a subtitle of "How Adventure and Thrills Develop Leadership Skills.""

"For how long do you want me to speak?" I asked.

"Probably about an hour."

I thought to myself, "Well I've often spoken that long with questions and answers. But this is an unusual topic. Can I really speak that long on this topic? I'm not sure."

I told Larry, "I'd like to think about it."

Larry called about two days later and said, "Omer, have you given thought to my proposal?"

I said, "Yes, I will go ahead and do it."

Larry said, "Great. What I would like to do then is to send a courier over from San Francisco to pick up material which I will use for the introduction. The items I want are photographs and/or video of things you have done only during the last six months because it's the age at which you have continued to do some of the things which are most compelling to me."

As a result of this event, Larry had a video put together that he used for the introduction at the event at which I spoke. One item, the aforementioned airplane wing walking, was not done during the six month period but was something specifically that Larry wanted to include. Anyone who wishes to view the video that was prepared for purposes of introduction can do so by visiting either of two websites: www.backtothesummit.com, or www.senorains.com (click on multi-media).

I was first introduced to camping as a Cub Scout and thereafter as a Boy Scout. My first night around the campfire captured me forever. And anything that gets me into nature appeals to me. It draws me like a magnet. Faced with the grandeur of nature, one's cares and concerns can drop like leaves from a tree.

John Muir wrote in 1901:

Climb the mountains and get their good tidings.
Nature's peace will flow into you as sunshine flows into trees.
The winds will blow their own freshness into you,
and the storms their energy, while cares will drop off like autumn leaves.

I would almost defy anyone to truly go into nature and not experience a feeling of great humility as well as reverence.

But I suppose that doesn't answer the question of why does one take risks? When George Leigh Mallory was asked why he wanted to climb Mount Everest, he replied, "Because it's there." That's probably as good an answer as any. Facing challenges is built into our DNA. It is something primal. It's a base instinct to just go for it. If you don't go for it, then in all likelihood you are living one of those lives of quiet desperation.

America itself has always been defined by risk. I think it may be a rather predominant national characteristic. Our country was founded by risk takers—those willing to buck the odds, and to take perilous chances. And given the sterilization and robotic lifestyle of modern society, people are increasingly desensitized unless they force themselves to go out and do something to make themselves feel again self-reliant and independent. I certainly don't want to be those who, on my deathbed, thinks, "What were my limits? If only I had tried."

To quote the poet Dawna Markova: "I will not die an unlived life."

42

Extreme Adventure
(More Sports; More Injuries)

"Strength is a matter of the made up mind."
— John Beecher

Indeed, throughout my 50s, I remained active in sports. While playing baseball midway through that decade, I broke my shoulder in four places and busted six ribs. I thought I was still twenty years old; my body knew otherwise.

Every chance I got I continued to do whitewater rafting. Sometimes I had some pretty hairy experiences. On one such occasion, my wife was with me. The water was Class V and "boiling" all the way. I thought it was great. Diana didn't. She never went rafting again. I also did some more paragliding, something that I had come also to enjoy greatly. On one occasion as I soared off some mountain cliffs in the American Southwest, when I came down I landed on a Saguaro Cactus. There's nothing like sailing smack dab into a cactus to appreciate the old joke about the difference between a caucus and a cactus is that a cactus has the pricks on the outside.

Ordinarily as a family we would go skiing several times a year. We would generally be joined by Mark and occasionally by Kelly and sometimes by my nephew Carter. Sometimes we would ski at Mammoth, California, more often at resorts around Lake Tahoe, and on a couple of occasions around Park City, Utah where Carter by this time lived.

At fifty-eight years of age, I drove to a place called Whitney Portal on the east side of the Sierras. Whitney Portal is the end of the road driving up toward Mount Whitney. At close to 8,000 feet, Whitney Portal is also the trailhead for the climb to the summit of Mount Whitney. The summit at 14,496 feet is the highest mountain in the "Lower 48." Ordinarily people take two or three days to climb the additional 6,500 feet.

On this occasion, I was determined to climb from Whitney Portal to the summit and back to Whitney Portal all during the same day. Although I had climbed Whitney twice before, I had never tried to do it up and back in one day. I accomplished my objective and thought, "Wow, at fifty-eight I am still feeling my oats."

But then later that same year one of those things happened that you simply don't expect to happen and it was something over which I really had no control. I was driving in Sacramento. A traffic light turned to red, so I came to a stop behind three or four other cars. In my rearview mirror I spotted a car coming at me at a high rate of speed. The driver was looking at a girl and she was looking toward him. Sure enough I was rear ended. Hard. It was a significant crash witnessed by several observers. I suffered severe whiplash, along with several herniated discs. It turned out that the driver was a young Mexican lad whom I later learned was in the country illegally. The girl jumped out of the car and kept screaming, "Please, please, please tell the cops I was driving." Needless to say, the driver had no insurance.

At the hospital, an orthopedic surgeon looked at the x-rays and MRIs and informed me that I had suffered a lot of cervical damage. I had pain in my back, my right arm, and my hand. I was told that it would be necessary for me to have what's known as an anterior cervical discectomy with a bone graft fusion. This is major surgery of the neck. I had known others who had undergone this surgery and they had all had a bad result. So I tried everything under the sun to avoid the surgery. I underwent physical therapy, massage therapy, nutritional treatment, carefully administered chiropractic treatments, and so on and so forth. None of it worked. In fact my right arm was going completely numb and I was losing all feeling in my hand. Along with the tingling and numbness came an almost complete loss of strength in my right arm. It got so bad that I couldn't even take the cap off my gas tank. I finally had no option so regrettably I told the surgeon to go ahead and schedule the surgery.

By this time I could not move my neck right or left and I was wearing a neck brace to help alleviate the pain. About a week before the date for surgery I was at a health food store and spotted a book entitled "Pain, Pain, Go Away" written by a Professor of Medicine at the University of Wisconsin. I bought it and read it in one sitting. It discussed something called "prolotherapy." The book was mainly one of testimonials. Many of them resonated with me because they sounded very similar to my problem. Through prolotherapy treatments a number of people had stated that they were able to avoid surgery.

At the back of the book was a list of doctors who had been trained by this physician in prolotherapy. The list was really quite short and there was only one in California. His name was Harish Porecha and he practiced in Modesto, only about an hour and a half drive south of Sacramento. I phoned his office and they faxed me some material which, truth be told, was not really that helpful. But again, I was intrigued by one of the testimonials as it came from C. Everett Koop, the Surgeon General of the United States. Koop basically said that he didn't quite understand prolotherapy or how it worked but that, "By God, it does." So I called Porecha's office back and scheduled an appointment. At the same time I postponed my date for surgery.

As soon as I met Porecha, a naturalized citizen from India, I could tell that he was one of those physicians truly concerned about the welfare of his patients. He did not really push prolotherapy at all and, in fact, told me, "If you want to do this, I have to tell you in advance that it is not for the faint of heart." I was still prepared to try anything to avoid surgery so I told him that we should give it a whirl. He told me that it would take him fifteen or twenty minutes to prepare the concoction and in the meantime I was to strip down from the waist up and be seated on a stool in the middle of the room until he returned. I agreed, and he left.

When he came back he had the largest syringe I had ever seen in my life. He told me he was going to give me several injections in the neck where the C4, C5, and C6 discs had been severely herniated and were bulging way out. He gave me a topical anesthesia in the neck and in other areas of the back. He then went behind me and said, "I'm going to now start making injections."

He made one injection. Then another. And another. And yet another. They just kept coming. After a while and after experiencing a lot of pain I started counting. There were more than twenty after I began my count. Finally, he finished. Porecha then said, "Well we are going to see what happens now. If you feel this helps, you're going to have to go through it for some substantial amount of time." That night I thought I had made some horrible mistake. My God, it hurt like hell. It felt like somebody had taken a chainsaw to my neck.

But to my amazement, the following morning I was able to move my neck. Not very much, but I had moved it. Thereafter I went down to see Porecha once a week for twelve consecutive weeks, going through the same thing every time. Then I began to do it every other week for several months, and then once a month.

What exactly is prolotherapy? Strangely, after all of my experience I still do not believe I can exactly define it. In the case of Porecha, it was a "cocktail" made up of about twenty-five different natural elements and enzymes. The therapy actually does not change the underlying pathological condition. However, the numerous injections, properly done, cause so much trauma to the relevant areas of the body that the body triggers a massive immune system response as it marshals its natural curative and defense forces.

So after about five or six of these treatments I was beginning to regain mobility of my neck. Then I was getting to use my arm effectively as well. Things just kept getting better and better. Before long I was out playing tennis, doing trekking and engaging in other types of activity I had been unable to do for several months. So if one looks at x-rays, the herniated condition still exists. But, man, I was able to do everything again that I had done before from skiing to playing basketball and softball to rafting.

As for Porecha, now retired, he is a saint as far as I am concerned—one of several I have been blessed to know and without whose help I would not be able to still be doing the things I do today.

So, with a bit of help, can't the body pretty much heal itself? Not always.

43

Black Diamonds

One day, I walked into my physical therapist's office in Incline Village and handed a piece of paper to Elayna Hocking, a pretty woman at the reception desk with whom I had become friendly during my regular visits. Elayna, who was twenty-some years younger than me, had piercingly beautiful blue eyes, a gentle smile, and impeccably styled wavy, chestnut hair. Whenever I came into the office for an appointment, she greeted me warmly; she smiled at my jokes. We had pleasant conversations.

I wondered if Elayna would be interested in going on a date with me. The piece of paper—a humorous questionnaire I created to keep the situation light—asked her as much. It gave her the chance to say yes to a movie, dinner, tea, or a talk by the fire or to opt out because she thought I was (a) an idiot and a buffoon, (b) ugly, (c) a doddering old man with drivel coming from his mouth, or (d) all of the above. If I got rejected, at least I would be rejected with a good laugh.

Elayna, it turned out, did not mind our age difference or the fact that I was recovering from an aneurysm and stroke. As a result, she and I went on a date that night—and on many others in the weeks and months that followed.

While onlookers might have marveled that a man like myself, struggling to re-master basic physical tasks like balancing on a bike or hitting a backhand, would have had the time—or the "cahonies"—to ask a beautiful woman more than two decades his junior to go out on a date, such a thought never occurred to me. My goal was to get back to life after all, and that meant among other things pursuing female companionship. The truth was that I was still attracted to women and, thank God, all my equipment in "that department" still worked!

One day in late spring, Elayna asked me if I would be interested in going skiing with her before the end of the Tahoe ski season. Having now spent a good deal of time with me, Elayna was well aware that I still lacked full strength and balance. She certainly didn't want me to get hurt, but she also had a spark urging her to get out on the slopes one more time before the resorts shut down for the year. We were spending more and more time together, so why shouldn't we try skiing together?

Being macho, I said, "Sure."

It wasn't like I hadn't been skiing, yet. After all, by this time, George and I had been out on the slopes a few times and I was progressing rather well I thought. Nevertheless, George definitely wouldn't have approved of me going skiing without him because he knew how I liked to push my limits—all the more so around a woman.

Each time I had gone skiing after returning to Tahoe, George acted as my "guide," making sure I took things at a slow pace and progressed in reasonable increments.

"Let's just have a nice time and get fresh air," George would say.

A world-class skier, George was ever gracious and accommodating. He could have zipped ahead and met me at the bottom of the mountain; instead, he always stayed close to me, leading the way and making sure that there was adequate visibility and that I wouldn't end up in areas that would foil me.

Then, there would always come a time each day when George would say, "Got to quit, Omer." "George, I'm having a good time. Let's not stop yet. I think I'm making progress," I'd say. "No," he would reply, "Given your condition, you're having to work harder than anyone else on the mountain. You're tired and that's when people get hurt. We're stopping now."

And so a successful day of improved skiing would be concluded, with me having advanced my recovery. More significantly, I had returned home each time without further injury.

So, when Elayna asked me to go with her, I answered yes. I figured I could handle it. After all, I'd been improving thus far by constantly pushing myself to do new things. This would just be one more of those opportunities.

———————

The next day, Elayna and I headed over to the Alpine Meadows Ski Resort, the one that Elayna seemed to most enjoy. At Alpine, without George to hold me back—and determined to keep up with a "mere" woman—I began skiing more aggressively than I ought to have done. It was just one more adventure—and one more victory—as I progressed through harder runs than I'd yet tried with George.

Although I was having an incredibly difficult time "edging" the skis with my weakened legs, the day was still unfolding pleasantly as Elayna and I sat down on yet another chairlift and relaxed during our ascent toward the top of the mountain to do a more challenging "black diamond" run. It felt good to be skiing on trails I had enjoyed before my aneurysm; it felt great to be out with a woman; and the white snow beneath the lift and carpeting the pine trees on the mountainside all made for a picture-perfect day.

As the chairlift crested at the top of the trail, Elayna and I readied ourselves to get off: ski tips up, poles ready. Just another run. But then, as we both started to stand and the chairlift continued to move along, Elayna stumbled and appeared to be falling. I reached down low to my right to help her regain her balance. But in so doing, my own skis got caught in the snow—while the chairlift kept moving forward. The young lift operator did not immediately see what was happening and my knees were forced to accommodate two forces that, by the natural laws of physics, wanted to tear my body in two. Against my will, my skis remained dug into the snowy ground behind me while the chairlift itself continued to barrel forward dragging me along beneath it. By the time the chairlift operator noticed me being dragged and wrenched along, the damage had been done to my body.

How badly, I did not yet know.

44

Mt. Everest

"A successful expedition is not measured by conquest of a summit, but rather by every member returning home alive and with fond memories of the journey."
— Anonymous

Yes, the mid-90s had been special. My marriage was still intact. My body was strong. My family members were seemingly in good health, and my spirit of adventure was as high as ever.

Wishing to see and experience the reality of the world—and all of it—no one would ever call me a normal or regular tourist. Chaotic, turbulent and challenging areas didn't repel me. Rather, they attracted me. I suppose 1995 evidences that as much as any year possibly could. A number of things happened that year that would have been unusual in the life of any person. For the most part they were positive though there were a few things that were uncomfortable—in one case, very uncomfortable.

I was now deeply involved in international business. I had scores of visitors from all over the world coming to see me both for business and personal reasons. As a result, I was trying to finish up most of my lingering legal cases, including representation of the Sacramento Kings. Although I continued to attend NBA All Star games and Super Bowls from time to time, I knew that that phase of my life was rapidly drawing to a conclusion as it was becoming increasingly difficult to do my international work and to provide day by day service to my domestic clients at the same time.

In late 1994, my son-in-law, Colin Lynch, invited us to become part of the 1995 American Everest expedition. Technically the expedition was headed by a man called

Paul Pfau, although Colin on the mountain took over a number of the leadership responsibilities. I prepared for both Nepal and Tibet in various ways. Long an avid mountain climber, by this time I had climbed in the Sierras, the Andes, the Rockies, the Cascades, the Alps, and in Alaska. Now, with an eye toward acclimatization, I climbed as many peaks over 10,000 feet as I could in the Sierra Nevada Mountains in California. I also worked out in a local gym with eighty pounds on my back and otherwise got myself in shape as best I could. I was fifty-five years old. I knew that you could be in Olympic shape at sea level but it meant nothing if you weren't acclimatized at altitude.

Complicating matters was that I had the ongoing professional responsibility of trying the National Medical Care (NMC/BMA) case in San Diego. I asked the Judge to postpone our trial date but he said he could not do that. This meant that by mid-April I had to be back to prepare for trial.

Near the end of February I left for Nepal with Diana. The expedition was called "The 1995 American Everest Expedition." Other than Nepali Sherpa's everyone involved with the expedition was an American with one exception, a relatively young man named George Mallory. His grandfather was, next to Sir Edmund Hillary, the most famous mountaineer in history. He had first attempted Everest in 1920-21 and again in 1924. This was thirty years before Hillary was to summit Everest in 1953. The greatest mystery in mountaineering to this day is whether George Leigh Mallory and/or his companion, Sandy Irvine, ever made it to the top of Everest because they were lost near the summit. Although Mallory's body was found just a few years ago, it was impossible to determine whether he died ascending or descending the great mountain.

The idea was for our group to rendezvous at Kathmandu, Nepal and to eventually climb up the North Col on the Tibetan side of the mountain, as opposed to the Nepalese side. Hillary had climbed the South Col on the Nepal side and it had become the more traditional route. But the goal of this expedition was to climb the North Col, the same one George Leigh Mallory had attempted. As it turned out avalanches had closed the only road north and we could not immediately get into Tibet. However we did not want to lose critical time. Climbing aboard a Soviet-built helicopter, we flew into Lukla in Nepal, a no-abort landing strip where Sir Edmund Hillary's wife and daughter had been earlier killed in a plane crash. We had decided to do acclimatization work on the south flank of Mount Everest. We started out toward base camp on the Nepalese side.

On the chopper flight from Kathmandu I developed giardia, a bacterial infection one gets from contaminated food or water. We landed at Lukla and the giardia was just terrible. In my case it caused constant belching and it was like belching up sulfur or raw eggs. It really weakened my body badly. By the time we landed I was so weak I could hardly walk. For about three or four days it was really affecting me, but I was determined not to let it deter me. And it didn't.

We began to trek up the south side of Everest. Soon we came to Namche Bazaar, the main Sherpa village on the south side of Everest. Sherpa's are the famous people who do so much of the carrying (and cooking) on these expeditions. From Namche we went higher to Tengboche, a scenic village on the trail about half way up to base camp. The monastery at Tengboche is famous throughout the Buddhist world. It is exquisite. One of the most beautiful mountains in the world, Ama Dablam, is right next to and commands the village of Tengboche. Above Tengboche is Pheriche, and the Sherpa villages get smaller and smaller the higher one climbs.

Finally, we received word that the road going into Tibet from Kathmandu had been cleared of the avalanched snow. So we trekked back down to Lukla, re-boarded the chopper and returned to Kathmandu. In Kathmandu we loaded our trucks and headed north. Another expedition (Japanese) was doing the same thing. When we reached the river that separates Tibet and Nepal, we got hassled by the Chinese communist guards. We had all of our permits in place, but they still gave us a hard time. Nevertheless, we had some funny experiences there. We had one Chinese-American climber on the expedition. His name was Hsieh. He was the youngest member of the expedition and one of the strongest. When we were at the bridge and being hassled by the guards, we asked Hsieh to translate for us. He said in English "We climbers. We go high mountain." It turned out that he spoke no Chinese at all. The guards then went through all our bags, and seemed awfully disappointed when they found absolutely nothing incriminating.

We went across the bridge and stayed in a "hotel" on the other side of the border in a small village called Zangmu. The "hotel" was simply a concrete building. Extremely primitive. Vermin and rats crawling everywhere. It was awful and we couldn't get out of there quickly enough and we did the next morning. Early.

We headed east toward the Rongbuk Monastery, a monastery below Mount Everest on the Tibetan side. There we reconnoitered and made sure everything was in place. We had yaks waiting for us at Rongbuk and we loaded the yaks with as much of our goods and equipment as we could. We then began to trek up to base camp on the Tibetan side.

Base camp at Mount Everest, whether on the north or south side, is at approximately 17,500 feet. The human body cannot be sustained at altitudes above that point for long periods of time. Above there, the danger of either a cerebral edema or a cardiac edema is constant.

All told, there were over twenty-five people in the expedition group, but that included physicians, sherpas, trekkers and others. Less than half of the group expected to challenge the summit. In fact, even the expedition leader, Paul Pfau, did not expect to climb high. Because I'm a realist and knowing my schedule, I was comfortable knowing that I wouldn't have an opportunity to summit.

I got to know one of the Sherpa's really well. His name is Kaji Sherpa and to this day we are good friends. A few years after the 1995 expedition, Kaji set a world record as the fastest man ever to summit Everest. His record has since been broken, but Kaji still remains a legend. He has since then migrated to America and now lives close to me. We see each other with some degree of regularity. I cherish his friendship.

By the time we had acclimatized by going up and down to and from base camp, Randy Carnahan, son of Governor Mel Carnahan of Missouri, had the same problem as me—not much time. He had to get back to the States, too. It had to do with his father's administration.

We heard that bad weather was coming in and Randy and I discussed what to do. Randy decided to stay at base camp until we departed, but I discussed matters with Kaji and he and I set out alone for one last high level experience. We went further up than we should have since we didn't have anyone else from our team with us. But seeing the storm approaching, we retreated in time to base camp. Everest is so huge that it creates its own weather, and it can be notoriously severe. As the storm began to hit, Randy and I, along with Diana and Kelly (my oldest daughter), accompanied by a Chinese "escort," got out just in time.

As the Chinese government controls Tibet, they required that we have a person with us whose job was basically to monitor our travels. We were lucky. The escort with us turned out to be a pretty cool guy because, as we continued east towards Lhasa, I wanted to do a lot of off-road things like see monasteries and speak with people. He didn't complain. We were careful not to do anything to alienate him or cause problems for the expedition. After a while, we arrived in Lhasa, the capital of Tibet. It was under military occupation by the Chinese. The Han population of China was being imported and was displacing the native Tibetan population. I'd seen some things on the way across Tibet that distressed me greatly.

On the way to the Rongbuk monastery, we had already been reminded a couple of times of the occupation. Shengazi is a village on the main road going east west in Tibet. Existing there was a significant Chinese military encampment. The Chinese had the only motorized vehicles. If two Tibetans were talking on the roadside, they would be broken up. The Chinese would come out and ride motorcycles around them stirring up a lot of dust in order to break up meetings or even social discussions. Their garrison would come out several times a day and march up and down the streets in the village just as a show of force.

I had travelled a lot in China by this time, had come to have many friends there, and had gotten to know the country rather well. It's a wonderful country with a great history and a strong culture. But the Tibetan situation was different than anything I had seen in China proper and the situation disturbed me greatly. Eventually we did get to Lhasa where Randy and I went to the Potala, the Dalai Lama's historic residence. We spent a few days in Lhasa, climbing up and down monasteries and exploring the city.

Although Randy was an attorney, his first love was farming. He took care of the Carnahan's family farm outside of Rolla. After returning from Mount Everest, Randy and I were to spend a great deal of time together over the next six years.

I got back to the States just in time to prepare for my pending trial. The same was true in Randy's case. Over the next few years, Randy became one of my best friends.

In 1997 after school let out, Jessica and I went on a trip together to the Midwest to give her a better idea of my heritage and to introduce her to a few of my friends in that part of the country. We travelled to Missouri, Iowa, Arkansas, and Illinois. We initially flew into St. Louis. We then drove over to Rolla to see and spend time with Randy.

Two years later, there was a tragic occurrence involving Randy and his father, Governor Mel Carnahan. In February 1999, I had gone back to St. Louis where I had again met up with Randy. After a day at Rolla, we flew up to Jefferson City to stay in what Randy called "people's housing" (the Governor's Mansion). His father, the Governor, was getting ready to run for the United States Senate against the Republican incumbent, John Ashcroft. Randy was an accomplished pilot, and generally flew his father to various venues in the state for campaign appearances. This was to ensure that public money was not inappropriately spent for campaign purposes. On that occasion, and thereafter both by telephone and in person, I discussed the Governor's race with the Governor and provided him with the names of a number of people whom I thought would be likely to contribute to his campaign.

I went back to visit Randy and his father again in the early fall. At that time Randy showed me a brand new plane they had purchased. They loved it. He and I flew over to St. Louis and then to Jefferson City where we again spent the night. Then we returned to Rolla the next day.

Shortly after returning to California, I received news that Randy while flying his father to a campaign event had encountered bad weather. The plane had crashed. The Governor, Randy and everyone else aboard were killed. This was a huge personal loss as Randy in only slightly over five years had become one of my best friends. A short time later when the election was held his father defeated Ashcroft. I believe it was the only time in United States history where a dead man defeated an incumbent United States Senator.

45

Pakistan, the Taliban and Paco Tech

"The successful person makes a habit of doing what the failing person fears to do."
— Thomas Edison

Later that same year, 1995, I began to represent a South African company known as Paco Tech. Paco Tech, headed by a white South African named Brian Harmer, took almost any type of organic material, whether wheat, straw, rice hulls, coconut husks, or any other type of organic crop and compacted it through a patented process. What was left was building material that could be used to construct homes, office buildings and all sorts of other structures. Harmer at the time was afraid that South Africa was going to go up in flames and that his family would be placed in jeopardy and his businesses burned. As a result, he wanted to relocate his business to another part of the world. Initially, I contacted Jimmy Carter and Habitat for Humanity because I felt that they might have an interest in the technology of Paco Tech. I also spent considerable time in DC speaking with the International Finance Corporation (IFC), to the Overseas Private Investment Corporation (OPIC), to the International Monetary Fund (IMF), and even to the Rockefeller Winrock office in DC and later at their hands-on center in Arkansas.

About the same time I began to represent a Pakistani-American named Rashid Saeed. Saeed had dual citizenship as he had been born in Pakistan and still maintained a home there. He also had business interests both in Pakistan and in America.

When I explained how Paco's technology could reduce the cost of housing and provide other benefits to lesser developed nations, Saeed took a personal interest. Through Saeed's connections, I received an invitation from Pakistan's Minister of Commerce representing the recently elected Prime Minister, Benazir Bhutto, to visit Pakistan.

The newly elected government was trying to entice foreign investment in Pakistan, especially in an area that Pakistan referred to as "Free Kashmir" (that portion of Kashmir that Pakistan occupies rather than India). In effect, Pakistan was prepared to offer full tax dispensation to a foreign company that invested and developed a business in "Free Kashmir" for twenty years if the company was prepared to locate in that area. I left for Pakistan not long after I returned from Nepal and Tibet and after I had successfully concluded the trial that caused me to return early from the Everest expedition.

I initially flew into Lahore, the capital of the state of Punjab. Harmer was arriving from South Africa later that same day. I was picked up at the airport and driven to an enormous home that belonged to a man who had recently retired as the doctor to the royal family of Saudi Arabia. This home was an incredible mansion with high walls all around the grounds. There were guard posts at each corner manned by men with automatic weapons. We drove in through the gates and I saw yet more armed guards. It was like an armed fortress. I was no shrinking violet when it came to luxurious surroundings, but this place was a real eye opener.

After I was introduced to the doctor, my host, I asked "My Lord, why all the guards?" His answer was, "Anyone who is rich in this country is in danger."

My curiosity was piqued. "How many guards do you have here?"

"About twenty-eight."

"Why so many?"

He laughed. "Actually my wife wants more. How many do you have?"

Jokingly I said, "Only two."

He looked surprised. "Oh, is that enough?"

I started laughing and told him that truth be told I had none. "I wouldn't be comfortable with armed guards."

"If wealthy, you couldn't get along here without armed guards." And he was deadly serious.

Harmer arrived at the complex later that same day. The following morning we were driven across the border into Kashmir to the town of Bhimber, the region in which Pakistan wanted to see development take place. Although the tax advantages were great, when Harmer saw how close his facilities would be to two huge nuclear-armed enemies facing each other a short distance away from one another, he gave up the idea entirely. Not exactly a great environment for business. So Harmer returned to Lahore and flew home to South Africa. However, I had planned to stay in Pakistan for awhile as I had been invited to meet with Prime Minister Bhutto in Islamabad, the capital of Pakistan. She remembered that meeting when many years later I spoke briefly with her again at a reception at Lake Tahoe. This latter incident was only a few years before her assassination.

Although my meetings in Islamabad focused primarily on the possibility of future business opportunities, I intended also while in Pakistan to go north to see the Karakoram Mountains. The most significant is K-2, the second highest peak in the world. The Karakoram's in the far north of Pakistan are in disputed territory, parts of it claimed by China, parts by India, and parts by Pakistan.

The Prime Minister told me that she would have me flown to Skardu and from there have an army officer drive me north because, according to her, the guides in the area could not be trusted. I declined the invitation to fly to Skardu as I preferred to rent a car. I wanted to drive through the Swat Valley and northward from there in order to see the countryside and meet some of the people. Probably a mistake. The trip took me close to thirty hours and the Karakoram Highway is one of the more harrowing roads in the world. Nevertheless, I finally made it.

As I had gone north from Islamabad, I was looked on with great curiosity and I am sure with suspicion by people that I passed by. I would just smile and wave. When I made stops, I would ordinarily find someone who could speak at least a bit of English so that I could communicate my needs. When I arrived at my hotel in Skardu, an army officer was awaiting my arrival.

The following morning, the two of us set out in an army jeep. It was a good thing I had the driver because army checkpoints were all along the road. The Karakoram's themselves are even more beautiful than the Himalayas. The mountains tend to stand out alone, thus giving them a more dramatic silhouette. I was not equipped for any kind of mountain climbing although I had brought boots and warm clothing with me. We finally got to the point where I was able to peer up at K-2, the second highest mountain in the world and considered by most mountaineers to be far more dangerous to climb than Mount Everest. This is the region recently made famous by Greg Mortenson in his book, "Three Cups of Tea." Some of the people I met in this area had light skin and blue eyes and they claim to be descendants of Alexander the Great's troops. It is possible. It was an amazing peek into a strange part of the world that few ever see.

Because my trip to the Karakoram's had taken longer than anticipated, when I returned to Skardu I decided to fly rather than drive back to Islamabad. Arriving at my hotel in Islamabad I found a message waiting for me. It was from Rashid Saeed who had been monitoring my travels. The message said, "Please call me as soon as possible. It's important."

I called my friend Saeed who asked me to visit his home in Faisalabad in order to meet his family and a few friends. As he was a friend and client and as he had been covering many of my expenses in Pakistan, I felt obliged to do so. He arranged a flight for me from Islamabad to Faisalabad. I picked up the ticket at the airport.

On the flight, however, the plane ran into very bad turbulence. Finally, the pilot announced, first in Urdu and then in English, "We must divert because of the storm. We will be landing in Lahore."

When we landed in Lahore, to my surprise Saeed and his driver were there waiting for me. They had also learned about the diversion made necessary by the raging storm. Faisalabad is quite some distance west of Lahore. By the time I got my luggage and we were on the road, it was well past midnight. The wind and dust storm was horrific. The wind was so bad that it was literally bouncing the car around, and the driver was having trouble just staying on the road. Visibility due to blowing dust was almost nil.

We eventually reached Faisalabad around 4:00 am. The entire trip had been incredibly hot as there had been no air-conditioning in the car. When we entered the home, the first room was bare except for a bed near the back of the room. The room was rectangular in shape and very large. Ordinarily it was used as a reception area. Saeed said, "Senator (that's what he always called me), please lie down here on this bed and get some sleep. We will talk in the morning. I want you to meet my family and some people in the community tomorrow. I will go back now to join my wife and children."

I removed my sweat-soaked and dusty clothes and gratefully laid down on the bed and fell asleep immediately. A couple of hours later I was awakened. I opened my eyes and was startled to see a string of men coming through the front door. They were entering the room to the right and were slowly circling the room single file in serpentine style. Pretty soon they had filled each wall of the room and had sat down cross-legged on the floor.

I wasn't exactly ready for visitors. In fact, I was in my skivvies, and nothing else. Not to mention that I had no idea who these people were or what they were doing here. I sat up on the bed flabbergasted. Most of the men were older, though not all of them. They were squatting and most were speaking in a foreign language that I could not understand but knew to be Urdu. Some however — especially the younger ones — were speaking Pashtu. It was an incredibly awkward situation and I wasn't sure what to do. Seemingly, no one spoke English and no one looked friendly.

About this time Saeed bolted into the room from the back of the house. Unlike me he was fully dressed. "Senator, I apologize. I overslept. These are the town leaders of Faisalabad and some of their friends from surrounding areas and they have come to talk to you. They knew that you were coming and they are very honored to have you here and would like to ask you questions. I will translate."

At least sixty people were in the room by now. I was very uncomfortable for all sorts of reasons. I just woke up from a deep slumber and before I even had a chance to wipe the sleep from my eyes I began to be peppered with difficult questions. It quickly became evident that Saeed had told people in Faisalabad, a major Pakistani city, that he was hosting a United States Senator. I was pissed. He was speaking to them in Urdu so I could not understand what was being said but I clearly began to get the gist of it. Because I do keep myself conversant in world affairs I knew what was being discussed because of the questions I was being asked. For the most part I also knew the American position on the various issues that were being raised. The questions were all over the place and, by and large, they were very intelligent questions.

But it wasn't at all a pleasant kind of give and take. To the contrary, the mood was at times confrontational and I sensed that some of the younger men were sympathetic to or associated with the Taliban of neighboring Afghanistan. They wanted to know why we (the United States) were holding hundreds of millions of dollars of Pakistani money that their country had paid to buy war planes and why we were not allowing the planes to leave American soil and at the same time were not returning their money either. I knew that the official American position was that Pakistan had refused to sign the Nuclear Non-Proliferation Treaty. Of course, India, Pakistan's long-term adversary, hadn't signed it either. Nor had the United States. I had no good answer as to why we had not returned their money. Then again, I was not a duly appointed spokesman for the United States government, but they were certainly acting as though I was.

Their attitude was, "How can you say you are going to punish us for not signing the Nuclear Non-Proliferation Treaty when you yourselves won't sign it?" The American position, when you come right down to it, really in effect is saying, "We are the good guys. We are responsible." But I wasn't at that moment exactly in a position where I could articulate that very well.

The fellow who seemed to be the leader was extremely persistent and somewhat demanding. He began to talk about Afghanistan. "You wanted our help in running the Soviets out of Afghanistan," he said. "So all the supplies that the Afghans received came through our country. Now that the Soviets have been driven out you are buddying up to India. We were there for you, but you're not there for us."

I repeatedly told them that I did not speak for the United States government. I did not speak for the Clinton administration. I am not a United States Senator. I have no diplomatic passport. I am just a plain American citizen and I can't answer your questions with any kind of authority whatever.

I have a suspicion however that Saeed was not translating any of that. It was clear that he wanted to appear important and impress his countrymen. He had in fact told them that I was a Senator, and by that they thought that I was a current member of the United States Senate. It was one of the most uncomfortable experiences of my life and I was really pissed off at Saeed. After two hours or more, they all filed out and I was finally able to breathe a sigh of relief, take a shower, and get clothed. It had been a very intense and confrontational experience.

I am still friends with Saeed, but at the time I was really upset and yelled at him. Very uncharacteristic behavior for me. He was apologetic but it gave me no solace. After cleaning up, meeting his family and having a bite to eat, I rented a car and drove southwest across the rest of Pakistan through Hyderabad and on to Karachi on the Arabian Sea, the country's largest and, arguably, poorest city where after a day of "sightseeing" in a city where there isn't much to see other than extreme poverty, I took a flight back to the United States.

Notwithstanding the incident in Faisalabad, I continued to represent Saeed. I had also met some very nice people in Pakistan, including a man named Rashid Khan who owned hotels in Pakistan and when he later visited the United States began to invest in the States as well. In addition, some of my very best friends are Pakistani-American and I have great respect for them. In fact, one is an individual with whom I today serve on the READ Global Board of Directors.

As for Paco Tech, I also continued to represent Brian Harmer and the company, but they no longer had any interest in Pakistan. I couldn't blame Harmer. I would have made the same decision he did. After all, who would want to establish a business smack-dab between two nuclear armed enemies?

46

Turkmenistan

"Not all who wander are lost."
— Anonymous

Near the end of that same year, I was approached by a group of people who lived in the States, most but not all of whom were citizens, who wanted to do a project in the country of Turkmenistan. The group included an attorney, some engineers, and principals who had originally come from Turkmenistan but were now living in the United States. The latter continued to have family and other ties to Turkmenistan. Knowing that I was involved in international finance, they asked if they could retain my services because they had the idea of constructing a fertilizer facility in southeast Turkmenistan near the borders of Iran and Afghanistan. All of the "Stans," Uzbekistan, Turkmenistan, Tajikistan, Kyrgyzstan, and Kazakhstan were former Soviet Republics. These are historically Muslim countries but because of the Soviet-era influence, the Islamic religion is much less influential in those countries than in most other parts of the Islamic world.

Turkmenistan has one of the largest natural gas reserves in the world. It also has ammonia. Gas and ammonia are the two key ingredients needed to produce fertilizer. Turkmenistan also grows a cotton crop. That's basically it. Not a very diversified economy. To produce the cotton, they rely on irrigation coming from the Aral Sea, which is one of the most polluted waterways in the world and is now diminishing in size because of heavy overuse by the countries that draw from it.

Those driving this particular project knew that I had previously dealt with the alphabet soup agencies in Washington, DC. They had located a fertilizer facility in the State of Oklahoma which they wanted to dismantle and transport to Turkmenistan. I became intrigued by this project. The company wanted me to accompany principals of the company to Turkmenistan. Before leaving for Turkmenistan, I went to Washington, DC and began to talk with governmental agencies that I thought might be of help. The biggest problem was that the President of Turkmenistan, Saparmurat Niyazov, was one of the most oppressive dictators in the world. The personality cult surrounding Niyazov was so intense that the United States Department of State had the country of Turkmenistan blacklisted. I was trying to persuade the agencies in DC to allow the project to go forward with the use, in part, of their finances. They still had the matter under consideration when I left for Turkmenistan in October 1995.

Changing planes in Istanbul, one of my favorite cities in the world, we continued on to Ashgabat, the capital of Turkmenistan. Ashgabat lies only a few miles north of the Iranian border. However, the two countries are separated by a mountain chain called the Caput Range. Turkmenistan and Iran had very good relations and insofar as I know, they still do.

Now, I had been in countries with dictatorial regimes before, and I had seen the cult-like personality before as well, but this was far beyond what I had ever seen. Here every citizen walked around wearing a lapel pin bearing a photo of Niyazov. You could stand at any intersection in the city of Ashgabat and look in any direction and see huge banners of Niyazov hanging from the buildings. Ashgabat will never be a tourist destination. Yet, Niyazov built many beautiful hotels at great public expense. Very few people go there. The only visitors are the occasional international business people who are primarily interested in the natural gas reserves of the country.

Turkmenistan had no way of moving its natural gas to the rest of the world unless it did so through the use of Russian pipelines and the Russians exacted great sums of money as tribute for the use of their pipelines. That was not the reason that took us to Turkmenistan but it did seem to dominate the conversation in most of the meetings in which I was involved. Turkmenistan was looking for options to take its gas to other parts of the world at a lower price than they were able to do by shipping it through Russia. The most logical option was to build a pipeline down through Iran to the Persian Gulf. But that had its own problems because the mullahs and other clerics were in control of Iran. Therefore there was concern that the Iranians could take control of the pipeline at any time. Most of the American companies involved in this complex situation wanted a pipeline to go west over to the Caspian Sea and eventually into the area around Turkey. Anything to get the product to the western markets. At the same time the Chinese had become huge players and were leaning on Turkmenistan to have the pipeline go east to

China. As I said, it was a complex political situation to say the least and I was never quite sure why we were involved in such discussions.

At one time, Niyazov invited me to go to the national bank, which was called "The Peoples Bank of Turkmenistan," obviously a holdover from the days of Soviet rule. Turkmenistan has its own native language, closer to Turkish than any other. However, most government officials I met with still spoke Russian. But when I went to see the President of the Bank, he also spoke English. In a way it was a funny conversation but in actuality it was tragic and spoke volumes. I asked him, "How do you decide who gets a loan?" A rather baffled look crossed his face. He said, "Well, whatever the President says. If the President says they get a loan, they do. If he says they don't, they don't." That pretty much described the business and social environment of Turkmenistan.

I was in Turkmenistan with my colleagues for some time and the talks were seemingly proceeding fairly well. We were meeting with government officials but I know that my Turkmen clients, behind the scenes, did not want me to know too much because they knew that I would not violate our "Foreign Corrupt Practices Act." There were also other meetings taking place in which I was not involved. I am sure there was a lot of quid pro quo taking place. Nothing happens in that country and in those parts of the world unless the government approves it.

In any case, during the first week in November, the President instructed his staff to plan a celebration for us. We drove quite some distance to the west of Ashgabat. The road went right along the base of the mountain range separating Turkmenistan from Iran. Finally, we came to a park like setting. Our hosts, the government officials, had brought a huge lamb which they intended to barbeque for us as part of the celebration.

Although the mountains were quite high near the capital, Ashgabat, they were not at all high where we stopped for the picnic. There was an entrance at the base of the mountains that went to underground thermal pools beneath the Caput Mountains. They were renown for their therapeutic qualities. After being in the water for awhile and being intrigued by my surroundings, I left the others and advised my hosts that I was going to climb a "short distance" up one of the low mountains separating Turkmenistan from Iran. So I excused myself, got dressed and told the others I was just going to take a hike. They knew that I was an experienced outdoorsman.

I left the caves and started up the mountain. For me, it was an easy climb. At the top of the mountain I realized that I was in fact looking directly into Iran. I was looking down on desert type country with a village about a mile in the distance. I don't know what possessed me, but I decided I wanted to take a few steps into Iran. I made my way down the hill, trying to remain covert because the nearest Iranian village, as indicated, wasn't that far off. As long as I didn't see anyone, I advanced a good distance downhill. There was almost no foliage on the hillside but there were some relatively large boulders. I kept going downhill from boulder to boulder crouching behind each one as I got to it. I'm not sure why I kept going downhill, but I did. What was I going to do when I got to the bottom? I wasn't sure.

Then I saw a jeep charging toward me, dust flying. "Oh fuck! I've been spotted!" There were four soldiers in a jeep. I didn't try to run but simply raised my hands to show that I was unarmed. One of the soldiers spoke pretty good English. He asked me who I was and I identified myself by name. Knowing they had good relations with President Niyazov I explained that I was his guest and I was just out for a hike and I didn't realize I had entered Iran. I apologized for the intrusion. The fellow who spoke English translated all this into Farsi, the language of Iran. They all thought it was funny and began laughing.

Soon another jeep came up loaded with townspeople. There must have been ten of them loaded into a jeep that was really built for only four people. Surprisingly they began to tell me how much they liked Americans—it was just our government that they disliked. I told the English speaking soldier, who was also clearly the Commander, that my hosts would be worried about me and that I had to get back. He said, "No problem." He directed one of his men to take me up a trail that they knew of. I shook hands with each of the soldiers and said goodbye to the townspeople. As I left, the Commander said that he hoped that one day our two countries would again have good relations. I replied that I hoped so, too.

Back at the barbeque, my colleagues were indeed beginning to worry and were happy to see me. I had probably been gone for about three hours. Realizing that my actions could have precipitated an international incident, I wasn't about to tell them that I had unlawfully entered Iran. It was one of the many rash adventures that people who don't know me might find hard to understand. I don't always understand myself why I do certain things. My yearning to explore and discover new things for myself often seems to have no bounds.

We returned to Ashgabat that night, and flew out the following day. In Istanbul others proceeded on to the States. I had other business planned in Europe so my route took me from Istanbul to London and from London onto other places.

Not long after I returned from Europe, a small delegation came from Turkmenistan to the States. A project was eventually built, but it did not involve the matter of our visit. However, the delegation brought with them a painting as a personal gift to me from the President. The inscription on the plaque on the paintings frame said: "To Senator Omer Rains from his Excellency Sapamurat Niyazov, President of Turkmenistan."

47
A Setback

"Let's do some black diamonds," Elayna said to me the day we went skiing together at Alpine Meadows—my first time on the slopes without George since suffering my aneurysm and stroke.

"Why not?" I thought. Elayna and I had been skiing intermediate runs and it was time to do something more challenging—or so I thought.

But then came Elayna's wobble as she started to dismount from the chairlift and my macho instinct to reach over to prevent her from falling. In a heartbeat the chairlift knocked me down and began to drag me along with my skis caught beneath the moving chair.

My hubris was probably bound to eventually catch up with me. After all, I had successfully tried to walk, drive, swim, and mountain bike, when the doctors had told me it was unlikely I'd ever leave a wheelchair. I had started dating a woman in her 30s while I was in my 60s. Good or bad, self-serving or self-destructive, I always pushed the limits. This time I was to pay the price.

After being dragged along by the chairlift, the lift operator had called for the ski patrol to take me down the mountain on a snow mobile. Elayna urged me to do so as well, as she had just seen my body being dragged by the chairlift and the tangled mess of my legs cleaving to the ice and snow beneath me.

I assured them, however, that a snow mobile would not be necessary. In spite of excruciating knee pain, I insisted that I could handle it. And off I went downhill, followed closely by Elayna.

After skiing down to the bottom of the mountain—perhaps by miracle, given the shredded state of my knees—Elayna and I retreated to the car. She drove me to the office of an orthopedic specialist and within a short time the diagnosis came in.

I had severely torn both the lateral meniscus and the medial meniscus, as well as a ligament, in my left knee. I had also suffered less severe damage to my right knee. "Because of the nature of your injury," the specialist explained, "we aren't going to be able to address this problem orthroscopically."

"Shit," I thought. "On top of everything else, the last thing I need at this stage of my life is major surgery, especially if it's going to interfere with my recovery."

I decided to get a second opinion. So, a few days after the ski accident, I was driven by a friend to San Francisco to see another knee specialist at the University of California, San Francisco. However, this physician told me the same thing the first one did: It would take major reconstructive surgery to repair my left knee, after which I would have to undergo approximately two years of rehabilitation, much of it on crutches.

Two years more of incapacitation? Crutches and more rehabilitation? This was not an option in which I was interested. Not only was it distasteful to imagine traveling on crutches while living in the icy winter climate of Tahoe, but frankly I did not even know if I had two years left to live given the still-fragile state of my health.

I probed the doctor to learn more about what might happen if I chose to forego the surgery. Amazingly, he explained that I had already done so much damage to my knee that I probably couldn't do much more by using it. Although it would be unlikely that I could do much physical activity due to the severity of the injury to my left knee, the doctor said that whatever activity I could muster was unlikely to greatly worsen my condition.

It was a done deal then—I would skip the surgery. I had mastered pain before and I would simply have to do it again. Pain was just…pain after all. Pain was something that could generally be handled and endured. So, after a short stint of resting and a great deal of icing my knee, I resumed my post-aneurysm recovery program of physical activity. Even with the knee injury, I could still move in a straight line, so I started there.

I could trek, bike, and hike. Eventually, I even got back to a bit of tennis. The difference from before the skiing incident was that I now had to continually deal with pretty horrible knee pain when I tried to engage in many of my recovery activities.

The pain in my knee was pretty much constant, but it was bearable. It was when I twisted or torqued my knee, during activities like tennis or skiing, that I had to push through especially sharp, shooting pain. Oftentimes, especially during tennis, my knee would simply give out and I'd end up on the ground with scraped elbows and bloody kneecaps.

I must admit that the knee pain was frustrating and uncomfortable—and at times intense and terrible—but I could not let this pain stop me from doing most of the activities in which I wanted to engage. I had been given a second chance at life, and I was most certainly going to take advantage of it. Harkening back to my prolotherapy experience, I also kept telling myself that the body would heal itself if I kept active. That is only partly true.

The same is true of the heart. When broken, the passage of time helps heal some wounds, but not all of them.

48

Geneva and the Unraveling
of a Long Marriage

"Climb every mountain, search high and low, follow every byway, every path you know."
— The Sound of Music

All of a sudden life whacks you with a 2 x 4. That's been true more than once in my life. I tend to keep my feelings close inside because I always try to avoid confrontation, particularly with those with whom I live and love.

Although Diana and I were married in 1977 we had been living together for several years prior to that time. For the first twenty years or so that we were together, we had a rather idyllic relationship. Many of my friends and associates, most of them very unhappy in their own married lives, would often comment how lucky I was to have such a good and strong relationship. I agreed. I actually dreamed of spending the rest of my life in an unchanged relationship with the woman I did in fact deeply love.

During those years, Diana was my best friend and confidante. Still the old fashioned man when it came to the financial aspects of marriage, I paid for everything at all times. Diana had no financial obligations whatsoever even though she was often making a great deal of money. She was my best friend and I shared everything with her. "What's mine is mine and what's yours is mine," she would often say. We would both laugh. Eventually however I came to realize that she was deadly serious.

Although I always traveled a great deal and worried about how this might affect our relationship, she was without a single exception always invited to go with me, even on my business trips. Often she did, and on occasion she did not for whatever reason. Those decisions were always hers. My travels and being away from her from time to time did concern me but she never complained and seemingly understood the necessity for my travels as most of them did revolve around making money and meeting financial obligations for the family.

Diana had a group of women in the Sacramento area that she ran around with. They called themselves "The Happy Campers." It seemed like a strange name because most of them were divorced and seemed very unhappy. "The Happy Campers" would frequently take trips together to places like Santa Cruz Island off the coast of Santa Barbara, to Yosemite, to Lake Tahoe, to the Napa Valley, to Palm Springs to visit spas, and to various resorts in the Sierra's. Sometimes they would be gone for a day or two and sometimes for a week or more. This didn't bother me. I actually thought it was healthy that she was able to lead a life from time to time independent of me. Jessica and I always managed to get by quite nicely on our own but were very happy whenever she did return.

But somewhere along the way I lost my best friend. When Diana started draining bank accounts and embezzling large sums of money as well as cashing checks made payable to me, notwithstanding the substantial income she was earning on her own, it obviously bothered me greatly. When she denied doing those things and lied about doing them, it bothered me even more. Things became serious when I would find proof that she was lying and she would then have to admit that she had in fact been doing it and lying about it. Moreover, she refused to tell me what she was doing with the money.

This was especially true when she refused to discuss the reasons for her actions. It was evident, however, that whatever was wrong was deeply wrong and Diana no longer took the marriage seriously. For a long time I was in denial, but it was steadily getting more and more clear to me that things were going from bad to worse.

Nevertheless, a good front was put on to all, primarily for the benefit of Jessica. In addition, by 1993 we were hosting more visitors from various countries than at any other time in my life. Often our guests would stay overnight, and Diana would to her credit be very involved in the conversations and I don't think anyone ever detected the problems that were beginning to surface.

The front being put forward notwithstanding, it certainly did seem as though she was trying to goad me into ending the marriage. For my part, I definitely did not want to go through another divorce. My theory about her was that she had never sown any wild oats and was now determined to do it. Ironically, despite our marital difficulties we were still taking family vacations together. Some of these were domestic and some were foreign. We especially enjoyed going to Hawaii as a family. We also continued to sleep together and seemingly had a healthy conjugal relationship.

Nevertheless, it was unmistakably clear that she was trying very hard to try to get me to file for divorce. I assumed that this was because of her personality—she wanted it to appear to be my action rather than hers. But I decided that even if a divorce was inevitable, and I hoped it wasn't, it shouldn't happen with such a young child at home and still in school. I told her that I would not file for divorce and that with Jessica at a still sensitive age it would be unhealthy to split up Jessica's family if it could at all be avoided. Her response was simply that "She will get over it."

I think that this entire process would have been much more heart wrenching if it hadn't happened to me before. I was hurt by what was happening and by Diana's actions, but I had also become somewhat conditioned to and philosophical about it. I knew that half the couples in America were getting divorced and I had of course been through one myself, but nevertheless I was determined to stay the course.

There came a point in the mid-1990s where I was beginning to catch Diana in more and more lies, very significant lies. I had very generously funded bank accounts in our joint names. Diana, without my knowledge, began to remove vast sums of money from those accounts. From one account alone, she removed $40,000, taking care to hide the various bank statements that came to the house so that I wouldn't immediately notice what was going on. At first she denied removing the money. However, when I got proof from the various banks she was finally forced to admit it. Eventually I had to remove her name from my accounts as my trust in her, sadly, was quickly being diminished.

Eventually, and after many requests, Diana agreed to see a marriage counselor who was highly respected. I liked the counselor, and found him to be not only nice but extremely even-handed. It seemed that after counseling, for a short time things got a bit better. However, after a few visits, Diana started skipping appointments and when she did attend she sometimes refused to give answers to the counselor. When the counselor asked her about missing money or drained accounts, her stock answer was, "I don't know." The doctor's response was, "That's an incredible statement completely lacking in credibility Diana. You cannot look me in the eye and tell me you don't know what happened, for example, to the $40,000." Diana just shrugged.

By 1998 it had become absolutely and equivocally apparent that Diana was having an affair. During a one month period she was "out of town on social events" for twelve days. Virtually every night she was in town, she would come home late, often not returning until around 11:00 pm or later. I asked Diana once again if she was having an affair and she curtly said, "No." But all of her actions continued to point to that.

Then came a point in time where I signed Jessica up to attend a special course at Claremont College in Southern California. At this program she was to learn speed-reading and organizational skills and hopefully other skills that would help her develop good study habits. Diana said that she wanted to drive her down to Claremont.

"Why? Why don't I just fly her down, rent a car and drop her off, and then fly right back. It can easily be done in one day," I asked. It was a 450-mile trip that would take ten hours each way by car.

"No, no, I want to drive her down," Diana said. "It will be good mother-daughter time for us." Diana also said that she might see a girlfriend for a day or two in Southern California before she came back. One of us could then later fly down to get Jessica when her course was over. The suggestion sounded fine to me, so I simply said, "OK."

A day before the course was to start, Diana and Jessica loaded the car for the trip and drove off. Diana promised she'd call every day to check in. We had one of those early car phones that was built into the floorboard with the antenna in the back, so Diana and I would certainly be able to stay in touch, even while she was on the road.

But Diana did not call during the drive down to Claremont. I did not worry though, knowing that she and Jessica had probably had a long trip. Then, the next day, when there was still no word from Diana, even after I left her phone messages, I wondered if anything was wrong. I called Claremont College to check in. They assured me that Jessica had arrived safely and been enrolled, which temporarily allayed the fears I was starting to have.

But as the days continued to pass without a single call home from Diana, I thought, "This is not good." True, there had been a few times that Diana hadn't called while gone on a weekend trip, but it was always in a situation, like camping, where no phones were available. This time was different. She had told me she'd check in daily, which should have been easy given the car phone and phones that would have been available either at a friend's home or at any hotel/motel where she might be staying. She had also told me she'd only be gone for a few days, but time was passing. I began to worry that some harm might have come to her.

I got hold of a good friend of Diana's, one of the so-called happy campers, who said, "Oh, Renee went with her." So I called Renee's husband to see if he knew where they were.

From time to time Diana would take trips with the happy campers just as I would from time to time go camping or white water rafting with my friends. But she had never mentioned taking Renee with her on this trip.

"Well, Renee's right here in town," her husband said. "She's out working with the horses right now."

I wasn't sure whether to be worried or suspicious. Maybe I should call the CHP and have an "all-points bulletin" (APB) put out, I thought. But first I called a mutual friend named Jeff who worked in Diana's office complex.

"Omer," Jeff said. "Well, um, I just think you and Diana have to work things out because, ….well I just uh, Omer she's just kind of doing her own thing, but I'm uncomfortable saying anything more than that."

"Well I'm thinking about calling the highway patrol and putting out an APB," I said.

"No, don't do that. She's with a friend," Jeff admitted.

"Well, I know, she was supposed to be with a girlfriend," I said, referring to Renee.

"Omer, I think you can read between the lines. She's not with a woman," Jeff said.

With that disclosure, in a strange way, I felt comforted. At least it meant that Diana was not in danger.

I had a good idea of the man whom Diana was having an affair with, even though I had not suspected they would be together on this particular trip. As had been the case with Judy, Diana had decided to have an affair with a married man—and it was to cost him his marriage. I have never quite understood why both men and women frequently have affairs with married people, especially when there are so many attractive unmarried people around. Nevertheless, I've come to learn that this is more frequently the case than not.

So I called a few numbers where I thought the man could be reached, as he worked out of the same office as Diana, and I was told he'd be out of town for seven to ten days.

After hanging up the phone, I thought to myself, "Screw it, I should have them both pulled over. She's married; he's married. They'll be embarrassed." Then I came to my senses, realizing that that would be a childish move. Instead, I called Claremont College and asked them to call me when Diana had picked Jessica up. When the call from them came, I breathed a sigh of relief to know that each of them was safe.

When Diana finally arrived home with Jessica, after being out of contact for over ten days, I asked her if she was with the other man.

"No, I was just visiting friends," she said with a shrug.

"That's hard to believe," I answered. "And it's absolutely hard to believe that you did not call once while you were gone. It's clear that you want me to know what's happening and you want me to file for divorce."

"Well you're free to do that," she replied. It was not the first time she had reminded me of my "freedom" to end our marriage.

"I'm not going to do that," I said. "I'm going to see this thing through. I think you will come to your senses, and I hope you do. If you don't, *you* are free to file for divorce." I still loved Diana, and I had no interest in filing. Furthermore, I still did not believe in divorce. If Diana didn't want to be married to me, then she would have to be the one to ask to end the marriage.

To be clear, I wasn't avoiding divorce to be vindictive to Diana. I truly hoped—and even prayed—right up until the end that the affair would be a passing phase and that she would come back to me, realizing that she really did want to stay married and the grass was not greener on the other side of the fence after all. Diana had been quite young when we had married and I firmly believed that she, like all of us, had some wild oats to sow. Maybe this was all just a passing phase? Obviously, I was still dreaming.

That being said, with all of the insensitivities, exclusions and rejections, I definitely had reached the conclusion that my role had become only that of Daddy Warbucks—

that of a Sugar Daddy. The household expenses amounted to well over $20,000 per month, and I paid them all. In addition, I even paid Diana's income taxes and funded for her an IRA during our twenty-year marriage.

So long as I felt wanted, needed and loved, then this arrangement didn't really bother me all that much. But things were changing dramatically. By this time I had also raised or invested over a quarter of a million dollars in various business endeavors of Diana's and I had "loaned" her father tens of thousands of dollars, made payments on her parent's home, and given them trips to Australia, England, and elsewhere. I always did these things gladly and without questioning because Diana asked me to do so.

Diana had been my partner and my lover, but most of all, my best friend for a long time. Everything was somehow acceptable so long as this was the case. But it no longer was. I'm not sure why or how I lost my best friend, but I certainly had to take responsibility for whatever I did or didn't do.

Finally, I told Diana that I was going to open an office in Geneva, Switzerland. In response she just shrugged her shoulders and said, "OK." No emotion was reflected on her face or by her tone of voice. I did assure her that I would be back and forth between Geneva and Sacramento and that I would go out of my way to make sure I never missed a single event of Jessica's, however difficult it might be given my business obligations and commitments. I told her that I was going to give her every opportunity to sow her oats. In doing so, I hoped that she would take the time to decide what she wanted to do with the rest of her life. A decade younger than me, she was still young. And, though yet quite beautiful, inevitably the years catch up with everybody.

So I went ahead and opened an office in Geneva on Avenue de Champel above the old city. A typical Swiss business building, it was spic and span clean, but rather non-descript on the outside. The same was true as one entered the building and went down the hallways of any floor. However, inside my office, it was large and absolutely gorgeous. There I partnered with a Swiss citizen who had a long-term lease on the complex. The entire time I was in Geneva I went without a car. I didn't need a car. When I left Geneva, as I would do virtually every weekend and often during the work week, I would travel by plane or by train. If I needed a car I would either lease it or I would borrow it from friends.

Geneva itself is not a big city. People think it's a large city but that's because it's the home of the International Red Cross, the World Health Organization, the International

Labor Union, the European Headquarters of the United Nations, and multiple other international organizations and entities. It's truly an amazing place. And quite beautiful. On a daily basis Geneva arguably hosts as many significant and important international meetings as any place in the world and that includes New York City and London. Nevertheless, you can almost walk the entire city.

Although I could have located in any major money market or financial center in the world, I loved the ambience, beauty, and history of Geneva. Whenever I didn't walk wherever I wanted to go in Geneva, I would generally take the bus. Amazingly enough it is on the honor system. Virtually everyone buys a ticket, simply because it is the right thing to do but I have never seen anybody check a ticket in Geneva. Can you imagine that working in New York City?

Shortly after my arrival in Geneva, I began working on a project with and for the Mitsubishi Corporation. Mitsubishi had spent hundreds of millions of dollars working on a liquid crystal display (LCD) technology. They had built a large plant and begun to manufacture in the city of Kumamoto in the far west of Japan. However, they came to the realization that with the Japanese economy going south at the time, it was important that they refocus their energies and finances on their core industries of shipbuilding, automobile manufacturing, and so on, as opposed to fighting for market share in what was then a newly emerging industry.

My Swiss partner and I were contacted by the Tokyo branch of Citibank which was representing Mitsubishi in connection with this matter. Citibank in effect was serving as a "go-between" because Mitsubishi did not want the word to get out that they were selling the technology on which they had spent a great deal of money. Eventually the business was sold, though not to the French combine that we thought to be the best fit.

A hotel near my office, The Adriatica, was where I stayed in Geneva. While the hotel was not fancy, it was clean and quite close to my office. It provided me with everything I needed and was perfect for my purposes—all at a special rate that I negotiated.

All during this time, Diana continued to keep me off balance. I was scheduled to make a climb of Mont Blanc, the highest mountain in the Alps, with some others who came over from the States. Diana said that she would like to travel around Chamonix during and after my climb. So I rented a nice Chateau near Chamonix in Megeve for Diana and Jessica, very close to Mont Blanc. They had a great time sightseeing and recreating in the area. When I came down from the mountain, the three of us took off and did a number of things together. It was a great trip. Back in Geneva, I introduced Diana and Jessica to a number of my Geneva friends. One of the individuals that Jessica met there was a German humanitarian named Klaus Ruhenstroth. Klaus was from Munich, though he had come to Geneva to visit with me. Jessica and I were later to see him again at one of his offices in Cairo, Egypt.

As Jessica had just graduated from her elementary school, I suggested to Diana that we put her in the International School in Geneva. It is the most famous high school in the world. It would have given her an incredible opportunity to meet people that she would never otherwise have met and provided her with many wonderful opportunities upon graduation. I offered to rent a place for us within a block of the school so that it would not at all feel like she was away at boarding school. Nevertheless, Diana said that she did not want to be separated from her own friends in Sacramento, so at Diana's insistence we enrolled Jessica in an all-girls' private high school in Sacramento.

Diana seemed to have enjoyed our time together in the French and Swiss Alps, but when I returned to the States shortly thereafter things were much as they had been before. Bad. Oddly enough and out of the blue, in 2001 Diana came to me and said, "You know I have always wanted to go to India and I would also like to go on a safari in Africa. You have been to some of those places but I haven't."

I said, "OK, I will put it together and we will go." I still had hopes of saving the marriage. So early in the year we went to India, the Maldives, the Seychelle Islands, Zanzibar, Kenya, and Tanzania. It was a neat trip and Diana and I again seemed to enjoy each other greatly throughout the trip.

As we returned home, I was once again seemingly secure in the knowledge that our marriage had at last survived the various problems that had been developing and I was greatly relieved. I was also again wrong in my thought process. In fact, as soon as we returned, Diana reverted to her prior conduct. I finally had to conclude that Diana had simply wanted to take one last fling to parts of the world she had not yet visited and had taken this opportunity to do so.

Within a day of returning home, the phone began to ring—constantly. It would ring several times a day and whenever Jessica or I answered, the caller would quickly and automatically hang up. Ultimately I found out that it was Diana's lover so when she answered the phone this did not happen.

Finally I was able to trace the call and it was a man whom I already knew to be her lover. Thereafter, when she came in to the house and I had received a "hang-up call" I would simply tell her, "You got a call from Rick." She would immediately go out to her car and use her cell phone. I never said anything to Jessica about what I'd learned but I again confronted Diana: "You know, it's so transparent. Why do you keep denying what is obvious? I thought the trip we just took together might have changed things, but clearly I was mistaken. You are completely out of integrity both with me and with your friends whom you mislead on a daily basis. So, if it be your wish, I will keep my office open in Geneva, but still come back every month to pay bills and to be sure not to miss any of Jessica's events. I will do my best to continue to give her my moral, as well as financial, support even when I'm away. Again, you are going to have all the freedom you want. But as I have already told you, you are making a big mistake. You are having an affair with a married man. It is going to cost him his marriage and if you wish it is going to cost you your marriage. You make up your own mind. I still want to save this marriage and I am still willing to see you through this a while longer."

So at least once a month and often several times a month, I continued to return from Geneva to Sacramento to attend events for Jessica and to take care of whatever needed to be taken care of in and around the Carmichael home. I was still willing to continue to endure the ongoing humiliation and hurt as long as possible. Strangely, and as I have said before, Diana and I were always civil to teach other, living under the same roof and sleeping in the same bed. But, nevertheless, she was also still doing her own thing and I had no idea what she would eventually do.

Although the majority of places I visited during the time I had an office in Geneva were visited for business purposes, I also took the opportunity to do sightseeing and exploration in various countries if I had time to do it. Because of connections and knowledge I was acquiring overseas, I actually shipped one of my cars in America from Oakland, California to Vladivostok, Russia where I sold a seven year old Cadillac, though in wonderful condition, for more than three times what I would have gotten for it in the United States. Friends of mine in the States thought I was crazy to containerize a Cadillac and send it to Russia for sale but I knew what I was doing and it worked out as planned.

On those rare weekends where I was not travelling elsewhere in Europe, Asia, or Africa, and not returning to the States, I would generally go to Ireland. I found a place in County Waterford near Dunmore East. It was not far from the mouth of the River Suir and on the grounds of a noted mansion where horse stables had been converted to apartments. I was renting one of the apartments whenever it was available. County Waterford is next to County Wexford where my good friends, the Codd's, lived in a village called Clearystown. There they raised and trained race horses, including one in which I had a 50% interest. Good bloodline, but a bust on the track.

49

The Snake Pit

"What you spend your life building, someone may destroy overnight.
Build anyway."
— Mother Teresa

Our marriage, such as it was, continued to stumble along. As the year 2000 rolled around, I returned to Carmichael from Geneva on one of my monthly trips to see Jessica and to pay the household expenses and bills. Again, the phone at the house was ringing constantly. However, this time the callers were generally creditors of Diana's!

Having been born in the latter part of the depression years, I had made a lifelong habit of paying for everything I bought in full at the time of purchase. That has even been true of every single car I have ever purchased including the several I purchased for Diana over the years. Throughout my life, if I couldn't afford something, I simply didn't buy it. Though I had occasionally used a credit card to make certain purchases such as airline tickets and the like, without a single exception the balance was paid off in full at the end of each month.

Therefore, I was truly stunned to learn of companies demanding payment for debts that Diana had incurred. There was no reason for her to incur any debt.

I didn't recognize by name any of the people calling or the companies they represented. One was even a home finance company. I was panicked that a second mortgage might have been placed against the home. But it had not. Diana said that the person she dealt with in connection with that loan simply told her that they would make an exception in her case and give her an unsecured loan—and a big one at that. Strange.

I began to add up the debts she had incurred and it appeared to be in the hundreds of thousands of dollars. I demanded to know from her what was going on. "Diana, you make about $150,000 a year working part-time. For twenty-five years you have led virtually an expense free life. I even pay your income taxes. Why are you borrowing money and incurring debt?"

"Why shouldn't I take advantage of opportunities when they are offered to me?"

"But these aren't gifts. These people are demanding payment and they have a right to expect repayment from you. What have you done with all of this money?"

"Mainly I've invested it."

"In what?"

"I don't have to answer that. It's my business. Besides, I have spoken to a bankruptcy attorney and I can get all of this eliminated and it will only cost about $3,000."

I was pissed, but at Diana's request I went to see the bankruptcy attorney and he confirmed that for approximately $3,000 and after a "short" meeting with the creditors, all of Diana's debts could be discharged. He added that since California is a community property state and since Diana and I were still legally married, I was also liable for all of her debts and would have to be named and so declared on the Petition. I knew that to be true. So in the year 2000, a Petition was filed in Bankruptcy Court "In Re D.W. Rains, et al." This turned out to be easily the worst non-personal decision I ever made in my life. The "short" creditors meeting ended up going off and on for over four months—and the entire proceeding lasted for seven years!

I tried without success to have the petition withdrawn, but the court would not allow it. I was required to produce literally thousands upon thousands of documents including every check I had written for many years into the past, along with all other banking account information, tax returns, and multiple other items.

Because our attorney said that we should list on the Petition everyone, contingent or otherwise, who at anytime in the past made a claim or who had ever had a potential claim against either of us, we did so. Among those listed was a long-ago deceased attorney who had represented us on a contingent fee case in an unsuccessful suit he had brought on our behalf approximately seventeen years before. Little did we know that both the deceased attorney and his widow were good friends of the Bankruptcy Judge.

In addition, the decedent's estate was represented by an attorney who was to go to work for the Judge immediately after our matter was completed some seven years later!

After suffering my brain aneurysm and apparently less than an hour before my brain surgery, while totally incompetent, Diana and the bankruptcy trustee had me sign a document that ostensibly allowed them to eventually penetrate my otherwise ERISA qualified and totally protected retirement fund that I had established in 1972, long before my marriage to Diana. From this "protected" fund alone, the Judge allowed the removal of $312,500.

Because I was so near death at the time they had me sign the document, they did not know what to do with the piece of paper. The following year, probably after discussing the matter with the conflicted Judge, the bankruptcy trustee actually filed a motion to enforce the "Agreement." As part of their motion, both the Trustee and Diana filed affidavits in which the stroke and aneurysm were not even mentioned.

The Judge in the case, Judge Klein, had a huge conflict of interest, as well. The widow of Mel CoBen, the long since deceased attorney and friend of the Judge, wrongfully claimed monies were due CoBen's estate. Rejecting irrefutable expert evidence to the contrary, the Judge found that the affidavit of Diana and of the bankruptcy trustee were "persuasive" because they were present when I affixed my signature to the document waiving my rights to my otherwise protected assets.

Unfortunately, in the Federal Court System, Federal judges are like "Gods." You can't challenge them and you can't dismiss them. On occasion, one finds oneself in an impossible position and this was such an occasion. Whatever order the Trustee and the trustee's attorney advanced, Klein signed it. It was an absolute charade. Doctors and other experts provided evidence to the Bankruptcy Court that I was totally incapable of conducting any business or understanding anything I was doing at the time that this document was placed in front of me. Nevertheless the Judge said that he would not accept the irrefutable medical declarations because the doctors were not physically present when the document was put in front of me.

What happened to the $312,500 I don't know. I don't know because, although I was to receive a copy of the distribution order, I never received it. I requested a copy from the bankruptcy trustee, from the bankruptcy trustee's attorney, from Diana's attorney, from CoBen's attorney, but did not receive a copy from anyone.

Finally, I went to the Federal Courthouse in Sacramento and asked for a copy from the file. The court clerk looked and looked and looked and finally said, "It's strange, but that document is missing from the file." It is clear that someone with the power to do so removed that document or had it sealed. My strong suspicion is that it would evidence that the entire money collected by the trustee was distributed to the Trustee himself, to his attorney, to CoBen's widow, and possibly even to Diana for her "cooperation." I know for certain that none of this money went to pay off any of Diana's creditors because they had all previously been paid off—by me.

A bankruptcy attorney once told me that when a "porker" ends up in bankruptcy court, the various attorneys get together and decide how the porker will be sliced up. I fear that's what happened in my case. Bankruptcy court is indeed a snake pit designed primarily to enrich the various attorneys and trustees involved. It is to be avoided at all costs.

At the end of the day, the bankruptcy nightmare had cost me well over $1,000,000 in addition to the $312,500 taken from my retirement account. This was to retire all of the real and phantom creditors, as well as our own attorney's fees.

Eventually I retired the debts owing to every one of Diana's creditors. Of greater significance is that I had to a large degree lost approximately seven years of my life because that's how long this entire process took. Diana never lifted a finger.

So Diana was at long last a true "Happy Camper" because she was free and clear of all debt, not having ever to account for what she had done with the money that she had borrowed from various companies or the debt she had incurred and not herself ever putting up a single dollar for the retirement of any of those debts. What a nightmare!

I never once over the entire seven year period heard the bankruptcy attorney or the trustee talk about the need to protect any creditor. All of the debt that I had retired of Diana's creditors I did on my own, separate and apart from the bankruptcy trustee and/ or his attorney. My advice to anyone—when it comes to Bankruptcy Court, don't go there —ever.

In discussions with Diana she had already told me that when she first saw me the day the document was signed she knew that I was near death. When I asked her why she had signed the affidavit she signed she simply stated, "We thought it important that we got your signature in the event you died." A cruel admission, but honest, I guess.

50

Tragedies in the 21st Century

"All that live must die, passing through nature to eternity."
— William Shakespeare

The year 2001 marked the opening of the new millennium. As things turned out it would also be the first two years of a string of personal tragedies. My only sibling, my brother Roy, had developed a very lethal, virulent, and almost always fatal form of cancer known as Merkel Cell Carcinoma. I was in Geneva when Roy called to tell me about his cancerous condition. I immediately rushed back to California flying directly into San Diego and driving to his home in Encinitas just north of San Diego. Before I left Geneva and each time I stopped on the way over I did research online. I reached full panic mode when I discovered the life span for one with this condition was almost invariably less than six months after detection. I also found that it is almost always caused by exposure to nuclear radiation. Roy, having been professional Navy, had been at Bikini Atoll when they tested the first hydrogen bomb. He had volunteered to be the only person topside on his ship in order to take water and air samples. He had no protective gear. All of the scientists and high ranking officers were sealed well below deck.

Little was known about the effects of radiation at the time and I found out that one of the reasons for exposing military personnel was to learn the effects. The ship he was on at the time was a destroyer escort. Roy was later to serve as the Chief Sonar man on a nuclear fast attack submarine and during the Cold War period was sometimes at sea, underwater, for months at a time.

After speaking with Roy, I decided to spend the next four days with him. He was seeing an oncologist in Encinitas, but the treatment was simply traditional chemotherapy and ironically radiation. So I began to phone doctors and healthcare centers all over the world. It was a benefit to me having a wide range of friends and associates who could help and guide me in this endeavor.

Almost from the time of the initial treatment, Roy was not reacting well to the radiation. He was of very fair complexion and during most of his life had red hair. The hair had turned grey over the last few years but his skin was so fair that it would erupt after radiation treatments. As a result, they had to periodically discontinue the radiation treatments.

After several more days of research and telephone discussions, I flew to Montreaux, Switzerland and from there on to London. I visited renowned medical centers hoping to find somebody with expertise with this virulent and seemingly incurable form of cancer.

In Europe, I met with some wonderful physicians and scientists but was not given any cause for optimism. From London, I flew to Mexico where a lot of experimentation was being done with alternative forms of treatment. Most of the doctors with whom I met in Mexico were actually American trained physicians who couldn't practice or experiment in the United States because of FDA restrictions. In Mexico, the centers I visited were quite state of the art and surprisingly well staffed. It's the kind of place that my friend, Steve McQueen, went to in his own final and desperate days.

I next traveled to Houston to visit the M.D. Anderson Cancer Center, a medical arm of the University of Texas. M.D. Anderson is today probably the most renowned cancer center in the United States. Nevertheless, once again, I was not given much reason for hope. However, a scientist at M.D. Anderson did refer me to a lady who represented herself (falsely as it eventually turned out) to be on the faculty of Columbia University in New York City. He said that by phone she had told him that she was working with a group doing non-conventional research on different types of cancers and that I might want to investigate the possibility that they were on to something. I immediately flew to New York City and met with her.

The lady with whom I met in NYC was beginning to realize that the incidence of cancer in South and South East Asia was dramatically lower than the incidence in North America. Clearly, this was not due to biology or genetics. If those same people came to the United States, their incidence of cancer shot up and paralleled the incidence in Caucasians, African Americans, Hispanics and other groups in America. So she had concluded that it must be something that Americans are ingesting and something beyond genetics. Therefore, she said that she had begun to experiment with products that were being ingested in certain parts of Asia on a regular basis. Two that stood out were fermented soy and curcumin, the latter being the active ingredient in turmeric. Research scientists at M.D. Anderson and elsewhere were beginning to draw the same conclusion. Thereafter, she began to send Roy products and formulas on which she was working. But it was too late, and my brother died shortly thereafter.

––––––––––

Roy's situation probably precipitated another personal tragedy. My mother was an angel. Somehow she had endured my father during sixty-six years of marriage. How she did it is beyond me but through thick and thin her two sons always came first. Ironically, that was one of the problems because I always sensed that my father was jealous of the attention that she gave Roy and me. But she many times had told me how seriously she took her wedding vows and, thus, never felt that the situation was so bad that divorce was an option. Had Dad even physically abused her, it might have been different. To his credit, however, there was never a single incident of physical abuse of which I was ever aware during their long marriage of sixty-six years.

In all the time we were apart, with but a limited number of exceptions when no telephone service was available, I unfailingly called my mother each and every Sunday. I knew that this was very important to her. As the Christmas season approached in 2001, my mother, though eighty-nine, was in remarkably good health. I always enquired about her health when I called her on Sunday and her answer was always the same: "My left knee is hurting me."

I would only half jokingly say, "So is mine, as well as my left shoulder, my neck, my back and often numerous other maladies, injuries, hurts, and pains." Then we would both laugh.

Roy had intentionally not mentioned his condition to Mom or Dad. He and I discussed this several times, both in person and by phone. He did not want to say anything because he feared that it would literally kill mother. I told him that this was very unfair; that it was wrong not to tell ones parents. They had a right to know. Ultimately, Roy agreed.

I asked Mom and Dad to join Diana, Jessica, and me in Encinitas to celebrate Christmas together with Roy and his family in 2001. Jessica and I had gone down early to pick up Mom and Dad at their home in Huntington Beach and proceeded to drive them south to Encinitas, just north of San Diego. Diana flew down a few days later.

On December 28, Roy and I sat down with Mom and Dad and told them of Roy's condition. Their initial reaction was one of stunned silence. We papered over the severity of the situation and did not mention that the condition was in all likelihood fatal. Without uttering a word, tears began to flow down mother's cheeks. That night, Jessica and I took Mom and Dad back to their home in Huntington Beach where we also spent the night. The last words that my mother uttered that night were, "I can't stand the thought of one of my boys dying before me."

The following morning Jessica and I arose early and proceeded north by car intending to stop in San Luis Obispo, California to say hello to my friend Jack O'Connell and his family. When we arrived at the O'Connell home in San Luis Obispo, Jack's wife, Doree, told me that it was urgent that I call my parent's home in Huntington Beach. I did so and, to my surprise, Roy answered the phone. He told me that mother was dead. I was grief stricken and at a loss for words. Jessica and I jumped in the car and we headed south. I think I broke every speed limit along the way.

Arriving in Huntington Beach, I found Roy and his wife sitting with Dad. Mother had already been taken away. Dad was in a state of shock.

When I asked Roy what had happened, he told me that from all appearances mother had just willed herself to death. It appeared that no pills had been taken and nothing was amiss. It was not a suicide.

The Bible was lying next to mother in bed when she died. She had scored with a yellow marker Isaiah, Chapter 40, verses 7-8: "The grass withereth, the flower fadeth, because the spirit of the Lord bloweth upon it. Surely people are like grass; but the word of God shall stand forever."

In speaking to the physicians who had examined mother's body, they confirmed that mother had simply died of what they termed "a broken heart." They confirmed that it was not a suicide in any conventional sense of the word. However, she had simply willed herself to death.

My mother was a beautiful woman and she had always taken great pride in her appearance. She had lived a life by the mantra that "cleanliness is next to Godliness." She had left a box with the clothes in which she wished to be buried, all neatly folded. In the box was a handwritten note that when buried she would like to have socks placed on her feet because her feet were always cold.

December 29, 2001 was the date of mother's death. A service was held for her on Friday January 4, 2002 and she was buried in the Garden of Meditation at Westminster Memorial Park not far from my parent's home. The large chapel where service was held before the burial was full of people. I don't think my mother had an enemy in the world. The casket was open and mother looked absolutely beautiful. Clothed as she wanted to be clothed. Socks were on her feet.

To my surprise, Judy showed up at mother's funeral although thirty years had elapsed since they had last seen each other. I was quite surprised to see her but I gave her a hug and thanked her for coming. After the funeral, Judy spent the rest of the day visiting with Diana. I was far too busy to think much about it at the time.

Unlike mother, my father was not in good health. He had a variety of maladies. He had had operations for cataracts, detached retinas, and late in life had developed glaucoma. His balance was poor and he had developed diabetes which had led to severe gout.

I moved in with him for a short time in Huntington Beach where I proceeded to pay many months of back bills and take him to various medical appointments, especially the ophthalmological appointments which were critical due to the condition of his glaucoma. In the meantime, Roy came back to Huntington Beach from Encinitas and, given his condition, he helped to the best of his ability. We took Dad to see his attorney in Orange County to make sure that all of his affairs were in order.

Although Dad was failing badly from a physical standpoint, he still had all of his faculties. He understood everything that was said and was able to lucidly reply to questions. We were fortunate in that Dad was able to provide his attorney with virtually all information that the attorney would need once he did pass on.

Next, Roy and I had to decide what to do about Dad. Although he was insistent that he could stay alone in his house, that was ridiculous. He couldn't see and thus couldn't drive. In fact, grief-stricken and frail as he was, he was incapable of living alone and would require care twenty-four hours per day. As I had to return to Geneva to close my European office, Roy's wife, June, prevailed upon us to move Dad into an assisted care facility in Encinitas only a few blocks from their home. June, in absolute good faith, felt that she and her daughter and grandchildren would be able to visit Dad on a regular basis. Given Roy's own personal medical problem, I was reluctant to do this but ultimately I agreed.

This arrangement worked out OK for a few months, but ultimately Roy's own condition began to deteriorate. He died in early August. I had been back and forth between Encinitas, Sacramento, Huntington Beach, and Lake Tahoe where I had taken an apartment. When I learned that the end was near for Roy I flew into San Diego but arrived at my brother's home twenty minutes after he died.

We had a memorial service for him on August 5, 2002 with full military honors. It was very moving. He was interred at a beautiful site at Point Loma overlooking the Pacific Ocean. Again, Judy showed up. Other than obligatory expressions of sympathy to other members of the family, she again spent the entire time talking to Diana.

51

Divorce Again!

"God, grant me the serenity to accept the things I cannot change....
The courage to change the things I can... and the wisdom to know the difference."
— St. Francis of Assisi

Jessica, Diana, and I returned to Sacramento from San Diego shortly after the memorial service for my brother. Knowing that divorce was increasingly likely at some point in the future, I had previously, though only briefly, spoken to a divorce attorney. Although I had not retained him, he did inform me that he would accept service on my behalf in the event Diana did at some point decide to file for divorce. I gave Diana all of the attorney's particulars, including his name, his office number, his cell number, his address, his email, his fax number, etc. Everything. I informed Diana that if she ever did decide to file for divorce that it was only necessary that her attorney contact the attorney with whom I had spoken.

The morning after my brother's service, I had an important 8:00 am breakfast meeting with associates and potential clients in Sacramento itself. When I arose the following morning, I went in to take my morning shower. When I got out Diana began to ask me all types of questions like, "Where are you going this morning?" "Who will you be meeting with?" "Is your meeting at an office or elsewhere?" At this stage of our lives this was rather unusual but I didn't give it any more thought and I told her of the planned breakfast meeting with business associates and clients.

When I got to the restaurant I spotted one of my associates so I went to join him in a booth. I saw only one other person in the restaurant. He was seated in a booth across the room. I joined my friend and sat down. Soon the others we were expecting also arrived.

We ordered our food and began to talk business. At that time, the man seated across the room got up and approached our table. He looked at me and said, "Good morning Mr. Rains." I didn't recognize him but replied, "Yes."

He shook his head as if in dismay. "I got to tell you. Sometimes the work I do is really shitty. And I don't understand people. I have divorce papers to serve on you and I am doing so at this time. The orders I had were to wait until you were in the presence of your entire group and then to serve the papers."

My jaw dropped. I was truly embarrassed. Diana or her attorney had chosen this diabolical method to humiliate me. I didn't get it. There was no bitterness on my part, only hurt and deep confusion. There had been stability in our relationship even with our separation and given the fact that divorce was probably on the horizon. We were still living together, sleeping together. I was still paying all the bills. We had been together for over twenty-five years. What would possess her to do this? And all of this the very morning after my brother's memorial service.

I didn't blame the process server. He was just doing a job and was clearly embarrassed about the way in which he had been told to do it. I tried all day to reach Diana by phone but without success. Finally I left her a note and drove to Lake Tahoe where I holed up in my rented apartment. The pressures of all that was happening (my mother's death, my father's condition, my brother's death) and now this, were all building up and I felt like a teakettle about to start screaming. I waited until the very last day to file an Answer to Diana's Divorce Complaint but on September 6th I drove from Lake Tahoe to Sacramento and did file my Answer. I still had not officially retained counsel and was at the time representing myself.

Diana and I had a meeting—very businesslike in nature. I presented her with a very generous settlement offer. She agreed that it was generous, but said that she had to discuss it with her attorney. However, there was no further response and she did nothing further for years until eventually forced to do so by the court.

––––––––––

Before I could get on with my life I still had to conclude both the bankruptcy proceedings and the dissolution of marriage proceedings. Regarding the divorce proceedings, Diana was still not cooperating and was refusing to file any documents with the court whatsoever. This included a Declaration of Income and a Schedule of

Assets and Debts as required by California law. She just wouldn't do it. I actually knew why. The reason was that she didn't want to reveal the extent of her holdings, some of which came from her earnings over the years and some from joint accounts that she had drained.

Diana also knew that I would not evict her from the Orange Hill Lane house in Carmichael so long as Jessica lived there. So Diana did not pay any rent or contribute to any mortgage payment even after she was ordered to do so by the court shortly after she filed the Dissolution of Marriage Petition. Then she started selling off or giving away many of my possessions, including a car, paintings, artifacts and other things—all without my authorization. Eventually the court ordered her to stop dissipating assets that were on the premises.

This included paintings that had been gifted to me by my friend, Evel Knievel. Again, for six years after Diana filed for divorce, she failed and refused to file any further documents, including most specifically the "Disclosure of Assets Statement." She was not about to make any mortgage, rent, tax or any other household related payment so long as she could avoid it and, more significantly, she was terrified of having to reveal both her very substantial onshore and offshore assets.

However, desperate after six years of making requests of Diana and her various attorneys and wanting to get on with my life, in late 2006 I sought and received a Court order that she comply, however belatedly, with the disclosure requirements of California law. Along with the order, she was sanctioned for refusing and failing to comply with law over the six-year period.

In addition, the Court ordered her to provide her 2005 income tax return. In her disclosure statement, she admitted to a net asset worth of $908,000. However, that was clearly a gross understatement and that between onshore and offshore investments and holdings (most of it being held offshore) it was evident that her net asset worth in fact exceeded $2,000,000. Her individual income for the last five years that I paid her income tax ranged from a low of $142,403 to a high of $205,257 per year.

Diana definitely did not want to disclose in open court where she had obtained such sums of money and such assets (hidden from the bankruptcy trustee). This also made her very amenable to talk settlement—quickly. The settlement agreement was virtually identical to the one I had offered her years before just shortly after she had first filed her divorce papers. In short, being debt free and apparently possessed of over $2,000,000 in assets, not to mention a lot more that she received by virtue of the settlement agreement, she was and is set for life. Knowing Diana, however, this is not something she would ever voluntarily admit. The lifelong pretension of a dearth of assets is simply too genetically ingrained.

52

A House of Cards

"We no longer make things; now we make things up."
— Arianna Huffington

By this time I had become very conversant with banking procedures and what went on in the "back rooms" of banks on the continent as well as in America. I was becoming alarmed at the way in which larger banks were carrying debt obligations "off balance sheet." Because of this it was becoming increasingly obvious that large international financial institutions, including those in the United States, were not as strong as appeared to be the case on the surface.

In the States, major institutions led by Citibank, which wanted to acquire Traveler's Insurance Company, lobbied Congress for a repeal of the Glass-Steagall Act which had been passed as part of the New Deal legislation in the 1930s during the Great Depression. The repeal of this act led to merger mania amongst different types of financial institutions that had historically been separated, at least in the United States. With that repeal strange and exotic types of financial instruments such as swaps and credit derivatives began to be traded. In America, historically an industrial colossus, we were no longer making things. Rather, we were making things up. A house of cards using fiat commodities of exchange were being developed in all sorts of weird ways. I did not see how this could sustain itself and from a public policy standpoint it could turn into a catastrophe. Several years later, that's exactly what happened.[3]

---

3   To learn more about "swaps," "credit derivatives," and other exotic financial instruments that in large measure led directly to the current recessionary meltdown, visit www.backtothesummit.com

So I began to spend more and more time back in the States where I had been working with a woman named Greta Marshall. I first met Greta near the end of my tenure in the California Senate. Greta was the Executive Director and Asset Manager of CalPERS, the world's largest public pension fund. She retired to Lake Tahoe, less than a two-hour drive from my home in Carmichael on the outskirts of Sacramento. As I became concerned about the way in which large banks were creating what I called "fiat money," money literally being created out of thin air, I began to have extensive discussions with Greta. To maintain my involvement in international finance but to avoid the more exotic and casino-like environment that was emerging, Greta and I began to discuss a more traditional approach where we could provide a service and at the same time help to finance projects in the lesser developed world.

By this time, I was quite familiar with the various bourses (stock exchanges) in London, Frankfurt, Paris, Milan, Zurich, and other money market centers in Europe. I was also familiar by this time with the International Financial Services Center that the European Union had established in Dublin. So, in concert with Greta and a few others that we got interested in the project, we began to develop a venture capital fund which we were going to start and, in all probability, run out of Dublin. In this regard, I also went to New York City to meet with representatives of the Federal Reserve of the United States. We began to have meetings in New York, California, and elsewhere.

Although the program in a much more modest way eventually came to fruition it was not as robust as many of us had anticipated because of the unexpected death of some of our principals. Not only that, but one problem after another was making the program far too complex, too expensive, and too burdensome as we were dealing with many different governments and institutional bureaucracies.

The death that was of the greatest significance was that of Greta herself. She had suffered a form of cancer about ten years before but now thought that she was in complete remission. But soon it was to come back with a vengeance. Nobody knew how bad her cancer was going to be. She was a dear friend to all, and when visiting Lake Tahoe many would stay at her large home which was known as "The Marshall Hotel."

At first, Greta thought that she could beat the cancer once again so we continued to do planning. I came up with the idea of calling the program "The Marshall Plan" which, for obvious reasons, was a catchy title. The idea was that we would invest where others would not dare to go. We intended to fund very unusual projects in the lesser developed world. Although we hoped to go on an exchange, that was not an imperative. I did draft multiple documents to comply with exchange rules, whether it was the Irish Stock Exchange, the London Stock Exchange or a new one that was opening in the Channel Islands between England and France.

However, as it turned out, Greta's health took a turn for the worse. She absolutely dreaded going through chemotherapy and radiation again, something she had endured ten years beforehand.

On October 10, 2000, the "Lake Tahoe Marathon" was held. I told Greta that I was going to participate. Many other friends of Greta's also entered. Greta herself obviously couldn't run but we encouraged her to do a portion of it. We told her to take her time. She walked in her weakened condition the last 1,000 meters. When I got within about 100 feet from the finish line I sat down on the grass and waited for Greta. Many others did the same. When Greta appeared, the group of us, arms locked, crossed the finish line together. It was great. And then we took her out to lunch. It meant so much to her that we had all crossed the finish line together. She said, "I'm so grateful for the wonderful friends I have." Her friends couldn't help but love and respect Greta. I think it was Greta's last time outdoors as she died shortly thereafter.

53

Aftermath of an Aneurysm and Stroke

"The longer I live, the more I realize the importance of attitude on life."
— Charles Swindoll

Shortly after Diana filed for divorce and sometime during the night of September 20, 2002 I suffered the ruptured brain aneurysm and associated hemorrhagic stroke that has been chronicled in this book. The following day, September 21, I did not show up for a meeting with my accountant in Sacramento. This was not like me. That day a lady came to my house to feed my dog. I told her I wasn't feeling well. I was completely disheveled. I complained to her about having a horrible headache. The next day, September 22, I had intended to attend my grandson's birthday in Marin County. Again, I failed to show up. Highly unusual for me. My daughter, Kelly, called to see what was wrong. I told her that I was not feeling well and had a raging headache.

On Monday, September 23, a divorce conference was to be held with Diana, her attorney and the bankruptcy attorney. Again, I did not show up until after I received a telephone call from Diana demanding that I appear since people were waiting. Again, I have no memory of this whatsoever, but apparently I told her I would get dressed and travel to the office address she gave me. According to witnesses, when I showed up at the offices my face was flushed and I was dragging my right leg. I couldn't understand basic questions asked of me. A document was placed in front of me and I was told to sign it. Apparently, I did.

After my signature was obtained on the document in question, I was taken to the hospital in critical condition. I required an immediate 7½ hour brain operation and was in critical condition in intensive care for over a month.

Sometime later, and after I had been transported to my home in Carmichael and while I was still confined to bed, out of the blue I received a phone call from a man in Orange County, California wanting to buy my parent's home. How he had obtained my name and phone number I wasn't sure, but I agreed to the terms and conditions contingent upon my father's approval.

I realized that one way or the other I had to make a recovery if I was to take care of my youngest daughter's future and to do whatever I could to provide assistance for my father during the latter part of his life.

When I was finally able to return to Lake Tahoe, I had additional pressure placed on me when I received a telephone call from my sister-in-law who informed me that her mother was ill in Hawaii and that she would have to go there to take care of her mother. I fully understood. However, one of my nieces who lived in my brother and sister-in-law's home with her own children only a few blocks from where my father was staying in the assisted care facility had not visited him a single time. Another niece who lived close by the facility had also not visited him. Yet another niece who lived in Utah visited the family home in Encinitas and also failed to go see her grandfather. Only my nephew, also an out of State resident, went to see him when he visited the family home. The manager and employees of the old age home in Encinitas where my father was staying were increasingly concerned about his welfare and said that my father was very depressed as he had not received a single visitor with the exception of the one visit by my nephew.

So, within a one-year period, I had lost both my mother and my brother. My wife of twenty-five years had filed for divorce. My father was ailing and fading fast, and he needed my help. And, to top it off, I had suffered a ruptured brain aneurysm and an associated hemorrhagic stroke. Nevertheless, it was obvious that I had to push even harder because there was no one else to carry on.

Thank God, I still had my best friend, Spartacus.

54

Spartacus

*"The one absolutely unselfish friend a man can have; the one that
never deserts him; the one that never proves ungrateful or treacherous…
is his dog. When all other friends desert, he remains."*
– Senator George Vest

I have had dogs most of my life, but none that have come close to matching my dog, Spartacus, when it comes to intelligence, gentleness, emotional depth, and loyalty.

Spartacus was born March 17, 2001. March 17 is also St. Patrick's Day so throughout his life we have had dual celebrations—both birthday and St. Patrick's Day parties on March 17. Spartacus is a Weimaraner with an incredible bloodline. He was one of a litter of six and a gift from a business associate of mine. I was given the pick of the litter. I chose well.

Although the gentlest dog ever, Spartacus is also very well muscled. This results in part due to the fact that he and I shortly after his birth began to take daily hikes and climbs in the Sierra Nevada Mountains around Lake Tahoe.

I was especially blessed that all during the time of my hospitalization and thereafter when I was initially forced to remain in Carmichael, Spartacus had another home—that of my friend George and his significant other.

I don't believe I've ever met a finer human being or had a finer or more trustworthy friend than George Galante. In saying that I'm sure that I simply echo the feelings of literally hundreds of others whom George has helped over his lifetime.

When I returned to Tahoe, Spartacus was deliriously happy to see me as I was to see him. He may be the largest Weimaraner in the world. He had already grown to full size—105 pounds of solid muscle and with the thickest chest you will ever see on a dog. He is quite a specimen. However, he did still have a lot of puppiness in him.

There was a store in Incline Village that was "new agey." They advertised that they had a person who could teach you to communicate better with your dog. I met the psychic. We went into a backroom and sat at a card table that was covered by a long white tablecloth. She began by asking me many questions about the dog and I answered her questions. Then she closed her eyes like she was in a séance. Pretty soon she opened her eyes and said, "We are very fortunate."

"Why?"

"Spartacus speaks English."

"Oh?"

"He calls you Daddy."

By this time I am thinking, "How hokey is this?" She then said, "Spartacus is frustrated with you because you won't let him put his paws up on the car console."

I said, "Yeah, I guess I knew that since I just told you that."

It gets nuttier and funnier. During one of these "séances," Spartacus went under the table while she was sitting in her trance-like state and as he stood up he raised the table off the floor and started walking across the room. When her eyes blinked open she saw the table levitating across the room. She looked like she was witnessing a mystical movement. What a hoot! I laughed so hard that I wasn't even irritated over the $50 that I had wasted.

What is most important though about the role Spartacus played during this crucial period of my life is that through thick and thin, he was always with me as I struggled to regain the full use of my body. He understood that something bad had happened to me, but he didn't care. He would give me comfort and love and do whatever he could to help me recover and, thus, return to my former self. I owe him a lot. Senator Vest was right. A dog is the one unselfish friend a person can have—one that never deserts him and is unfailingly loyal. To this day, Spartacus and I are together taking on challenges together. He was, is, and will always be my best friend.

55

Death of a Father

"People are often unreasonable, illogical and self-centered. Forgive them anyway."
— Mother Teresa

By the summer of 2003, I realized that I had to do something about my father's situation. I had had a strange and strained relationship with my father throughout my life. As indicated, my grandpa Cochran had a far greater influence on my life than did my father with whom I was never very close. Nevertheless, I knew it was my responsibility to take care of him as soon as my health permitted. This became a matter of increasing concern when my sister-in-law moved back to Hawaii to take care of her mother. My nieces, though close by, did not visit their grandfather at all. Because of my own health challenges and being over 500 miles away, I also had been unable to visit him.

From the facility in which he was housed, I learned that my father was becoming severely depressed. So in mid-August I went to Reno and rented a huge mobile home with a bed and other amenities arranged to transport an ailing person. I drove to Carmichael where I picked up Jessica and then drove several hundred miles further south to Encinitas.

We picked up my father at 6:00 am on August 20, 2003. The trip back was really frightening because of a severe case of hiccups that I had even before picking him up. This may sound like a minor thing, but it was not. The bout was definitely the worst case of hiccups I have ever had. I had them nonstop for over eighteen hours. And this while I'm still in recovery mode from my aneurysm and stroke.

The mobile home unit I was driving, thirty feet long, was designed to provide maximum comfort for my father who was bedridden. He was in the bed and was secured at all times. I was driving and Jessica was in the passenger seat up front. It is difficult to drive this kind of vehicle under any circumstance but especially in the congested metropolitan areas of California. I tried everything under the sun to get rid of my hiccups. I drank gallons of water. I tried every remedy I had ever heard of but nothing would stop them.

When I finally dropped Jessica off in Carmichael I still had ninety miles to go. When I got to the assisted living community which was attached to a hospital in Truckee, California, it was about 2:00 am. After taking care of my father, the attending physician also hospitalized me for the night. I was given several injections and ultimately managed to get the hiccups under control but did not leave the hospital until the following day. I thank God that I didn't harm Jessica, my father, or anyone else on the road during that terrible journey north.

Thereafter, I made an effort to visit my father every day. During the waning days of his life I felt a powerful obligation to do all I could to make sure that he sensed love in my heart. Whatever our lifelong differences, he was my father and it was critical that he knew that someone really cared for him because there was no one else there to do it.

I was with him on October 9 for several hours before and when he passed away. By that time, he was no longer verbally responding but I did talk to him and I think he was both hearing and understanding me. I think he died as peacefully as was possible under the circumstances.

I made arrangements to have Dad's body taken to Huntington Beach where, on October 15, he was buried next to my mother. Whatever his shortcomings as a husband he and my mother had been married for sixty-six years—a rarity in today's world.

His death brought home the importance of living in the now, of enjoying each day and appreciating the loved ones that surround each of us. My father's death didn't impact me as strongly as did my mother's. In part this was no doubt due to the fact that I was closer to my mother than to my father, but it was also in part due to the fact that it was no great shock when my father passed on as he had been growing increasingly weak since the death of my mother.

In any event, at times like this, one inevitably ponders the mysteries of life and of life beyond the grave. I have never claimed to have all of the answers. All I knew for certain was that, at least as far as this life was concerned, in very short order I had now lost all members of the family into which I had been born. And that really hurt.

Years before, I had become a practitioner of Transcendental Meditation (TM), and my daily meditation helped me immensely at this time in my life. It's not that TM provides answers to questions to which there really are no certain answers, but to quiet the mind through meditation during periods like this helps immensely to cope with such hurtful experiences.[4]

Fortunately, after my mother's death but while my brother was still alive, Dad had asked my brother and me to go with him to see his attorney to make sure that his Will was as he wanted it. Knowing that my brother was very ill and did not have long to live, Dad wanted to leave whatever he had to me. I said no, that would just cause problems with my brother's family. So Dad said OK and the Will was drafted accordingly. As a result, one half of whatever estate he did have was left to my brother's children. After Dad's funeral, I contacted the attorney who had me close Dad's bank accounts so that the cash could be placed in the attorney's trust account for distribution. Dad also had some stock with a brokerage house in Newport Beach, California. Whatever stock he had I assumed was in Chevron as he had worked for Chevron during the latter period of his business life. However, I was to discover that he had converted most of his Chevron stock to WorldCom, which turned out to be one of the great stock disasters in US history.

Dad had a portfolio manager who supposedly was overseeing his limited stock investments but the Manager took no steps to protect the portfolio after my father's death. As a result, the value of my father's WorldCom stock had plummeted from its peak at $63.50 to $0.21 by the time Dad's attorney and I learned of the stockholding.

But this was not of great consequence. I felt that I had done the best that I possibly could for my father under the circumstances. But I was beginning to feel very much alone. By this time, I was also increasingly of the realization that, for whatever reason, the Creator was not finished with me yet. Even more than earlier in life, I knew the importance of giving myself in service of others. The enrichment I would gain by helping others would be my reward as I approached the so-called "golden years" of my life.

---

4   To learn more about the therapeutic effects of transcendental meditation, and meditation in general, visit www.backtothesummit.com

56

The Flume Trail

Soon I would be celebrating my sixty-second birthday. At that point in time, one year would have passed since I had suffered my brain aneurysm.

What was the state of my recovery? What were my underlying limitations? I still wasn't certain. But I had to find out.

"You know, George," I said to my good friend one day. "I want to bike the Flume trail."

The Flume trail may not be the Tour de France, but it is one of the more famous and challenging mountain bike trails in the States. It is sufficiently difficult that it will test even a skilled and conditioned athlete's limits. Due to the trail's steep, narrow, and curving nature on the downhill side, occasionally riders have lost their lives or been badly injured on the dangerous descent.

"Oh God, you're not ready for that," George said. "I've done the Flume Trail before, but it was a long time ago. And I remember it being pretty hellacious."

"That's okay, you don't need to come with me," I said.

"No," George said. "If you're going, so am I." And that is how it was decided that we would attempt to bike the Flume Trail on my 62nd birthday, exactly one year after I had suffered my aneurysm and stroke.

So on September 25th, the morning of my birthday, George and I parked one car at the Ponderosa Ranch—made famous in the Bonanza TV series— and drove a second car with our mountain bikes secured on the back down State Highway 28 to Spooner Lake, where we parked and disembarked. If we finished the Flume Trail successfully, we'd complete the ride at the Ponderosa and drive back to Spooner Lake to retrieve the second vehicle.

I was in good spirits as we began the ascent— knee pain and all, it felt good to put my body in motion. As George and I peddled our way up the steep path toward Marlette Lake, the ride quickly grew intense so that I had to focus every ounce of my energy on turning those peddles.

The first half of the Flume trail—a steep upward climb of nearly 1,500 feet—called on every muscle. It's not uncommon for riders to stop and rest, or walk one's bike, on this the "easy" portion of the ride. I had everything to prove and nothing to lose, so I pushed and pedaled—sweated and gritted—my way to the top. And as I ascended the trail, determined to master the course, my body did not fail me.

After a short water break at Marlette Lake, it was time to tackle the real challenge: the descent. The route down—with its slippery foliage, loose scree, dirt, and potential for excessive speed—was sure to try my skill, focus, and ability to ride through the inevitable pain.

George and I steered and peddled our bikes up over the summit and headed down toward Lake Tahoe. The drama of the natural scenery immediately struck me. Red, yellow, and orange leaves glistened on tree limbs, and wind whispered through the aspen trees. The crystalline waters of Lake Tahoe beamed up at me from the lake basin below.

At the very same time that I was marveling at this incredible scenery, I clenched the handlebars and applied all my energy to keeping the bike on course. "Shit," I thought. Could I stay upright on this angular dirt descent from the rim of the Sierra's above Marlette down the mountainside to Lake Tahoe? I wasn't sure, but I was hell-bent to try.

With each and every yard of ground I covered, I fought the earth: the constant potential to skid out of control on loose gravel, jerk forward on a sand patch, or lose my balance. One false move and I might simply slide and tumble off the trail and right over the nearby rocky edge. It was a long way down.

Yet even with my constant attention to the trail in front of me, I could not miss the majesty of Lake Tahoe as I biked nearer and nearer to it. The shallow waters around Sand Harbor shimmered a translucent green; as the water grew deeper, its hue changed to a brilliant blue. What a special place on earth!

From all around, the earth seemed to speak to me—through the sky, through the wind, through the water, through the trees. I was myself again, cutting down a mountainside, the sun on my face, the breeze at my back, marveling at the beauty of nature. The pain was there, but it was the last thing on my mind.

When George and I rolled down the bottom stretch of the Flume trail, past the Ponderosa Ranch and into the parking lot where one of our cars awaited us, I exhaled and set my legs down.

"Thank you for joining me, my friend," I said to George. "This was the greatest birthday present I've ever had."

Exactly one year had passed since I had suffered my aneurysm and stroke—less than a year since doctors had told me that I would likely never walk again. And here I was leaning on my bike at the end of the famous Flume Trail.

As I gave George a bear hug, I truly felt that I was on top of the world. My damaged knee had just become part of me and, in any event, I knew that I would someday get it taken care of (and years later I did). The fact is that I was "back." Bad leg and all, as far as I was concerned, I was all the way back!!! Back to the summit—the greatest one I had ever climbed. With this gift, it was time to pass on my gift to others—and to that end I would now dedicate my life.

57

Nicaragua

"It's so cold here at Tahoe."
— Osorno (a Miskito Indian)

Sierra Nevada College at Incline Village is the only private college in the State of Nevada. The State line between California and Nevada goes through the center of Lake Tahoe and the college is just a few miles on the Nevada side and sits right above the lake in a very picturesque setting.

A Professor at the college, Tim Brown, was trying to create a unique international studies program at Sierra Nevada College (SNC) and knowing of my background in international affairs requested that I assist him in this endeavor.

Although I was not an ideological companion of Professor Brown, I did respect him. He had good contacts because he had been involved with the State Department during most of his professional life. Between the two of us, we were lining up some wonderful speakers and establishing some new programs that I found to be quite exciting from an academic standpoint. Tragically, the program was abandoned because of a dispute that arose between Brown and the administration of the college.

However, before abandonment I had met a student named Emilio Vaca who had worked his way up the hard way. Emilio had been raised by a single father, a field laborer. As I heard the story, when Emilio's parents had come to the United States, his mother was already pregnant. As a result, Emilio was born in the States and thus is an American citizen. His mother subsequently returned to Mexico. Emilio was a bright student and became the President of the student body at the Winnemucca, Nevada High School.

He then travelled to Modesto, California where he lived with his cousin and his aunt and uncle. He enrolled in Modesto Junior College and once again became Student Body President. He subsequently became President of the Junior College Association of California.

Because of the international studies program that Tim Brown and I were helping to start at SNC, Emilio transferred there where once again he became the Student Body President. Most students at SNC come from wealthy families. Most attend SNC because of the skiing opportunities. Partly as a result of having too much money some get into the drug environment.

Emilio was different. He was dedicated, hardworking, and had pulled himself up by his own bootstraps. I was impressed. With an internship from the Organization of American States, Emilio was assigned to work in Managua, Nicaragua during the summer of 2004.

Emilio and I stayed in touch with each other during the summer by email and land phone. In August, he asked if I could come down to Nicaragua. Knowing that I had been in Nicaragua for a few days in 1990, Emilio wanted me to see the changes that had taken place. He also wanted me to meet a young Indian lad that he had met named Osorno (nicknamed "Miskut").

Emilio knew that after the Sandinistas and Contras signed a Peace Accord in 1989, thus ending the Civil War that had been raging for years in Nicaragua, I had travelled to Nicaragua with others as one of the 1990 International Election Monitors. He also knew that I had not been back since then.

When I arrived in Managua in August 2004, I was stunned at what I observed. There had been some amazing changes. During the three days I was in Nicaragua in 1990 I was only in the capital, Managua, and the city of León. The 1990 election was between the Sandinista leader, Daniel Ortega, and the opposition candidate, Violetta Chomorro. I travelled to various polling places in those two cities to see if there was any obstruction or harassment and to ensure the ballots were properly sealed and delivered. Seemingly, it was a fair election and Chomorro prevailed.

But now, fourteen years later, Managua and León had been cleaned up and I observed a considerable amount of building construction. I went south to Granada which I had not visited in 1990 and found it quite beautiful, having maintained its historic colonial architecture.

A lot of people were coming to the realization that Nicaragua was becoming the new Costa Rica. There were droves of Americans, Canadians, Brits, Dutch, Spanish, Italians, Germans, and others poking around and buying up property. I did as well, a parcel near the Costa Rican border. A couple from Holland had acquired some jungle land above a beach. The property was strikingly beautiful with an incredible view overlooking Bahia Salinas (Salinas Bay). The islands in the middle of the bay contributed to the charm of the whole area. Monkeys and beautiful birds were all around us. Turtles nested on the beaches below us. On my first visit, I had to chop my way through the jungle like setting with a machete. Today I have a lovely home there.

As for Osorno, the young man that Emilio wanted me to meet, he is a Miskito Indian. Emilio felt that Osorno, or Miskut as he prefers to be called, if given a chance could become the first of his tribe ever to graduate from an American college. Miskut comes from the very northeast corner of Nicaragua. There are mountains and jungles between the heavily populated western side which is almost exclusively Spanish speaking and the eastern or Caribbean side where multiple languages, some indigenous, are spoken.

Miskut's home in Puerto Cabezas was historically reached only by rivers and by trekking, but now it can be reached by air. However, I first met Miskut in Managua and I was so impressed that I took him with me when I returned to the States and helped him get enrolled in Sierra Nevada College. While that College is almost exclusively white, he had the companionship of Emilio Vaca and Emilio's cousin, Christopher Rodriguez. Miskut became like a member of my own family and remains so to this day.

Needless to say, living in Nicaragua, Miskut had never seen snow. The day he arrived at Tahoe was a heavenly August day, blue skies and mild temperatures of about seventy-five degrees. It could not have been more gorgeous anywhere in the world. Yet Miskut was shivering saying, "It's so cold here at Tahoe." I realized then and there that I had better get a wardrobe for Miskut to prepare him for a Lake Tahoe winter. I am proud to say that in 2010 Miskut received his college degree from SNC. He is going to acquit himself well in years to come.

———————

Another outgrowth of my involvement in Nicaragua is helping to construct a much needed orphanage and school near the remote southwestern town of Tola in the State of Rivas. What is particularly rewarding to me about this recent project is that it involves my entire family, especially my son and his wife who have now in large measure taken over the lead. But the entire family—my children, their spouses, and my grandchildren are all involved. Working with a wonderful INGO, Paso Pacifico, that had been previously established in Nicaragua to preserve the forests and to protect the various species of turtle populations that nest on the beaches of the southwest, the project is now well underway and will hopefully be completed within a relatively short period of time. I expect to visit the facility many times in the years to come and I'm sure that my children and grandchildren will as well. We will all be spiritually richer for it.

58

READ and a "Pistol of a Lady"

"Only a life lived for others is a life worth living."
— Albert Einstein

I met Dr. Antonia ("Toni") Neubauer shortly after I started my recovery program at Lake Tahoe. She soon became a very close friend.

Toni is a bundle of energy. I call her a "pistol." Standing no more than five feet tall and I suspect not many years younger than me, she founded and heads an adventure travel company, Myths and Mountains, rated by National Geographic as one of the ten best in the world. She leads many of the trips that Myths and Mountains puts together herself. When not overseas, she seems to be constantly inviting people to her home for song circles, play reads, and book clubs. One can get dizzy trying to figure out how she packs so much energy into her small frame.

Of greater significance is that in the early 90s, Toni had founded an organization known as Rural Education and Development, an international non-profit organization initially designed to bring literacy and economic development to the country of Nepal. The organization, better known by its acronym of READ, had a Board of Directors but the members were not much engaged and Toni pretty much soldiered on by herself for many years.

As we got to know each other, Toni began to ask me to join the Board of Directors of READ Global. I told her over the course of several years that as much as I respected what she was doing, I simply could not commit myself to accept her request. Not only was I still going through a physical rehabilitation effort but I finally, for the first time in my life, was learning to say "no." A problem that I have always had is that when I say yes I completely throw myself into a project. I feared that it would be too much for me to undertake yet further responsibilities with READ given the state of my health and everything else that I had on my plate.

By the summer of 2004 I had made a remarkable recovery by any measure or standard. Nevertheless, my wakeup call had convinced me that I might not have long to live. So I decided that I would put together a trip to visit the only region of the world that I had not previously visited. For the most part, that was the former French Indo-China consisting of Vietnam, Laos and Cambodia. I also wanted to see what Myanmar (formerly Burma) was like.

So I put together a two and a half month trip which started in Vietnam. Travelling alone, as more times than not I have done, I left in early September for Vietnam. I travelled everywhere in the country that I wanted to see starting in the far south and continuing to the farthest point north. I found the Mekong Delta in the south to be incredibly hot and humid and I could certainly understand how frightening warfare must have been in that area. Narrow waterways and thick jungle, perfect for hiding ambushers. I travelled up the Delta to Ho Chi Minh City, formerly Saigon. It is a huge city and remains the economic center of the country.

As I travelled north, the country became quite lush and very beautiful. I crawled through a major tunnel that had been dug by the Viet Cong. It was a difficult ordeal but a Vietnamese lad told me that he would guide me through it. He was young, quite small, very nimble, and he scooted right along. However, as a westerner I am substantially larger than the average Vietnamese and with my bad knee to boot I was in pain and had a very hard time making my way. It was one of only two times in my life that I remember being claustrophobic. The tunneled maze seemed to go on forever and it was unbelievably hot. Eventually I got to an area within the tunnel that had been used by the Viet Cong for a hospital. There I was able to stand up for a few minutes.

Then we continued on, still underground. It would have been impossible for an American G.I. laden with military gear to get through those tunnels. There was simply not enough room in the passageways and the sweltering heat and humidity was insufferable. Eventually the tunnels led to a river which in effect was the escape route if one was needed. After a good forty-five minutes or so, was I ever happy to stand upright and to breathe fresh air. I was dripping wet with sweat.

Continuing farther north past Hue, DaNang and Marble Mountain, I eventually came to Hanoi. Hanoi is a beautiful city. It is much smaller than Saigon and still retains its French architecture which the Vietnamese greatly prize. They may not have liked the French occupation of their country but they did and still do appreciate French architecture and cuisine.

From Hanoi I continued on to Halong Bay on the Chinese border. It is one of the most beautiful spots to be found anywhere, startling in its beauty with small, lush chiseled islands all over the bay.

During the month I was in Vietnam, I attended a lot of religious ceremonies. Although my visit was only a generation after the end of the Vietnam War, not once as an American did I encounter any hostility. I found that extraordinary because I had been in Europe a generation after the end of World War II, and the animosity towards Germans in most parts of Europe at that time was still quite palpable. The Buddhist philosophy embraced by most Vietnamese values among other things living in the present and not unduly dwelling on the past. As one Vietnamese told me, "If one dwells on the past it is generally with regret, and if one dwells on the future it is generally with anxiety. Better to live in the present." Very Buddhist.

I found that quite interesting because on two prior occasions I had been privileged to meet the Dalai Lama. My first meeting with the Dalai Lama had been in the United States in a group setting but I was later to meet with him again in Geneva with only a few others present and with the opportunity to have face to face discussions with his Holiness. My respect for the Dalai Lama is enormous and, later in life, I have myself taken refuge in Tibetan Buddhism.

Although the Vietnamese do not hold the same reverence for the Dalai Lama that one finds in Tibet and in many parts of northern China, Nepal, Bhutan, Northern India, and elsewhere, he is greatly respected and many Vietnamese still look to him for spiritual guidance.

When I left Vietnam I flew to Bangkok for a pre-arranged meeting with an Englishman named John Sanday O.B.E. (Order of the British Empire). Toni Neubauer had arranged for me to meet with Sanday in Bangkok and we met right on schedule. John is a tall, somewhat stuffy man who has done some extraordinary things including helping with the building of hospitals in Nepal. However, he is best known for his work in restoring wats or temples of the ancient Khmer civilization. During the time of the Khmer Rouge and the Killing Fields in Cambodia, John was one of the very first westerners to go back in and to start reconstruction of the great antiquities at Angkor Wat and of other wats or temples of the Khmer civilization. I had the honor and extraordinarily rich educational experience of travelling with John through northeast Thailand, Laos, and Cambodia.

There are literally hundreds of wats in this part of the world. Most are difficult to find since they have been overgrown by jungle. Some of the more fascinating ones are far removed from Siem Reap, the city where Angkor Wat and Angkor Town are located. John has done so much archaeological and reconstructive work throughout the ancient Khmer world that almost everywhere we went people referred to him as "Mr. John." His knowledge of the Khmer civilization, one of the greatest of the ancient empires, is unsurpassed.

After visiting well over one hundred wats I saw the results of the "Killing Fields" near Phnom Phen, Cambodia. It was sickening. I had been to a lot of other atrocity sites including several holocaust sites in Europe as well as the holocaust museum in Israel but I had never seen anything like what I saw in the killing fields where up to 40,000 skulls were stacked in one huge pile. There were all kinds of victims. Those who wore glasses. Those who could read or write. The insanity of Pol Pot and his regime was unbelievable.

Mine fields are still being cleared in various regions of Cambodia. I am an adventurous guy. When people tell me not to go somewhere, I'm generally the first to say I'm going there, but I will be the first to admit that in Cambodia when I was told not to venture into a mined area I did not. There were places where Cambodians were down on their hands and knees with proper instrumentation checking for mines and instructing people where they could safely step. I listened intently and stepped exactly where I was told it would be safe to step —and nowhere else.

Leaving Cambodia, I flew into Yangon, Myanmar (Burma). Myanmar has one of the most repressive governments in the world. Nevertheless, I fell in love with the people and with the beauty of the country even though I spent only one week there. Elayna flew to Asia to join me for that week.

The government required that we have a guide. She was quite small and very intelligent. We became good friends with her over that short period of time and she confided in us that every single evening she was required to report all of our movements. This was true when we were in Yangon, Pagan, Mandalay—everywhere. She was also to inform authorities what was being said during conversations with people we encountered. The authoritarian government is reprehensible in every respect.

Myanmar is incredibly rich in resources—diamonds, rubies, sapphires, oil, and much more. The sanctions imposed by the European countries as well as by the United States might have an effect but for the Chinese who openly exploit trade opportunities that enrich the Generals who rule Myanmar. The Buddhist monuments in Myanmar are perhaps as significant as any I have found in the world and lend themselves to the mystique of the country. I could write a book about Myanmar even though I spent only a week there. It is a country where virtually everything is based on astrological forecasts, and where women "paint" their faces white with the bark of a tree and chew beetle nut which causes their teeth to eventually turn dark brown. A strange and mysterious country, full of people begging to be free.

I had now been away from the States for two months travelling in South and Southeast Asia, but I knew that Toni Neubauer wanted me to join her in Nepal to see firsthand what READ is all about and to visit some of the libraries READ had already developed.

I agreed and after seeing Elayna off for her flight back to the States, I caught a flight into Kathmandu and from there onto Pokhara, Nepal. In Pokhara I met up with Toni and with the Director of READ Nepal, the entity in Nepal that works under the umbrella of READ Global. After a day and night in Pokhara, taking in the spectacular views of the Himalayas including the famous mountain known to westerners as "Fish Tail" (also known as Machhapachhare) we caught a Buddha Airlines flight further north to Jomsom in the Kingdom of Mustang, which is a kingdom within what was then the kingdom of Nepal.

Virtually all INGOs had left Nepal because of the Maoist insurrection. Both the Maoists and the government forces were committing horrible human rights abuses. Somewhat remarkably, personnel working for READ were never bothered because READ had assiduously stayed out of politics. Its goal was simply to inspire literacy and economic prosperity in rural and remote parts of the country.

After visiting the READ library in Jomsom, we began to trek up the Kali Gandaki, the deepest gorge in the world bordered to the south by the Annapurna Range and to the north by Dhaulagiri, one of the world's highest mountains.

Trekking to various villages was fascinating because as we approached each village we would see teenage kids up high on the cliffs signaling where we were. The villagers all seemed to know we were coming. By the time we reached the village most of the people would be lining the streets waiting to put floral garlands around our necks. It was quite moving.

In the village of Tukche, after visiting the library, we went to view the small furniture plant they had established as their sustaining project. They had enjoyed so much success that they had built two more stories on what had started out as a one-story library. The furniture made at their furniture plant became greatly sought after by, among others, the monasteries in the region.

With their surplus money, not only were the villagers able to sustain the library but they were able to build a bridge across the Kali Gandaki, a great river. Before the bridge was built, the people on the other side would have to trek miles upstream to cross over and miles back down to get to the village. A full day round trip.

Now, not only could people on the other side of the river cross to visit the library and to visit the village of Tukche itself, but it also benefited people on the village side of the river as the land on the other side was more arable. Fruit orchards were planted and a small brandy industry followed. One could not help but be impressed—and I was. It was a classic example of what READ was accomplishing.

Toni, having knowledge of the region, had also timed our visit to Tukche so that we were able to witness the most important ceremony of the year. The ceremony which took place in the monastery was one that involved casting the demon from the village so that land would be rich and crops plentiful. Although I had witnessed similar ceremonies before, none had been as colorful as the one in Tukche, nor had any been as prolonged and ornate. Two days and nights in duration, eventually a processional formed and the demon was cast into fire some distance from the monastery.

From this region in the Himalayas which had been settled by people from Tibet hundreds of years ago, we trekked across the Kali Gandaki and took a different route back to Jomsom. Trekking both to and from Jomsom had allowed us to stay overnight in several small but memorable tea houses in villages along the trails.

Back in Jomsom, we flew back to Pokhara. From Pokhara we drove south from some of the highest country in the world in the Himalayas to close to sea level in the Chitwan area next to India known as the Terai. There was a stark contrast in flora and fauna as in this jungle area one can find Bengal Tigers, elephants and other jungle life not found in the high country.

At the village of Jhuwani, we got the same type of reception we had received at Jomsom and Tukche. The reception actually became humorous as eventually the garlands had covered my entire head and I had to push with one hand the garlands up above my eyes and with the other the garlands down below my eyes in order to see. Everyone laughed, myself included. The villagers put on a big show for us as they did in every village.

As mentioned, Toni had asked me several times to serve on the READ Board of Directors and I had continued to say no, but the night after we arrived in Jhuwani when I was again asked, I said: "Toni, I am so moved by the good that READ is doing in this country I cannot say no any longer." So I agreed and I became a member of the READ Global Board of Directors and, as is always the case, threw myself wholeheartedly into the work. That is my custom. Today, I serve as Chairman of the Board of READ Global.

The first request Toni made of me was that I use my connections to expand and strengthen the READ Global Board of Directors. That I did. Today we have an outstanding Board and a small but very dedicated and talented staff, all deeply engaged and committed to the future of READ and the work that READ is doing in the lesser developed world.

By 2007, READ was ready to expand into another country. In fact, READ had received a grant from the Bill & Melinda Gates Foundation on condition that its program be taken to additional countries. The first was India, a country that both feeds the soul and tears at the heart at the same time. Toni and I and another Board Member went to India and established READ India, hired a staff and selected the first village that we would work in.

The first village in which we began to work was the village of Ullon, about ninety miles south of Kolkata (previously known as Calcutta). The village of Ullon is on the Bay of Bengal in the Sunderbans area, one of the last sanctuaries of the Bengal Tiger. As one drives south of Kolkata it is seemingly a never ending congested road marked by squalor and poverty. It takes approximately five hours to travel the ninety miles by car from the airport in Kolkata to Ullon. For hours on end, the road is congested by cars, buses, trucks, cattle, rickshaws, and thousands upon thousands of people.

With a driver holding his hand on the horn the entire distance, after several hours all of a sudden we came upon a litter free road bordered by trees. It was a real contrast to everything that we had previously seen on our way south from Kolkata. We had arrived in the village of Ullon. Here is located an entity known as VSSU—a microfinance/microcredit program headed by a man named Kapilanda Mondal. VSSU is modeled after Grameen Bank, which was founded by Nobel Peace Prize winner Muhammad Yunus.

VSSU now works in over 400 villages in West Bengal regardless of caste or religion. The villagers in Ullon wanted READ to establish the first READ India project in Ullon. They had put together one of the best business plans that had ever been brought to READ's attention. As a result, we made a decision then and there to start our Indian program in the village of Ullon.

Later that same year I again visited India and, among other things, travelled to Ullon to lay the cornerstone and do the groundbreaking for our library and economic development center there in the village. It was dedicated the following May and since then has attracted visitors from all over the world. From that start in 2007, READ now works in several States in India. However, the country is so vast that, with a population of over one billion people, it will take scores of years to reach all of the impoverished villages and peoples that seek our help.

With additional funding from the Bill & Melinda Gates Foundation and recognition received not only from that foundation but other international entities as well, READ now has also taken its program to Bhutan. This occurred in the latter part of 2008 when Toni and I travelled there not only to establish READ Bhutan but also at the invitation of the King to observe the ceremony by which the new King was being coronated.

Bhutan is the only country in the world that measures progress not by the customary standard of Gross National Product by rather by the standard of Gross National Happiness. Surprisingly, most of the people speak not only Dzonga, the national language, but also English which is taught throughout the school years. The Bhutanese treasure their architecture, their dress and their culture and have been able to preserve them well so far.

Until recent times, Bhutan was pretty much closed to the outside world. Therefore, I was somewhat surprised and very impressed at the caliber of people that applied for the position of Executive Director of READ Bhutan. Toni and I interviewed over ten people and the vast majority were well qualified for the position. I was enormously impressed with Bhutan and felt privileged to have gone there as it was one of a limited number of countries in the world that I had not yet visited.

The work of READ and the good it does is gratifying and enriches my soul beyond words. I was blessed when I said "yes" to Toni in the village of Jhuwani, Nepal in late 2005.[5]

---

5   To learn more about the enrichment derived from doing humanitarian work, visit www.backtothesummit.com

Epilogue

"I have to say it now; it's been a good life all in all;
it's really fine to have a chance to hang around."
— John Denver ("Poems, Prayers & Promises")

To be sure, I have led a rugged, adventurous, and blessed life. I am blessed to have been born in the United States, a country which I dearly love, where opportunities abound for anyone who is willing to work hard and persevere through hardships.

I have been blessed to have seen and experienced parts of the world that most people never dream of seeing—and I managed to see most of them before the world became "flat" and homogeneous.

I am blessed to have had English as my native tongue because this richly diverse country—the United States—has been such a beacon to the world that wherever I have traveled, within minutes I have invariably been able to find someone with whom I could communicate.

I am blessed to have lived in an age of medical marvel and miracles. At no other time in the history of mankind could I possibly have survived some of my ordeals. Of that I am certain.

I have been blessed to have fathered beautiful children who, sometimes in spite of my absences and lapses, have turned into caring and contributing adults. They, in turn, have provided me with three adorable grandchildren and, who knows, there could always be more in the future.

Each morning, I open the paper first to the obituary page. If my name is not there, I think "Isn't this day off to a great start! Now, accept the blessing and make the most of it."

So while I've not yet "gone fishing," I have only my own hard charging personality to blame. My suspicion is that, while I may preach to the contrary, till the day I die I will keep busy (and never regret a moment of it).

So what's next for me? That chapter has yet to be written. Yet, one constant remains as certain in my life as the rising of the sun tomorrow. Whatever fate may have in store for me and whichever road I choose to follow, most assuredly there will be something new around the next bend. The insatiable quest for knowledge burns as brightly today as ever.

Robert Frost put it best when he wrote:

> *The woods are lovely, dark and deep,*
> *But I have promises to keep,*
> *And miles to go before I sleep,*
> *And miles to go before I sleep.*

About the Author

During his tenure in the California Senate, Omer Rains represented over a million people in the Central Coast Area of California (principally the Counties of Santa Barbara and Ventura). In that capacity, among many others, Rains served as Chairman of the Senate Majority Caucus (the youngest in State history), as Chairman of the Senate Judiciary Committee, and as Chairman of the Senate Committee on Political Reform.

Rains has fought tirelessly throughout his adult life for environmental protection, for political reform, and for civil and human rights—both at home and abroad. He has also served as a prominent international lawyer, financier and investment advisor with extensive experience in all major world markets and finance centers.

After a life-threatening stroke and aneurysm at age sixty-one, Rains beat incredible medical odds to walk again and thereafter to once again lead an active life of service to others. He continues to engage in humanitarian and charitable work in all parts of the lesser developed world with special emphasis on projects in Nepal, India, and Bhutan, as well as on more recent projects in Latin America. Among other responsibilities, he currently serves as Chairman of the Board of READ Global. When not abroad, he makes his principal residence at Lake Tahoe (California/Nevada).

Mr. Rains is an experienced and frequent lecturer and mentor on virtually all topics covered in *Back to the Summit* including, but not limited to: overcoming brain injuries and paralysis; doing international legal and finance work; and speaking on the enormously important and gratifying work being done to promote world literacy by Rural Education and Development (READ) Global. He is also available to speak on the therapeutic effects of Transcendental Meditation (TM) and the calming practice of Tibetan Buddhism. He can be contacted through his websites: www.backtothesummit.com or www.senorains.com.

Index

BUY A SHARE OF THE FUTURE IN YOUR COMMUNITY

These certificates make great holiday, graduation and birthday gifts that can be personalized with the recipient's name. The cost of one S.H.A.R.E. or one square foot is $54.17. The personalized certificate is suitable for framing and will state the number of shares purchased and the amount of each share, as well as the recipient's name. The home that you participate in "building" will last for many years and will continue to grow in value.

Here is a sample SHARE certificate:

HABITAT FOR HUMANITY

THIS CERTIFIES THAT
YOUR NAME HERE
HAS INVESTED IN A HOME FOR A DESERVING FAMILY

1985-2010
TWENTY-FIVE YEARS OF BUILDING FUTURES
IN OUR COMMUNITY ONE HOME AT A TIME

1200 SQUARE FOOT HOUSE @ $65,000 = $54.17 PER SQUARE FOOT
This certificate represents a tax deductible donation. It has no cash value.

YES, I WOULD LIKE TO HELP!

*I support the work that Habitat for Humanity does and I want to be part of the excitement! As a donor, I will receive periodic updates on your construction activities but, more importantly, I know my gift will help a family in our community realize the dream of homeownership. **I would like to SHARE in your efforts against substandard housing in my community!** (Please print below)*

PLEASE SEND ME _____ SHARES at $54.17 EACH = $ $_____

In Honor Of: _____

Occasion: (Circle One)   *HOLIDAY*   *BIRTHDAY*   *ANNIVERSARY*

     OTHER: _____

Address of Recipient: _____

Gift From: _____ *Donor Address:* _____

Donor Email: _____

I AM ENCLOSING A CHECK FOR $ $_____ PAYABLE TO HABITAT FOR HUMANITY **OR** PLEASE CHARGE MY VISA OR MASTERCARD *(CIRCLE ONE)*

Card Number _____ Expiration Date: _____

Name as it appears on Credit Card _____ Charge Amount $ _____

Signature _____

Billing Address _____

Telephone # Day _____ Eve _____

PLEASE NOTE: Your contribution is tax-deductible to the fullest extent allowed by law.
Habitat for Humanity • P.O. Box 1443 • Newport News, VA 23601 • 757-596-5553
www.HelpHabitatforHumanity.org

CPSIA information can be obtained at www.ICGtesting.com
Printed in the USA
BVOW021123231011

274256BV00002B/1/P

9 781614 480945